First World War
and Army of Occupation
War Diary
France, Belgium and Germany

I0345526

36 DIVISION
Divisional Troops
Royal Army Medical Corps
109 Field Ambulance
5 October 1915 - 14 June 1919

WO95/2499/2

The Naval & Military Press Ltd
www.nmarchive.com
Published in association with The National Archives

Published by

The Naval & Military Press Ltd

Unit 10 Ridgewood Industrial Park,

Uckfield, East Sussex,

TN22 5QE England

Tel: +44 (0) 1825 749494

www.naval-military-press.com

www.nmarchive.com

This diary has been reprinted in facsimile from the original. Any imperfections are inevitably reproduced and the quality may fall short of modern type and cartographic standards.

Contents

Document type	Place/Title	Date From	Date To
Heading	WO95/2499/2		
Heading	36th Division Medical 109th Fld Ambulance 1915 Oct-1919 Jun		
Heading	36th Div F/195/2 Oct Nov Dec 1915 109th F.A. Vols. 1, 3		
Heading	War Diary Of 109th Field Ambulance From 5th. Oct 1915 To 31st Oct 1915 Volume I		
War Diary	Havre	05/10/1915	06/10/1915
War Diary	Longeau	06/10/1915	06/10/1915
War Diary	Bertangles	06/10/1915	19/10/1915
War Diary	Coisy	19/10/1915	20/10/1915
War Diary	Beauval	20/10/1915	31/10/1915
Heading	36th Div F/195/1 Nov. 1915 109th F.A. Vol 2 121/7928		
Heading	War Diary of 109th Fd Ambulance From 1st Nov" 1915 To 30th Nov" 1915 Volume 2		
War Diary	Beauval	01/11/1915	27/11/1915
War Diary	Longvillers	28/11/1915	28/11/1915
War Diary	Pont Remy	29/11/1915	30/11/1915
Heading	War Diary of 109th Fd Ambulance From 1st Dec 1915 To 31st Dec 1915 Volume III		
War Diary	Pont Remy	01/12/1915	31/12/1915
Heading	109th Field Ambulance Jan Feb 1916 March April 1916-Dec 1918		
Heading	109th F.A. Vol: 4		
Heading	War Diary of 109th Fd Ambulance From 1st January To 31st January 1916 (Volume IV)		
War Diary	Pont Remy	01/01/1916	19/01/1916
War Diary	Berteaucourt	19/01/1916	31/01/1916
Heading	War Diary of 109th Field Aml From 1st Feb 1916 To 29th Feb 1916 (Volume) 5		
Heading	109th F.A. Vol 5		
War Diary	Berteaucourt	01/02/1916	09/02/1916
War Diary	Val de Maison	10/02/1916	22/02/1916
War Diary	Vauchelles.	22/02/1916	29/02/1916
Heading	War Diary of 109th Fd Ambulance From 1st March 1916 To 31st March 1916 (Volume) VI 36th Div		
War Diary	Vauchelles-Les-Authie	01/03/1916	04/03/1916
War Diary	Bertrancourt	04/03/1916	29/03/1916
War Diary	Varennes	29/03/1916	31/03/1916
Heading	War Diary of 109th Fd Ambulance Volume 7 From 1st April 1916 To 30th April 1916 36th Div.		
War Diary	Varennes	01/04/1916	30/04/1916
Heading	War Diary of 109th Field Amb. From 1st May 1916 To 31st May 1916 Volume (VIII) 36th Div.		
War Diary	Varennes	01/05/1916	31/05/1916
War Diary	Clairfaye	31/05/1916	31/05/1916
Heading	War Diary of 109th Field Amb 1st June 1916 To 30th June 1916 Volume 9		
War Diary	Clairfaye	01/06/1916	30/06/1916

Heading	War Diary of 109th Field Ambulance From 1st July 1916 To 31st July 1916 Volume X		
War Diary	Clairfaye	01/07/1916	05/07/1916
War Diary	Val De Maison	05/07/1916	10/07/1916
War Diary	Vacquerie	10/07/1916	11/07/1916
War Diary	Auxi Le Chateau	12/07/1916	12/07/1916
War Diary	Thiennes	12/07/1916	12/07/1916
War Diary	Compagne	12/07/1916	13/07/1916
War Diary	Quelmes	13/07/1916	14/07/1916
War Diary	Culem	14/07/1916	21/07/1916
War Diary	Bollezeele	21/07/1916	23/07/1916
War Diary	Hondeghem	23/07/1916	24/07/1916
War Diary	Bailleul	24/07/1916	31/07/1916
Heading	War Diary of 109th Field Ambulance From 1st Aug. 1916 To 31st Aug 1916 Volume XI		
War Diary	Bailleul	01/08/1916	31/08/1916
Heading	War Diary of 109th Field Ambulance From 1st Sept 1916 To 30th Sept 1916 Vol XII 36th Div		
War Diary	Bailleul	01/09/1916	30/09/1916
Heading	War Diary of 109th Field Ambulance From 1st Oct 1916 To 31st Oct 1916 Volume XIII 36th Div.		
War Diary	Bailleul	01/10/1916	31/10/1916
Heading	War Diary of 109th Field Amb From 1st Nov 1916 To 30th Nov 1916 Vol XIV 36th Div		
War Diary	Bailleul	01/11/1916	30/11/1916
Heading	War Diary of 109th Field Ambulance From 1st Dec 1916 To 31st Dec 1916 Vol XV 36th Div		
War Diary	Bailleul	01/12/1916	31/12/1916
Heading	War Diary of 109th Field Ambulance From 1st Jan 17 To 31st Jan 1917 Vol 16 36th Div		
War Diary	Bailleul	01/01/1917	31/01/1917
Heading	War Diary of 109th Field Ambulance From 1-2-17 To 28-2-17 Vol XVII 36th Div		
War Diary	Bailleul	01/02/1917	28/02/1917
Heading	War Diary of 109th Field Ambulance From 1st March 1917 To 31st March 1917 Vol XVIII 36th Div		
War Diary	Bailleul	01/03/1917	31/03/1917
Heading	April 1917. 140/2086 109th F.A.		
War Diary	Bailleul	01/04/1917	30/04/1917
Heading	War Diary of 109th Field Ambulance From 1st May 1917. To 31st May 1917 Vol. XX.		
War Diary	Bailleul	01/05/1917	31/05/1917
Heading	War Diary of 109th Field Ambulance From 1st June 1917 To 30th June 1917 Vol XXI		
War Diary	Bailleul (Magilligan Camp)	01/06/1917	30/06/1917
War Diary	Court Croix	30/06/1917	30/06/1917
Heading	War Diary of 109th Field Ambulance Vol XXII From 1st July 1917 31st July 1917		
War Diary	Court Croix	01/07/1917	05/07/1917
War Diary	Hondeghem	05/07/1917	06/07/1917
War Diary	Arques	06/07/1917	07/07/1917
War Diary	Bouvelinghem	07/07/1917	26/07/1917
War Diary	Winnezeele	26/07/1917	30/07/1917
War Diary	L.20.b.7.7 (Sheet 27)	31/07/1917	31/07/1917

Miscellaneous	B.E.F. Summary Of Medical War Diaries Of 109th F.A. 36th Div. 8th Corps. 5th Army. 19th Corps from 26th July. 4th Corps III. Army from 23rd August.	26/07/1917	26/07/1917
Miscellaneous	109th F.A. 36th Div. 8th Corps. 5th Army. Officer Commanding-Lt. Col. R. Magill. 19th Corps from 26th July.	26/07/1917	26/07/1917
Miscellaneous	109th F.A. 36th Div. 19th Corps 5th Army. Officer Commanding-Lt. Col. R Magill.		
Miscellaneous	109th F.A. 36th Div. 8th Corps. 5th Army. Officer Commanding-Lt. Col. R. Magill. 19th Corps from 26th July.	26/07/1917	26/07/1917
Miscellaneous	109th F.A. 36th Div. 19th Corps 5th Army. Officer Commanding-Lt. Col. R Magill.		
Heading	War Diary of 109th Field Ambulance From 1st Aug 1917 31st Aug 1917 Vol XXIII		
War Diary	Hillhoek (L.20.b.7.7. Sheet 27 1.20,000)	01/08/1917	04/08/1917
War Diary	Red Farm	04/08/1917	19/08/1917
War Diary	Hillhoek	19/08/1917	20/08/1917
War Diary	Winnezeele	20/08/1917	24/08/1917
War Diary	Caestre.	24/08/1917	24/08/1917
War Diary	Bapaume	24/08/1917	24/08/1917
War Diary	Barastre	25/08/1917	29/08/1917
War Diary	Maricourt	29/08/1917	31/08/1917
Miscellaneous	Summary Of Medical War Diaries Of 109th F.A. 36th Div. 8th Corps. 5th Army. 19th Corps from 26th July. 4th Corps III. Army from 23rd August.	26/07/1917	26/07/1917
Miscellaneous			
Miscellaneous	109th F.A. 36th Div. 19th Corps. 5th Army. Officer Commanding-Lt. Col. R. Magill.		
Miscellaneous	109th F.A. 36th Div. 19th Corps. 5th Army. Officer Commanding-Lt. Col. R. Magill. 4th Corps III. Army from 23rd August.	23/08/1917	23/08/1917
Miscellaneous			
Miscellaneous	109th F.A. 36th Div. 19th Corps. 5th Army. Officer Commanding-Lt. Col. R. Magill.		
Miscellaneous	109th F.A. 36th Div. 19th Corps. 5th Army. Officer Commanding-Lt. Col. R. Magill. 4th Corps III. Army from 23rd August.	23/08/1917	23/08/1917
Heading	War Diary of 109th Field Ambulance From 1st Sept 1917 To 30th Sept 1917 Vol XXIV		
War Diary	Maricourt	01/09/1917	30/09/1917
Heading	War Diary of 109th Field Ambulance From 1st Oct 1917 To 31st Oct 1917 Vol XXV		
War Diary	Maricourt	01/10/1917	31/10/1917
Heading	War Diary of 109th Field Ambulance From 1st Nov 1917 To 30th Nov 1917 Vol XXVI		
War Diary	Maricourt	01/11/1917	30/11/1917
Heading	War Diary of 109th. Field Ambulance. from 1st. Dec. 1917. to 31st. Dec. 1917. Vol. XXVII.		
War Diary	Maricourt	01/12/1917	05/12/1917
War Diary	Fins.	05/12/1917	05/12/1917
War Diary	Nurlu	05/12/1917	08/12/1917
War Diary	Metz En. Couture	08/12/1917	10/12/1917
War Diary	Metz	11/12/1917	15/12/1917
War Diary	Rocquigny	15/12/1917	16/12/1917
War Diary	Milly	16/12/1917	29/12/1917

War Diary	Domart Sur La Luce	29/12/1917	31/12/1917
Heading	War Diary of 109th Field Ambulance from 1st. January 1918 to 31st. January 1918 Vol. XXVIII.		
War Diary	Domart Sur La Luce	01/01/1918	07/01/1918
War Diary	Mezieres	07/01/1918	09/01/1918
War Diary	Marche-Allouard	09/01/1918	11/01/1918
War Diary	Ollezy	11/01/1918	13/01/1918
War Diary	Artemps	13/01/1918	31/01/1918
Heading	War Diary of 109th. Field Ambulance. from 1st. Feby. 1918. to 28th. Feby. 1918. Vol. XXIX		
War Diary	Artemps	01/02/1918	28/02/1918
Heading	War Diary of 109th Field Ambulance from 1st. March 1918. to 31st. March 1918. Vol. XXX.		
War Diary	Artemps	01/03/1918	21/03/1918
War Diary	Annois	21/03/1918	21/03/1918
War Diary	Brouchy	22/03/1918	22/03/1918
War Diary	Esmery Hallon	22/03/1918	22/03/1918
War Diary	Liber Mont	23/03/1918	23/03/1918
War Diary	Beaulieu	24/03/1918	25/03/1918
War Diary	Amy	25/03/1918	25/03/1918
War Diary	Warsey	26/03/1918	26/03/1918
War Diary	Grivesnes	26/03/1918	27/03/1918
War Diary	Chirmont	28/03/1918	28/03/1918
War Diary	Laward	28/03/1918	29/03/1918
War Diary	Namps au Val	30/03/1918	30/03/1918
War Diary	Saleux	30/03/1918	31/03/1918
Heading	War Diary of 109th. Field Ambulance. from 1st. April 1918 to 30th. April 1918. Volume XXXI.		
War Diary	Woincourt	01/04/1918	04/04/1918
War Diary	Rousbrugge	05/04/1918	05/04/1918
War Diary	Dirty Bucket Camp.	05/04/1918	06/04/1918
War Diary	Gwalia	07/04/1918	12/04/1918
War Diary	Gwalia Farm	13/04/1918	19/04/1918
War Diary	Gwalia	19/04/1918	30/04/1918
Heading	War Diary of 109th Field Ambulance. from 1st. May 1918 to 31st. May 1918. Volume XXXII.		
War Diary	Gwalia Farm	01/05/1918	31/05/1918
Heading	War Diary of 109th. Field Ambulance. from 1st. June 1918. to 30th. June 1918. Volume XXXIII.		
War Diary	Gwalia Farm	01/06/1918	06/06/1918
War Diary	School Camp 27/L.3.a.7.4.	06/06/1918	07/06/1918
War Diary	School Camp	08/06/1918	30/06/1918
Heading	War Diary of 109th Field Ambulance from 1st. July 1918. to 31st. July 1918. Volume XXIII.		
War Diary	School Camp	01/07/1918	03/07/1918
War Diary	Trois Rois Sheet 27.O.6.10.9	03/02/1918	03/02/1918
War Diary	Trois Rois	04/07/1918	09/07/1918
War Diary	27/P.26.d.7.8	09/07/1918	31/07/1918
Heading	War Diary of 109th. Field Ambulance from 1st. August 1918. to 31st. August 1918. Volume-XXXV.		
War Diary	Parkside (P.26.d.8.6.)	01/08/1918	09/08/1918
War Diary	Parkside 27/P.26.d.8.6	10/08/1918	31/08/1918
War Diary	Q.22.C.4.3 East of Eecke	31/08/1918	31/08/1918
Heading	War Diary of 109th Field Ambulance for Month of September. 1918. Vol. No. XXXVI		
War Diary	27/Q.22.C.4.3. (Eecke)	01/09/1918	03/09/1918

War Diary	Roch Farm	03/09/1918	11/09/1918
War Diary	Q.22.C.3.4.	11/09/1918	16/09/1918
War Diary	27/O.22.C.4.3	17/09/1918	30/09/1918
Miscellaneous	Regt. No. 182.		
Heading	War Diary of 109th Field Ambulance. from 1st. October 1918. to 31st. October 1918. Volume XXXVI.		
War Diary	27/Q.22.C.1.3	01/10/1918	01/10/1918
War Diary	28/A.23.a.1.0.	02/10/1918	26/10/1918
War Diary	Ledeghem.	27/10/1918	27/10/1918
War Diary	Belleghem	28/10/1918	31/10/1918
Heading	War Diary of 109th Field Ambulance for month of November, 1918. Vol. XXXVIII		
War Diary	Belleghem 29/N.27.C.	01/11/1918	03/11/1918
War Diary	Steerhoek. 29/M35.C.3.3	04/11/1918	30/11/1918
Heading	War Diary by Lieut Colonel H.S. Davidson. R.A.M.C. Commanding 109th Field Ambulance. December 1918.		
War Diary	Steerhoek	01/12/1918	31/12/1918
Heading	War Diary of 109th Field Ambulance by Lieut-Colonel H.S. Davidson, R.A.M.C., Period:- From 1st January 1919. To 31st January 1919. Vol 40 36 Div Box 2298		
War Diary	Steerhoek	01/01/1919	31/01/1919
Heading	War Diary. by Lieut-Colonel H.S. Davidson. R.A.M.C. Commanding 109th Field Ambulance. Vol 41		
War Diary	Steerhoek	01/02/1919	28/02/1919
Heading	War Diary by Lieut-Colonel H.S. Davidson. R.A.M.C. Commanding 109th Field Ambulance. March. 1919. Vol 42		
War Diary	Sterhoek.	01/03/1919	31/03/1919
Heading	War Diary by Captain S.P. Rea. R.A.M.C. Commanding 109th Field Ambulance. April 1919 Vol 41		
War Diary	Sterhoek	01/04/1919	30/04/1919
Heading	War Diary by Captain S.P. Rea. R.A.M.C. Commanding 109 Field Ambulance. May 1919 Vol 44		
War Diary	Sterhoek	01/05/1919	31/05/1919
Heading	June 1919 109th F.A. 140/3585		
War Diary	Sterhoek	01/06/1919	14/06/1919

36TH DIVISION

MEDICAL

109TH FLD AMBULANCE

~~JAN 1916-DEC 1918~~

1915 OCT — 1919 JUN

Confidential

War Dairy

Of

109th Field Ambulance

From 5th Oct 1915 To 31st Oct 1915

Volume

I

[illegible]
Capt R.A.M.C.
Cmdg. 109 Fd Amb.

Instructions regarding War Diaries and Intelligence Summaries are contained in F. S. Regs., Part II. and the Staff Manual respectively. Title pages will be prepared in manuscript.

WAR DIARY
or
~~INTELLIGENCE SUMMARY~~
(Erase heading not required.)

Army Form C. 2118.

Hour, Date, Place	Summary of Events and Information	Remarks and references to Appendices
1 AM. 5-10-15. HAVRE	The Unit arrived. Rm	
7 " " "	Disembarked. By order of a Staff officer blanket wagons & teams were handed over to A.S.C.	Rm
11-30 " " "	Marched off to Camp 5, where men had dinner. Remained in Camp till	Rm
10.30 PM " "	Left Rest Camp for Railway Station. Rm	
12.30 AM. 6-10-15 "	Commenced entraining. Rm	
3. AM " "	Train left. Rm	
2 PM 6-10-15 LONGEAU	Detrained and after watering & feeding horses marched off	Rm
8 " " BERTANGLES	Arrived in billets. Reported arrival to 109th Bde. The entire journey was uneventful. Rm	
7th Oct. " "	Established dressing Station. Rearranged billets. Rm	
8	7 motor ambulances & 17 N.C.Os & men M.T. A.S.C arrived and were taken on the strength.	Rm
9 " "	By orders of D.D.M.S. VII Corps. Two officers were detailed to report to 11th & 12th Fd ambulances for 4 days instruction in the advanced dressing stations — Lts Mulkern & Montgomery	Rm
10 " "	The officers & men attended Divine Service.	Rm
11 " "	Routine.	Rm
12	Routine	Rm
13	O.C. & Lieut Ferguson proceeded to 11th & 12th Fd Ambulances for 4 days instruction. Lieuts Mulkern & Montgomery rejoined.	Rm Rm
14 "	Routine	
15	Capt Pinion & Lieut Gray proceeded to 11th & 12th Field Ambulances for 4 days instruction. O.C. & Lieut Ferguson rejoined.	Rm.

Army Form C. 2118.

Instructions regarding War Diaries and Intelligence Summaries are contained in F. S. Regs., Part II. and the Staff Manual respectively. Title pages will be prepared in manuscript.

WAR DIARY
or
INTELLIGENCE SUMMARY

(Erase heading not required.)

Hour, Date, Place	Summary of Events and Information	Remarks and references to Appendices
16th Oct. 1916 BERTANGLES.	109th Bde Field day. The 109th Field Ambulance took part.	Rm
10.30AM 17 " "	The Unit paraded with 9th R. Innis. Fus to hear a lecture by 3rd Army ~~Gas Sup~~ Chemical adviser, after which the unit donned old pattern gas helmets and filed through a room in which a cylinder was discharging chlorine gas.	Rm
18 " "	Routine. Received orders to move to COISY ~~tomorrow~~ tomorrow.	Rm
2PM 19 " "	The unit marched off.	Rm
3PM 19 " " COISY	arrived. Established dressing station.	Rm
20 " " "	Capt Johnston & Lt Dickson proceeded to 11th & 12th Fd Ambulances for 4 days instruction. Capt Pinion & Lt Gray rejoined.	Rm
" "	Received orders to move off on following morning at 8.50 A.M. to new billeting area & to take part in Divisional Exercise.	Rm
8.50AM 20" " "	marched off across country in rear of 109th Bde to NADOURS where orders from 109 Bde were received to billet in BEAUVAL.	Rm
6PM " " BEAUVAL	arrived. Established dressing station.	Rm
21 " "	Routine.	Rm
22 " "	Routine.	Rm
23 " "	Capt Johnston and Lt Dickson rejoined. Routine	Rm
24 " "	Routine	Rm
25 " "	Lieut Russell proceeded to 11th Fd Amb. for 4 days instruction.	Rm
26 " "	Routine	Rm
27 " "	Routine	Rm
28 " "	Lt Russell rejoined	Rm
29 " "	Routine	Rm
30 " "	Routine	Rm
31 " "	Pte Quin struck off strength. Evacuated to C.C.S.	Rm.

Nov 1915

36th Div

F 195/1

109th F.A.
Vol 2

121
7928

Confidential

War Diary

of

109th Fd Ambulance

From 1st Nov 1915 To 30th Nov 1915

VOLUME ~~I~~ 2

R. Magill
Capt RAMC
Cmdg 109th Field Ambulance.

Army Form C. 2118.

Instructions regarding War Diaries and Intelligence Summaries are contained in F. S. Regs., Part II. and the Staff Manual respectively. Title pages will be prepared in manuscript.

WAR DIARY
or
~~INTELLIGENCE SUMMARY~~

(Erase heading not required.)

Hour, Date, Place	Summary of Events and Information	Remarks and references to Appendices
1. November 15 BEAUVAL	3 patients remaining Rw	
2 " "	" " " Rw	
3 " "	2 " " Rw	
4 " "	9 " " Lieut M. S. Boucher A.S.C. admitted & transferred to 4 C.C. station. (Gastritis). Rw	
5 " "	11 " " 40925 Private T. Bowden evacuated to Base, & Struck off. Rw	
6 " "	10 " " Baths for troops in BEAUVAL i.e. 2 Battalions 109th Bde and Field ambulance opened by this unit; capable of bathing 350 men per day. Boilers built in brick and all Equipment purchased locally. Provision is made by means of a force pump and sprays to give each man a shower bath of clean water. Lieut Gray in charge. No 54761 Private Smith J.R. is attached to Div. H.Q. unit for rations & accomodation. Rw	
7th " "	4 patients remaining. Rw	
8" " "	7 " " . Lieut Mulkern is detailed to attend Inspection Room at Pensionett JEAN D'ARC, RUE D'ARRAS, DOULLENS at 9 A.M. daily to see sick of Div. Supply Column and 48th Mobile Vet. Section Rw	
9" " "	13 patients remaining Capt to F. H. Pelly 9th R Innis Fus. admitted & evacuated to 4 C.C. St. (Bronchitis) Rw	
10th " "	14. patients remaining. Wire received from A.D.M.S. Begins Detail Lieut MULKERN H.C. to report himself forthwith to O.C. 9th R. Innis Fus. for medical charge vice Lieut CRAIG A.N. who is posted to 109 F. Amb. Handing and taking over reports and certificates to be sent to this office Ends. Rw	

[illegible] Capt RAMC

[illegible] FIELD AMBULANCE Station No. 185 36th ULSTER DIV.

Instructions regarding War Diaries and Intelligence Summaries are contained in F. S. Regs., Part II. and the Staff Manual respectively. Title pages will be prepared in manuscript.

WAR DIARY
or
~~INTELLIGENCE SUMMARY~~
(Erase heading not required.)

Army Form C. 2118.

Hour, Date, Place	Summary of Events and Information	Remarks and references to Appendices
11 November 1916. BEAUVAL	a laundry was opened by the unit capable of washing 350 sets of underclothing and arrangements made to provide each man using the baths with a clean set of underclothing. Capt Pinion in charge. 11 patients remaining	Rm
12 " "	The Divisional Commander inspected the unit & expressed himself as highly pleased. 12 patients remaining Rm	
13 " "	8 patients remaining. Rm	
14 " "	18 patients remaining Rm	
15 "	35 patients remaining Rm	
16 "	40 patients remaining. Rm	
17 "	31 " " Rm	
18 "	33 " [illegible]. Lt. W J K NOON 9th R. Inniskillings admitted and evacuated to 19 C.C.Stn. Rm	
19 "	30 patients remaining. Rm	
20	From this date 13th Corps takes over this Division. 27 patients remaining. Rm	
21 " "	19 Patients remaining. Rm	
22 " "	23 " " Rm	
23 " "	22 " " Rm	

R. ... Capt RAMC

1080 FIELD AMBULANCE Station No. 185 36th ULSTER DIV.

1247 W 3299 200,000 (E) 8/14 J.B.C.& A. Forms/C. 2118/11.

Instructions regarding War Diaries and Intelligence Summaries are contained in F. S. Regs., Part II. and the Staff Manual respectively. Title pages will be prepared in manuscript.

WAR DIARY

or

~~INTELLIGENCE SUMMARY~~

(Erase heading not required.)

Army Form C. 2118.

Hour, Date, Place	Summary of Events and Information	Remarks and references to Appendices
24th November '15 BEAUVAL	29 Patients remaining. The temporary Commissioned Officers of the unit attended a lecture by Bde Major 109th Bde on Procedure of F.G. Courts Martial & sentences in the field.	Rm
25th " "	24 Patients remaining. The Officers of the unit attended a lecture by the Chemical Advisor 3rd Army, at MONTRELET. Orders received to move on 27th November to PONT REMY billeting on the night of 27th–28th at St HILAIRE, and to evacuate all patients ~~[illegible]~~ unable to march to C.C.S.	Rm.
26 " "	Order received that as St HILAIRE would not be vacated by the troops quartered there until 28th. The Field Ambulance would billet the night of 27th–28th at LONGVILLERS. Patients remaining 27	Rm.
27 "	Marched off at 10.30 A.M. The O.C. going on in advance to arrange billets. The unit arrived at LONGVILLERS at 3 P.M. Patients remaining 5. Roads very good	Rm
28 " LONGVILLERS	Marched off at 9 A.M. arrived PONT REMY at 3.PM. Patients remaining nil. Cold dry weather Roads good.	Rm
29 " PONT REMY	Received orders to open Div. Rest Station. Patients remaining 1	Rm
30 " " "	Div. Rest Station opened in Cooperative stores, accommodation for 200 patients. Patients remaining 6.	Rm

R. Meville Capt RAMC

Confidential

War Diary

of

109th Fd Ambulance

From 1st Dec 1915 To 31st Dec 1915

Volume

III

R Moore

Capt RAMC

Cmdg 109 Fd Amb.

Instructions regarding War Diaries and Intelligence Summaries are contained in F. S. Regs., Part II. and the Staff Manual respectively. Title pages will be prepared in manuscript.

WAR DIARY
or
~~INTELLIGENCE SUMMARY.~~
(Erase heading not required.)

Army Form C. 2118.

Place	Date	Hour	Summary of Events and Information	Remarks and references to Appendices
PONT REMY	1.12.15		Under instructions of D.D.M.S. 13th Corps Lieut. Dickson + Corporal Porter are detailed for duty with Hd.Quarters of the Corps. Patients remaining 12.	Rm
	2.12.15		Cpl. Porter and 4 men transferred to 76th Sanitary Section. 5 men retransferred from Sanitary Section to this Unit. Patients remaining 32. Major J.E. Gunning 14 R.I. Rifles. Evacuated to C.C.S. Fract. Fibula	Rm
"	3.12.15		Lieut Montgomery detailed to proceed to LONG as M.O. i/c 153 Bde R.F.A. vice Lieut Gavin attached to this unit for instruction. Patients remaining 43	Rm
"	4.12.15		Routine. Ptes Sutcliffe and Matthews taken on the Strength. Capt. G.A. Hops. Staff Captain Ulster Divisional Artillery. Evacuated C.C.S. neurasthenia. Patients remaining ~~4~~ 44	Rm
"	5.12.15		Routine. Patients remaining 63	Rm
"	6.12.15		One N.C.O. and ten men proceeded to Highland C.C.S. for 14 days instruction. Patients remaining 66.	Rm
"	7.12.15		Baths and Laundry opened in ROUTE D'ABBEVILLE by the unit for all troops in PONT REMY Lieut Gray in charge. Bath capable of accommodating 150 men daily. Patients remaining 78.	Rm
	8.12.15		Routine. Dining Room at rear of Hospital opened for all personnel. 5 stoves purchased for hospital. Patients remaining 69.	Rm
	9.12.15		Routine. Band beat retreat through the town and attracted a large crowd of the inhabitants Patients remaining 75.	Rm

Instructions regarding War Diaries and Intelligence Summaries are contained in F. S. Regs., Part II. and the Staff Manual respectively. Title pages will be prepared in manuscript.

WAR DIARY
or
~~INTELLIGENCE~~ SUMMARY.

(*Erase heading not required.*)

Army Form C. 2118.

Place	Date	Hour	Summary of Events and Information	Remarks and references to Appendices
PONT REMY	10.12.15		Lt. A. N. Craig detailed to report to D.M.S. BOULONGUE & struck off strength.	
			Lieut Dickson returned from XIII Corps. Patients remaining 83.	Rue
"	11.12.15		Capt. Mercier reported his arrival and taken on the strength vice Lt. A.N. Craig.	
			Patients remaining 74.	Rue
"	12 " "		Lieut Dickson relieved Lt. Montgomery RAMC. 153 Bde R.F.A. Capt Pinion proceeded	
			to Div. Artillery Hd. Quarters to advise on baths. Patients remaining 83	RMM.
"	13 "		Medical inspection of the unit. The men were practised with gas helmets.	
			Patients remaining 64	Rue
"	14 "		Routine, Corporal Morton returned from XIII Corps. Patients remaining 61	Rue
"	15 "		Inspection by A.D.M.S. who expressed his appreciation of the appearance, smartness +	Rue
			cleanliness of the personnel and transport. also of the Hospital + billets. Patients remaining 63	
"	16 "		Lieut Gavin proceeded to 14th R. Ir. Rif for temporary duty as M.O. i/c. Authority A.D.M.S.	Rue
			Patients remaining 57.	
"	17 "		Routine. Patients remaining 66.	Rue
"	18 "		Capt Mercier granted leave from 18th to 2nd prox. Patients remaining 59.	Rue
"	19 "		L/cpl Hall granted leave till 29th Dec. Patients remaining 68	Rue

1577 Wt. W10791/1773 500,000 1/15 D. D. & L. A.D.S.S./Forms/C. 2118.

Instructions regarding War Diaries and Intelligence Summaries are contained in F. S. Regs., Part II. and the Staff Manual respectively. Title pages will be prepared in manuscript.

WAR DIARY
or
~~INTELLIGENCE SUMMARY.~~
(Erase heading not required.)

Army Form C. 2118.

Place	Date	Hour	Summary of Events and Information	Remarks and references to Appendices
PONT REMY	20.12.15		Lt & Qrmaster Chester granted leave from 21-12-15 to 30-12-15. 5 men proceeded to Highland CCS for 14 days instruction. 1 N.C.O & ten men returned from HIGHLAND C.C.S. patients remaining 57.	Rm
	21 "		Routine. patients remaining 53	Rm
	22 "		one man Pte Berry taken on strength patients remaining 37	Rm
	23 "		Routine. Patients remaining 29.	Rm
	24 "		Routine. Pte Wallace D. evacuated to CCS & struck off strength. Patients remaining 35	Rm
	25 "		Holiday. Hospital was tastefully decorated by a few of the patients. By the generosity of the British Red Cross the patients were provided with turkeys plum pudding, fruits and many varied luxuries. The personnel were provided by the Officers with like fare. a barrel of beer was also on tap from which the patients received their share. The A.D.M.S. kindly visited the patients & personnel at dinner when his health was enthusiastically honoured. Patients remaining 44	Rm
	26 "		Routine patients remaining 41.	Rm
	27		Lt Dickson proceeded to 16 R Ir Rif as M.O. i/c. patients remaining 49	Rm
	28		Inspection by Divisional General who saw that the unit was most excellent	

1577 Wt. W10791/1773 500,000 1/15 D. D. & L. A.D.S.S./Forms/C. 2118.

Instructions regarding War Diaries and Intelligence Summaries are contained in F. S. Regs., Part II. and the Staff Manual respectively. Title pages will be prepared in manuscript.

WAR DIARY
or
~~INTELLIGENCE~~ SUMMARY.

(Erase heading not required.)

Army Form C. 2118.

Place	Date	Hour	Summary of Events and Information	Remarks and references to Appendices
PONT REMY	28.12.15		Especially the transport which he characterised as the best he had ever seen. He also expressed himself as being very pleased with the arrangements which had been made for the comfort of the patients + personnell. Patients remaining 47.	[illegible]
	29.		Routine Patients remaining 38.	[illegible]
	30		Capts. Pinion + Ferguson granted leave till 12-1-16. Patients remaining 30	[illegible]
	31"		A/Sgt. Pugsley M.T.A.S.C. and Pt. Sloan evacuated and struck off strength. Patients remaining 30.	[illegible]

109th Field Ambulance

Jan }
Feb } 1916

March }
April } 1916

|
Dec 1918

109th 7a.
Vol: 4

Confidential

War Diary

of

109th Fd Ambulance

From 1st January

To 31st January 1916

(Volume IV)

R. Magill
Capt RAMC
Cmdg 109 Fd Ambulance

Instructions regarding War Diaries and Intelligence Summaries are contained in F. S. Regs., Part II. and the Staff Manual respectively. Title pages will be prepared in manuscript.

WAR DIARY

or

~~INTELLIGENCE SUMMARY~~.

(Erase heading not required.)

Army Form C. 2118.

Place	Date	Hour	Summary of Events and Information	Remarks and references to Appendices
PONTREMY	1-1-16		Revd J. KNOWLES C.F. reports his arrival for duty & is taken on strength. Lt & Quartermaster CHESTER reported his return from leave of absence. Corporal TOZER M.T. A.S.C. having reported for duty from 36th Div. Supply Col. is taken on the strength. Patients remaining. 40	[illegible]
..	2-1-16		The Band under Staff Sergt Gillespie proceeded to 3rd Army School of Instruction for duty for some days. Patients remaining 37.	[illegible]
..	3-1-16		1 N.C.O. and 9 men detailed to proceed to South Midland C.C.S for 14 days instruction. Capt. MERCIER reported his arrival from leave of absence, and is detailed to proceed to LONG as M.O. i/c 153 Bde R.F.A. vice Lieut MONTGOMERY who returns to this unit. The former is struck off the strength. Patients remaining 45	[illegible]
..	4-1-16		Lieut. MONTGOMERY reports his arrival for duty. 5 men returned from 14 days instruction at HIGHLAND C.C.S. Patients remaining 50	[illegible]
..	5-1-16		Routine. Patients remaining 47.	[illegible]
..	6-1-16		M. DESPICHT Interpreter granted 6 days leave. 57.	[illegible]
	7-1-16		Cpl McCurdy granted 9 days leave of absence. At the request of A.D.M.S. 55th Division this unit will collect & deal with all sick of that Division pending the arrival of	

1577 Wt. W10791/1773 500,000 1/15 D. D. & L. A.D.S.S./Forms/C. 2118.

Army Form C. 2118.

Instructions regarding War Diaries and Intelligence Summaries are contained in F. S. Regs., Part II. and the Staff Manual respectively. Title pages will be prepared in manuscript.

WAR DIARY
or
~~INTELLIGENCE~~ SUMMARY.
(Erase heading not required.)

Place	Date	Hour	Summary of Events and Information	Remarks and references to Appendices
PONT REMY	7-1-16		its medical units. Patients remaining. 56	Rm
	8-1-16		Routine patients remaining. 46.	Rm
"	9-1-16		Routine Patients remaining 54.	Rm
"	10-1-16		Cpl Morton takes over charge of baths vice Sergt. McCann. Patients remaining 62.	Rm
"	11-1-16		2 motor ambulances borrowed from X M.A.C. to assist in collecting sick from 55th Division. Patients remaining 47.	Rm
"	12-1-16		The band under Staff Sergt. GILLESPIE returned from duty with 3rd Army School. patients remaining. 40.	Rm
"	13-1-16		Captains PINION & FERGUSON returned from 14 days leave. patients remaining 41.	Rm
"	14-1-16		Capt. F.G. JOHNSTON granted leave of absence Patients remaining 38	Rm
	15-1-16		Routine Patients remaining 43 Capt. Pinion + B Section proceeded to BERTEAUCOURT to take over from 96 F. Ambulance	Rm
	16-1-16		Routine Patients remaining. 50. at BERTAUCOURT 51 patients.	Rm
	17-1-16		1 N.C.O + 4 men detailed to S. Md. CCS for 14 days instruction. 1 N.C.O + 4 men detailed to HIGHLAND C.C.S. for 14 days instruction. 1 N.C.O + 9 men returned from S. Md. CCS after 14 days instruction Patients remaining. 46. at BERTEAUCOURT 49.	Rm
.	18-1-16		Routine. Patients remaining. ~~4~~5 at BERTEAUCOURT 54.	Rm

1577 Wt. W10791/1773 500,000 1/15 D. D. & L. A.D.S.S./Forms/C. 2118.

Instructions regarding War Diaries and Intelligence Summaries are contained in F. S. Regs., Part II. and the Staff Manual respectively. Title pages will be prepared in manuscript.

WAR DIARY
or
~~INTELLIGENCE SUMMARY.~~
(Erase heading not required.)

Army Form C. 2118.

Place	Date	Hour	Summary of Events and Information	Remarks and references to Appendices
PONT REMY	19-1-16	10 AM.	Under orders from G.H.Q through A.D.M.S Lt + Q.Mst CHIESTER proceeded from LONGPRE' Rly station to report at MARSEILLES for duty with the 1/3 N. Md Field Ambulance proceeding overseas. Cpl McCurdy returned off leave.	
"	"	10.30 Am	The unit marched off. Lieut Montgomery + 6 men left as a rear party.	
BERTEAUCOURT	"	3 PM.	The unit arrived. Roads very heavy. Weather good. Patients remaining 70	Rm
"	20 "		Took over Co-operative store as Hospital in addition to existing accommodation. Lieut Dixon reported his arrival for duty, & taken on strength. Patients remaining 92	Rm
"	21 "		Inspection by A.D.M.S patients remaining 76	Rm
"	22 "		Capt PINION, + Lieut DIXON with 33 men + section equipment proceeded to CAYEUX to establish a hospital for the Divisional Artillery who are proceeding there for a few weeks. Patients remaining 83	Rm
"	23 "		The Primate visited the C.O this afternoon, having addressed the patients + personnel he had tea with the Officers. His Grace expressed as being very pleased with the appearance of the personnel and with the arrangements made for the comfort of the sick patients remaining 96	Rm.
"	24.		Routine. patients remaining. 76	Rm

1577 Wt. W10791/1773 500,000 1/15 D. D. & L. A.D.S.S./Forms/C. 2118.

Instructions regarding War Diaries and Intelligence Summaries are contained in F. S. Regs., Part II. and the Staff Manual respectively. Title pages will be prepared in manuscript.

WAR DIARY

or

~~INTELLIGENCE SUMMARY~~.

(Erase heading not required.)

Army Form C. 2118.

Place	Date	Hour	Summary of Events and Information	Remarks and references to Appendices
BERTEAUCOURT	25.1.16		Routine. Patients remaining 77 Capt Pinion reported having arrived at CAYEUX. 24.1.16	Rer
"	26 "		Routine. Patients remaining 80	Rer
"	27 "		Routine. Patients remaining 63	Rer
"	28		5 reinforcements reported for duty & taken on Strength. Patients remaining 63	Rer
"	29"		Sergt. Major HARLAND & Pte FEELY granted 9 days leave. Patients remaining 57	Rer
"	30"		Capt Johnston reported his arrival off leave. 1 N.C.O + 4 men returned from 14 days instruction at S. Mid C.C.S. 1 N.C.O + 4 men returned from HIGHLAND C.C.S after undergoing 14 days instruction. Patients remaining 60	Rer
"	31st		2 men Evacuated. Patients remaining 68	Rer

1577 Wt. W10791/1773 500,000 1/15 D. D. & L. A.D.S.S./Forms/C. 2118.

Confidential

War Diary

Of

109th Field Amb^ce

From 1st Feb 1916 To 29th Feb 1916

(Volume) 5

R. Magill
Major RAMC
Cmdg 109 Fd. Ambulance

109th 7a.

Vol. ~~4~~, 5

Instructions regarding War Diaries and Intelligence Summaries are contained in F. S. Regs., Part II. and the Staff Manual respectively. Title pages will be prepared in manuscript.

WAR DIARY

or

~~INTELLIGENCE SUMMARY.~~

(Erase heading not required.)

Army Form C. 2118.

Place	Date	Hour	Summary of Events and Information	Remarks and references to Appendices
BERTEAUCOURT	1.2.16		Lieut GRAY granted leave of absence from 3.2.16 till 11.2.16. Capt PESEL reported his arrival from 10th F.A. and taken on Strength. Capt FERGUSON detailed to proceed to CAYEUX as M.O. i/c 154 (HOW) Bde R.F.A. Patients remaining 57	Rm
	2.2.16		ROUTINE. patients remaining 45.	Rm
	3.2.16		Pte McCORMICK returned from duty with X Corps H.Q. patients remaining 54.	Rm
	4.2.16		Routine patients remaining 70	Rm
	5.2.16		Routine Patients remaining 70	Rm
	6.2.16		Cpl MORTON & 12 men detailed to proceed to VAL DE MAISON as an advance party. Patients remaining. 94. Privates Cairns & Black granted 9 days leave	Rm
	7.2.16		Routine patients remaining 99.	Rm
	8.2.16		Ptes Davidson & Bryson detailed for duty to 109th Bde Machine Gun Section and struck off strength Patients remaining 100	Rm
	9.2.16		S.M. Harland & Pte Feely returned from leave. The unit moved to VAL DE MAISON where accommodation for sick was found in an empty Farm House. Patients remaining 86	Rm
VAL DE MAISON	10.2.16		Ptes Tennant & Forbes granted 9 days leave. patients remaining 63	Rm

Instructions regarding War Diaries and Intelligence Summaries are contained in F. S. Regs., Part II. and the Staff Manual respectively. Title pages will be prepared in manuscript.

WAR DIARY
or
~~INTELLIGENCE SUMMARY~~.
(Erase heading not required.)

Army Form C. 2118.

Place	Date	Hour	Summary of Events and Information	Remarks and references to Appendices
VAL DE MAISON	11.2.16		Routine patients remaining 49	[illegible]
	12.2.16		Routine patients remaining 48.	[illegible]
	13.2.16		Lt. Gray returned from leave and is detailed as temporary M.O. i/c 16 R. I Rifs. at RAINCHEVAL. patients remaining 44	[illegible]
	14.2.16		Lt. Russell + 5 NCOs + men granted leave 9 days. Patients remaining 25	[illegible]
	15.2.16		Lt. + Qr. Mr. CHESTER reported his arrival for duty from 46th Div and is taken on Strength. Patients remaining 25	[illegible]
	16.2.16		One NCO + 12 men detailed under C.R.E. at VAUCHELLES-LES-AUTHIE patients remaining 27.	[illegible]
	17.2.16		Routine. patients remaining 24	[illegible]
	18.2.16		ROUTINE. patients remaining 19.	[illegible]
	19.2.16		Capt PESEL + Lieut MONTGOMERY detailed to proceed to CAYEUX to take charge of the Section of this Unit vice Capt PINION + Capt DIXON reporting sick. one reinforcement taken on Strength. patients remaining 23	[illegible]
	20.2.16		Routine patients remaining 27.	[illegible]
	21.2.16		2 men returned from leave. 1 W.O. 3 NCOs + 2 men granted leave 9 days. One NCO + Eighteen men detailed for duty with Town Major BEAUVAL	[illegible]

1577 Wt. W10791/1773 500,000 1/15 D. D. & L. A.D.S.S./Forms/C. 2118.

Instructions regarding War Diaries and Intelligence Summaries are contained in F. S. Regs., Part II. and the Staff Manual respectively. Title pages will be prepared in manuscript.

WAR DIARY
or
~~INTELLIGENCE SUMMARY~~.
(Erase heading not required.)

Army Form C. 2118.

Place	Date	Hour	Summary of Events and Information	Remarks and references to Appendices
VALDEMAISON	21-2-16		Patients remaining 5. Lt Q^r Mr CHESTER appointed Town Major of VAUCHELLES.	Rm
"	22-2-16		Lieuts ROSE + CAMPBELL reported their arrival for duty from ETAPLES.	
		2 PM	The unit moved at 2 P.M. to VAUCHELLES-LES-AUTHIE ~~[illegible]~~.	
VAUCHELLES	"	4.30 PM	arrived at VAUCHELLES. Patients remaining 6.	Rm
"	23-2-16		Capts PINION + DIXON evacuated to No 3 General Hospital LE TREPORT. Patients remaining 4.	Rm
	24-2-16		1 NCO + 18 men returned from BEAUVAL. Lt Russell + party returned from leave. Patients remaining 5	Rm
	25-2-16		Routine patients remaining 5.	Rm
	26-2-16		Routine patients remaining 3.	Rm
	27-2-16		One Motor Ambulance detailed to proceed to LA VICOGNE for duty under M.O i/c 36 Div. Amm. Col. Patients remaining 5.	Rm
	28-2-16		Routine. Patients remaining 6.	Rm
	29-2-16		Capt PESEL + Lieut MONTGOMERY with section from CAYEUX reported their arrival. This party left CAYEUX on 25-2-16 + billeted that night at PONT REMY a 25 mile march in a snow storm. Under orders from D.H.Q. they remained in PONT REMY till 28th the roads being under snow. They moved to PERNOIS on 28th marching to VAUCHELLES today. Patients remaining 3.	Rm

109 F Amb
Vol 6

36th Div

Confidential

War Diary

of

109th Fd Ambulance

From 1st March 1916 To 31st March 1916

March 1916

(Volume)
VI

J. G. Johnston Capt.
for O.C. 109th Field Ambce.

Instructions regarding War Diaries and Intelligence Summaries are contained in F. S. Regs., Part II. and the Staff Manual respectively. Title pages will be prepared in manuscript.

Army Form C. 2118.

WAR DIARY
or
INTELLIGENCE SUMMARY.
(Erase heading not required.)

Place	Date	Hour	Summary of Events and Information	Remarks and references to Appendices
VAUCHELLES-LES-AUTHIE	1. March 16		Routine, Thaw scheme in force, all lorry traffic stopped. Supply wagon drawing supplies from DOULLENS, Roads in very bad condition. No. of Patients remaining 7.	[illegible]
"	2 "		Routine. Thaw continues. No of patients remaining 7.	[illegible]
"	3 "		Routine " " Patients remaining 11.	[illegible]
	4 "	4.P.M.	Order received from A.D.M.S. to move tomorrow to BERTRANCOURT and to relieve 108th Fd Amb's advanced dressing stations at MAILLY-MAILLET and AUCHONVILLERS also to take over 4 collecting posts of the line held by the 107th Bde	
"	4.	9.A.M.	Capt. Johnston. Lieuts. Gray & Rose with B section proceeded to MAILLY MAILLET to take over from 108th F.A as per yesterdays orders.	
		12 noon	Remainder of unit left. Wire received from A.D.M.S notifying cancellation of Thaw scheme	
BERTRANCOURT		2. P.M	Remainder of unit arrived, Roads very difficult, Heavy snow. Established main dressing station in Estaminet vacated this morning by a Fd Amb of 48 Division.	
		6. P.M	C.O. proceeded to MAILLY to inspect arrangements. On his arrival Capt Johnston reported that the relief had been completed by 4 P.M, Capt. Johnston taking charge of A.D.S at MAILLY, Lieuts Gray and Rose at AUCHONVILLERS, One N.C.O & 3 men posted to WHITE FARM collecting post, one N.C.O. & 3 men to THE CHATEAU C.P. One N.C.O and 7 men to –	[illegible]

1577 Wt. W10791/1773 500,000 1/15 D. D. & L. A.D.S.S./Forms/C. 2118.

Instructions regarding War Diaries and Intelligence Summaries are contained in F. S. Regs., Part II. and the Staff Manual respectively. Title pages will be prepared in manuscript.

WAR DIARY
or
INTELLIGENCE SUMMARY.
(*Erase heading not required.*)

Army Form C. 2118.

Place	Date	Hour	Summary of Events and Information	Remarks and references to Appendices
		Continued		
BERTRANCOURT	4.3.16		C.P. Dug out at TENDERLOIN. 1 N.C.O at SERRE ROAD C.P. with 6 men.	
	"	7 PM	Wire sent to A.D.M.S. notifying move and all dispositions completed.	
		8 PM	C.O. returned to BERTRANCOURT finding road between MAILLY and BERTRANCOURT blocked by motor lorries stuck in snow. Patients remaining Nil.	[illegible]
"	5 "		Routine. Accommodation prepared for 150 casualties. Patients remaining 6.	[illegible]
"	6 "		Routine. Patients remaining 8.	[illegible]
	7 "		Admitted first wounded (1 officer and 6 other ranks). Lieuts Hennessy and Lindsay reported arrival for duty and taken on strength. Lieut Lindsay detailed for duty at A.D.S. MAILLY. M. DESPICHT Interpreter transferred by French Mission to VIII Corps. Patients remaining 16.	[illegible]
	8 "		Cpls. McCurdy R and Morton J promoted acting Sergeants with pay. A working party of 14 men detailed to excavate 2 dug outs on MAILLY–AUCHONVILLERS Road. These dug outs are intended as shelters in the event of the A.D.S at AUCHONVILLERS being rendered untenable by shell fire. Patients remaining 12	[illegible]
	9 "		Routine. Patients remaining 12.	[illegible]
	10 "		2 reinforcements received. Weekly conference of 7th Amb's O.C. at A.D.M.S office.	[illegible]

1577 Wt. W10791/1773 500,000 1/15 D. D. & L. A.D.S.S./Forms/C. 2118.

Instructions regarding War Diaries and Intelligence Summaries are contained in F. S. Regs., Part II. and the Staff Manual respectively. Title pages will be prepared in manuscript.

WAR DIARY
or
INTELLIGENCE SUMMARY.
(Erase heading not required.)

Army Form C. 2118.

Place	Date	Hour	Summary of Events and Information	Remarks and references to Appendices
	Continued			
BERTRANCOURT	10-3-16	–	patients remaining 11	[illegible]
	11-3-16		Lieut W. D. Rose detailed to proceed to 15th R. Ir. Rifles to take over temporary medical charge. Lieut Lindsay to relieve Lieut Rose at AUCHONVILLERS. Lieut Hennessy to relieve Lieut Lindsay at MAILLY. patients remaining 27	[illegible]
	12 "	10.30 AM	Personnel practised wearing gas helmets while working. Helmets worn for 2 hours.	
		11.30 AM	Taube dropped bomb close to A.D.S. MAILLY. no harm resulting beyond all windows smashed. patients remaining 34.	[illegible]
	13 "	10.30 AM	Medical Board consisting of C.O. and Capt. Johnston assembled at A.D.S MAILLY to examine 4 temporary Commissioned officers for commissions in regular Army. patients remaining 25	[illegible]
	14 "		Working party of 1 N.C.O. & 9 men attached to 11 R Innis. Fus at MARTINSART. Issue of 12 pairs Gum boots thigh approved by Divisional Commander.	
		12 noon	3 bombs dropped by enemy aeroplane close to SERRE ROAD C.P. breaking all the windows in building. patients remaining 31	[illegible]
	15 "		Routine. patients remaining 22	[illegible]
	16 "		Lieut. Rose rejoined from 15th R. Ir. Rifles. patients remaining 31.	[illegible]
	17 "		Routine. patients remaining 23.	[illegible]

1577 Wt. W10791/1773 500,000 1/15 D. D. & L. A.D.S.S./Forms/C. 2118.

Instructions regarding War Diaries and Intelligence Summaries are contained in F. S. Regs., Part II. and the Staff Manual respectively. Title pages will be prepared in manuscript.

WAR DIARY
or
~~INTELLIGENCE~~ SUMMARY.
(Erase heading not required.)

Army Form C. 2118.

Place	Date	Hour	Summary of Events and Information	Remarks and references to Appendices
BERTRANCOURT	18.3.16		Lt. Hennessy detailed for duty with 9th R I Rif as temporary M.O in charge. patients remaining 14.	Rm
"	19.3.16		Corporal Rowley + Pt. Fullerton proceeded to base for munition test. patients remaining 22	Rm.
	20.3.16		one NCO and 19 men detailed for duty as a working party with 7th R.E. Park ACHEUX.	
		2.15 PM	Inspection by D M S. of 4th Army of the unit H^d quarters and A D Ss patients remaining 32.	Rm
"	21. "		Capt Johnston detailed to take charge at BERTRANCOURT vice C.O proceeding on leave tomorrow, Lieut Gray to MAILLY vice Capt. Johnston. Capt Pexel to AUCHONVILLERS vice Lt Gray. patients remaining 29	Rm
"	22.3.16		Major R. Magill C.O. of Ambulance granted leave of absence from 23.3.16 to 1.4.16 Patients remaining 20	J.G.J.
"	23.3.16		Lieut. J.P. Montgomery, granted leave of absence from 24.3.16 to 1.4.16 Lieut R.B. Hennessey, rejoined this unit from temporary duty as M.O. i/c 9th Bn. R. Ir. Rif. and detailed for duty at the A.D.S. MAILLY. Capt Cumming, Lieut Forbes, + 3 N.C.O's reported arrival from 93rd Fld. Amb. for 3 days instruction. Patients remaining 20	J.G.J.

1577 Wt. W10791/1773 500,000 1/15 D. D. & L. A.D.S.S./Forms/C. 2118.

Instructions regarding War Diaries and Intelligence Summaries are contained in F. S. Regs., Part II. and the Staff Manual respectively. Title pages will be prepared in manuscript.

WAR DIARY
or
~~INTELLIGENCE~~ SUMMARY.
(Erase heading not required.)

Army Form C. 2118.

Place	Date	Hour	Summary of Events and Information	Remarks and references to Appendices
BERTRANCOURT	24.3.16		Lieut. R.B. Hennessy detailed for duty as Medical Officer in charge 9th Batt. R. Ir. Rif. vice Capt. T Grimson. Patients remaining 12	JGJ
"	25.3.16		Capt T. Grimson reported his arrival for duty with this Unit from 9th Batt. R. Ir. Rif.	
			Lt. W. Russell detailed for duty at the A.D.S. MAILLY vice Lt. H Gray who returns to Ambulance Headquarters at BERTRANCOURT. Patients remaining 14.	JGJ
"	26.3.16		Routine – Patients remaining 13.	JGJ
"	27.3.16		Capt Cumming, Lt. Forbes, & 3 N.C.O's of 93rd Fld Amb, attached for instruction returned to their unit.	
			Secret orders received from A.D.M.S. that this unit will move to VARENNES on 29th inst on being relieved by the 95th Fld. Amb. of 31st Division. Advance party of 1 Officer & 20 men to be sent in advance tomorrow. Patients remaining 14	JGJ
"	28.3.16		Capt Grimson & 20 other ranks ~~detailed to~~ proceeded as advance party to VARENNES, to take over & prepare accommodation for the unit.	
			Lt Russell rejoined Headquarters of the Ambulance from duty at A.D.S. MAILLY. Patients remaining 23	JGJ
"	29.3.16	11 AM.	Capt. Pesel, & Lt Lindsay with B. section rejoined Headquarters, after being relieved by the 95th Field Ambulance, & having handed over the A.D.S's at MAILLY-MAILLET and AUCHONVILLERS & the C.P.S held by this unit.	
"	"	12.30 PM	Unit left BERTRANCOURT, having handed over to 95th Field Ambulance	
VARENNES	"	2 p.m.	Unit arrived at VARENNES & took up quarters in Hutments. Patients remaining Nil.	JGJ

2353 Wt. W2544/1454 700,000 5/15 D. D. & L. A.D.S.S./Forms/C. 2118.

Instructions regarding War Diaries and Intelligence Summaries are contained in F. S. Regs., Part II. and the Staff Manual respectively. Title pages will be prepared in manuscript.

WAR DIARY
or
INTELLIGENCE SUMMARY.
(Erase heading not required.)

Army Form C. 2118.

Place	Date	Hour	Summary of Events and Information	Remarks and references to Appendices
VARENNES	30.3.16		Order received from A.D.M.S. to collect sick from VARENNES & HEDAUVILLE. Men employed in covering Hutments with tarpaulins, erecting cookhouses etc. Snowstorm. Patients remaining nil	J.G.J.
"	31.3.16		Routine Patients remaining nil	J.G.J.

J.G. Johnston Capt RAMC
for O.C. 109th Field Amb.

April 1916.

Confidential

War Diary

of

109th Fd Ambulance

Volume 1

From 1st April 1916 To 30th April 1916

36th Div

R. [illegible]
Major
Comdg 109th F.A.

109 Fd Amb
V 57

Instructions regarding War Diaries and Intelligence Summaries are contained in F. S. Regs., Part II. and the Staff Manual respectively. Title pages will be prepared in manuscript.

WAR DIARY
or
INTELLIGENCE SUMMARY.
(Erase heading not required.)

Army Form C. 2118.

Place	Date	Hour	Summary of Events and Information	Remarks and references to Appendices
VARENNES	1st April 1916		Lieut. H. Gray, detailed for duty as Medical Officer in charge of 9th Royal Inniskilling Fusiliers vice Capt. H. C. Mulhern, sick. Authy. – A. D. M. S. M. 157. 1. 4. 16.	
			1 Patient G. S. Wd. (accidental grenade sc[ex]plosion) died soon after admission. Patients remaining 2.	[illegible]
"	2.4.16		Lt. G. E. Lindsay detailed for temporary duty as Medical Officer in charge 172nd Bde. R.F.A. vice Lt. H. S. Smith, proceeding on leave. Authy. A.D.M.S. – M. 167. – 2. 4. 16.	
			Major R. Magill rejoined from leave of absence. Patients remaining 3.	[illegible]
	3"		Routine. Patients remaining 9.	[illegible]
	4"		1 NCO and 15 men returned from duty with C.R.E. Patients remaining 8.	[illegible]
	5"		Routine. Patients remaining 3.	[illegible]
	6"		Lt. Rose & party of 10 men detailed for road mending at MARTINSART. Capt. Grimson detailed to take over medical charge of 9th R. Innis Fus. vice Lt. Gray sick. Lt. Montgomery rejoined off leave. Cpl. Neville A.S.C. M.T. and one Pte. R.A.M.C. evacuated to No. 4. C.C.S. Patients remaining 4	[illegible]
	7"		Routine. Patients remaining 3.	[illegible]
	8"		9 men detailed for duty with 76th Sanitary Section. Patients remaining 4.	[illegible]
	9"		1 NCO + 5 men detailed to take over the Bde. Baths at MARTINSART. Patients remaining 10.	[illegible]
	10"		Capt. Pisel granted leave of absence from 11th to 19th inst to proceed to Scotland. Patients remaining 8.	[illegible]

Instructions regarding War Diaries and Intelligence Summaries are contained in F. S. Regs., Part II. and the Staff Manual respectively. Title pages will be prepared in manuscript.

WAR DIARY
or
~~INTELLIGENCE SUMMARY~~.
(Erase heading not required.)

Army Form C. 2118.

Place	Date	Hour	Summary of Events and Information	Remarks and references to Appendices
VARENNES	11th Sep 16		Lt Russell & 18 men proceeded to MARTINSART to take over the Advanced Dressing Station at that place from 108th F.A. Lt Montgomery and 16 men proceeded to take over the Collecting post at AUTHUILLE. The following arrangements were made for ~~the~~ collection & evacuation of wounded from the Right sector of the Divisional Front:- Four men in Regtl aid Post at GORDON CASTLE. This party to take over wounded from Regtl S.Bs and convey them to C.P. at PAISLEY AVENUE where 6 men are stationed The wounded are conveyed thence by wheeled stretcher to AUTHUILLE from which C.P. they are sent by wheeled stretcher to BLACK HORSE BRIDGE where they are met by motor Ambulance (stationed at AVELUY) and conveyed to 108th Main Dressing Station at FORCEVILLE Patients remaining 4.	Rm Rm
	12th		Lt Gray reported his arrival for duty from D.R. Station patients remaining 7	
			Lt Rose detailed to take	
	13th		Lt Russell detailed to take charge of road party vice Lt Rose detailed to take charge of A.D.S. MARTINSART. One N.C.O. & 12 men detailed to report to 109th Bde as a working party to complete the Regtl Aid Post in SPEYSIDE STREET on the East bank of RIVER ANCRE. Patients remaining 5	Rm Rm
	14th		Routine. Patients remaining 6. All leave stopped.	Rm
	15		Routine. Patients remaining 9.	
	16th		One NCO & 14 men detailed as a working party with O.C. 121st Co RE to complete the C.P. in S.E. corner of THIEPVAL WOOD. Patients remaining 5	Rm
	17th		Routine patients remaining 6	Rm
	18th		Routine patients remaining 6	Rm
	19		Capt Reed returned from leave. Patients remaining 5	Rm

2353 Wt. W2544/1454 700,000 5/15 D. D. & L. A.D.S.S./Forms/C. 2118.

Army Form C. 2118.

Instructions regarding War Diaries and Intelligence Summaries are contained in F. S. Regs., Part II. and the Staff Manual respectively. Title pages will be prepared in manuscript.

WAR DIARY
or
~~INTELLIGENCE SUMMARY.~~
(Erase heading not required.)

Place	Date	Hour	Summary of Events and Information	Remarks and references to Appendices
VARENNES	20.4.16		Lt Lindsay reported his arrival for duty from 172 Bde R.F.A. Patients remaining 10	Rm
"	21 "		~~[illegible]~~. C.P. at AUTHUILLE handed over to 32nd Div. Personnel & Equipment removed to SWALLOWS NEST in Q.36.c.6.6. (Ref Sheet 57 D) Patients remaining 11.	Rm
"	22 "		ROUTINE. Patients remaining 8	Rm
"	23 "		Routine Patients remaining 11	Rm
"	24 "		One Pte R.A.M.C. evacuated. Patients remaining 8.	Rm
"	25 "		Routine. Patients remaining 12	Rm
"	26 "		Lt Lindsay detailed as temporary M.O. to 11th R. Innis Fus. vice Capt Crosbie on leave. Lt H.E. Brown reported his arrival for duty. Patients remaining 4	Rm
"	27 "		Lt Rose detailed to proceed to ETAPLES to report to A.D.M.S there for duty and to be struck off the strength. Patients remaining 9.	Rm
"	28th "		Capt Pesel detailed to relieve Lt Rose at MARTINSART. Lt Brown detailed for duty with Lt Montgomery. Lt Gray detailed to see the morning sick at HAPONVILLE. Lt Gray is also detailed with a party to erect huts for the accommodation of wounded in view of eventualities at CLAIRFAYE. The necessary material to be drawn from R.Es. Patients remaining 7.	Rm
"	29 "		Personnel & Equipment of C.P. SWALLOWS NEST transferred to new C.P. at PAISLEY AVENUE. SWALLOWS NEST retained as an extra shelter. Patients Remaining 5	Rm
"	30		Routine, Patients remaining 4.	Rm

109. F. Amb
Vol 8
36th Div

Confidential

War Diary

of

109th Field Amb

From 1st May 1916 To 31st May 1916

Volume (VIII)

[illegible] Major RAMC
O.C. 109th F. Amb.

May 1916

Instructions regarding War Diaries and Intelligence Summaries are contained in F. S. Regs., Part II. and the Staff Manual respectively. Title pages will be prepared in manuscript.

WAR DIARY

or

~~INTELLIGENCE SUMMARY~~.

(Erase heading not required.)

Army Form C. 2118.

Place	Date	Hour	Summary of Events and Information	Remarks and references to Appendices
VARENNES	1-5-16		2 A.S.C Drivers sent for course of instruction to School of Farriery ABBEVILLE. patients remaining 4.	[illegible]
	2-5-16		3 men exchanged between Collecting Post at AUTHUILLE and A.D.S. MARTINSART. Patients remaining 9	[illegible]
	3-5-16		Routine patients remaining 8.	[illegible]
	4-5-16		One reinforcement received patients remaining 10	[illegible]
	5-5-16		Routine patients remaining 8	[illegible]
	6-5-16		Routine " 10	[illegible]
	7		Routine " 12	[illegible]
	8		One N.C.O. & 15 men detailed for duty with 150 Coy R.E. on work at Q.30 b 1.8. Sheet 57D. This work is for a R.A.P. for the left of Right sector. It is intended to make a dugout 36 feet long with elephants. Capt. Johnston granted leave from 10.5.16 to 18.5.16. patients remaining 16. A raid by the 9 Royal Innis Fusiliers on the enemy trenches ~~by the~~ last night was highly successful but on returning to their own trenches the raiding party was caught by the enemy's barrage fire and suffered 85 casualties of these 18 were killed the remaining 67 together with 10 of 10th Royal Innis Fus. & 5 of other units a total of 82 wounded were very efficiently dealt with & evacuated by Lieut Montgomery & his staff under heavy fire. In the afternoon the Brigadier General Cmdg 109 Bde complimented Lt Montgomery & thanked him for his good work.	[illegible]
	9-5-16		Routine patients remaining 13	[illegible]
	10-5-16		Lt Lindsay reported his arrival for duty from 11th R Innis Fus. Patients remaining 7.	[illegible]
	11-5-16		The following was received from A.D.M.S. this morning "The officer Commanding 108 F.A. with reference to the evacuation of sick from the line on the morning of the 8th and	[illegible]

Army Form C. 2118.

Instructions regarding War Diaries and Intelligence Summaries are contained in F. S. Regs., Part II. and the Staff Manual respectively. Title pages will be prepared in manuscript.

WAR DIARY

or

~~INTELLIGENCE SUMMARY.~~

(Erase heading not required.)

Place	Date	Hour	Summary of Events and Information	Remarks and references to Appendices
VARENNES	11-5-16	Cont.	Will you please convey to Lieut F.P. Montgomery and the N.C.Os and men under him, my great appreciation of the way in which the arduous duty was performed." Patients remaining 7.	[illegible]
	12-5-16		Routine. Patients remaining 12	[illegible]
	13-5-16		The G.O.C. 36 Division inspected the unit. The Transport in line. He expressed himself as highly pleased with the smartness + general arrangements of the Unit + asked that an expression of his appreciation be conveyed to all ranks. Patients remaining 4	[illegible]
	14-5-16		Routine " " 11	[illegible]
	15 " "		Routine " 9	[illegible]
	16 " "		Routine " 9	[illegible]
	17-5-16		Lt Lindsay detailed for duty at A.D.S. A special routine order by the A.D.M.S. was received this morning expressing his great appreciation of the work of the Divisional Fd ambulances. Patients remaining 12	[illegible]
	18-5-16		Capt. W. Russell granted leave of absence from 20.5.16 to 2.6.16. Patients remaining 11.	[illegible]
	19-5-16		Capt. Johnston reported his arrival from leave of absence. Lt Montgomery reported his arrival from duty at A.P. at AUTHUILLE on being relieved by Lt Lindsay. Patients remaining 8	[illegible]
	20-5-16		Routine Patients remaining 12	[illegible]

2353 Wt. W2544/1454 700,000 5/15 D. D. & L. A.D.S.S./Forms/C. 2118.

Instructions regarding War Diaries and Intelligence Summaries are contained in F. S. Regs., Part II. and the Staff Manual respectively. Title pages will be prepared in manuscript.

WAR DIARY

or

INTELLIGENCE SUMMARY.

(Erase heading not required.)

Army Form C. 2118.

Place	Date	Hour	Summary of Events and Information	Remarks and references to Appendices
VARENNES	21.5.16		Lt Gray detailed to attend a course of instruction at 4th Army Anti Gas School. Patients remaining 7.	[illegible]
	22.5.16		Capt. Grierson reported his arrival for duty. Patients remaining 10.	[illegible]
	23 "		Capt Grierson granted leave of absence from 25.5.16 to 2.6.16. Patients remaining 8	[illegible]
	24 "		Routine. 2nd Dug out at SWALLOWS NEST ready for occupation. Capt Johnston posted to SWALLOWS NEST to take over charge of A.D.S. vice Capt. Pesel. The N.C.O. 1 N.C.O. & 1 Driver A.S.C. transferred being surplus to new establishment. The surplus horses disposed as follows:– to A.S.C. ROUEN, the Driver to 36 Div. Train. 1 rider to 109 M.G. Coy. & 1 light draught and 1 H.D. to 48 mobile Section (A.V.C.). Patients remaining 7.	[illegible]
	25 "		Capt. W. McCREADY R.A.M.C. reported his arrival for duty on his transfer from the Infantry (10 R.I. Rifs). Patients remaining 11	[illegible]
	26	"	Routine. 10 men exchanged with personnel at C.P. SWALLOWS NEST. Pts remaining 7	[illegible]
	27	"	Capt. W. McCREADY detailed for duty at No 4 Stationary Hosp ARQUES. Lieut Gray reported his arrival from Anti Gas School. Capt Johnston reported his arrival from MARTINSART on being relieved by Lt Lindsay from SWALLOWS NEST. Patients remaining 2	[illegible]
	28	"	Routine. Patients remaining 8	[illegible]
	29	"	Routine. 8 Orders received from A.D.M.S. to move to CLAIRFAYE tomorrow. Patients remaining 6.	[illegible]
	30	"	The Unit moved to CLAIRFAYE during the day, owing to large amount of stores. The move occupied most of the day. The patients were transferred to 110th F.A.	[illegible]
CLAIRFAYE	31st	"	The move was completed by 7 P.M. The personnel being accommodated in tents.	[illegible]

109 F Amb
June
Vol 9

15

June/16

Confidential

War Diary

of

109th Field Amb.

109 F.A.

1st June 1916 — To 30 June 1916

Volume 9

[illegible]
Lt Col RAMC
Cmdg 109 Fd Amb.

Army Form C. 2118.

Instructions regarding War Diaries and Intelligence Summaries are contained in F. S. Regs., Part II. and the Staff Manual respectively. Title pages will be prepared in manuscript.

WAR DIARY
or
~~INTELLIGENCE SUMMARY.~~
(Erase heading not required.)

Place	Date	Hour	Summary of Events and Information	Remarks and references to Appendices
CLAIRFAYE	1-6-16		The day was spent in making shelters & bivouacs for personnel. Remaining in Hospital nil.	Rm
	2-6-16		Lt Gray detailed for temporary duty as MO i/c 10th R Innis Fus. Capt Johnston proceeded to A.D.S MARTINSART. to relieve Lt Lindsay granted leave from 3rd to 16th June. Patients 4.	Rm
			Capt Russell reported his arrival from leave. Patients remaining 9	Rm
	3		Capt Grimson reported his arrival from leave. No 45054 Corpl W. Hall evacuated sick to	Rm
	4		92nd Fd Amb. Patients remaining	
	5		No T/3031150 Dr W. Fullerton released for munitions work. Capt Grimson to relieve Lt Gray as MO i/c 10 R Innis Fus. Patients remaining 18.	Rm
	6		Routine. Patients remaining 20	Rm
	7		Special Xth Corps traffic map to come into use tomorrow at 4 A.M. Patients remaining 16.	Rm
	8		Routine patients remaining 17	Rm
	9		Capt Russell and Lt Montgomery with one section took part in Divisional Field day. Capt Sander & 2 N.C.Os 2nd W. Riding FA attached for instruction in evacuation from the line for 2 days. Patients remaining 15.	Rm
	10th		Capt Russell & Lt Montgomery with one section took part in Brigade Field Day. One A.S.C reinforcement reported arrival Patients remaining 13.	Rm
	11th		Lt Gray detailed as temporary MO i/c 252 Tunnelling Co. R.E. Patients remaining 18	Rm
	12		Routine. Patients remaining 9.	Rm

Army Form C. 2118.

Instructions regarding War Diaries and Intelligence Summaries are contained in F. S. Regs., Part II. and the Staff Manual respectively. Title pages will be prepared in manuscript.

WAR DIARY
or
INTELLIGENCE SUMMARY.
(Erase heading not required.)

Place	Date	Hour	Summary of Events and Information	Remarks and references to Appendices
CLAIRFAYE	13.6.16		The O.C. proceeded to C.P. at SWALLOWS NEST vice Cpl Crellin wounded & evacuated. Patients remaining 10.	[illegible]
	14.6.16		Special Conference at office of ADMS. to arrange finally the scheme for Evacuation of large numbers of wounded. This unit to furnish 2 bearer sub divisions, [illegible] 2 motor dispatch riders. 2 mounted orderlies to ADMS. remainder of unit to remain in reserve. Patients remaining 10.	[illegible]
	15.6.16		Routine. Preparations to receive large numbers of wounded continue. Q.M.S reported having sufficient supplies – Rations comforts dressings etc for all possible emergencies. Timber & materials for huts & shelters asked for from C.E. X Corps. Large hut 100' x 30' finished. It is proposed to build 9 other smaller huts 30' x 16'.	[illegible]
			Work on East Bank of River ANCRE inspected. Patients remaining 7.	[illegible]
	16.6.16		A.D.S. MARTINSART and C.Ps AUTHUILLE and PAISLEY AVENUE handed over to 110th Fd Ambulance who from this date will evacuate the right sector of the Div. Line. Capt. Pesel remains with Lt Brown & 103 O.R. in THIEPVAL WOOD to complete the work on Dugouts & Gas chambers. Patients remaining 14.	[illegible]
	17.6.16		THIEPVAL works inspected by DDMS X Corps accompanied by C.O. All works practically completed and Gas chambers being fitted to all doors (12). Lieut [illegible] rejoined from leave. Patients remaining 8.	[illegible]

Army Form C. 2118.

Instructions regarding War Diaries and Intelligence Summaries are contained in F. S. Regs., Part II. and the Staff Manual respectively. Title pages will be prepared in manuscript.

WAR DIARY
or
~~INTELLIGENCE SUMMARY.~~

(Erase heading not required.)

Place	Date	Hour	Summary of Events and Information	Remarks and references to Appendices
CLAIRFAYE	18.6.16		Operation orders received from A.D.M.S. to detail 2 bearer subdivisions to proceed on morning of "Y" day one to THIEPVAL WOOD (SPEYSIDE STREET) and one to HAMEL. Both to work under 108 Inf Bde. The Remainder of the Unit to remain at CLAIRFAYE & hold itself in reserve ready to advance and form a main Dressing Station at any place which may be selected. Lt Montgomery is detailed to command A Section bearer sub division and to proceed to THIEPVAL on "Y" day. Capt Johns is detailed to command B section bearer subdivision and to proceed to HAMEL on "Y" day. Patients remaining 6.	[illegible]
	19.6.16		Capt Pearl, Lieut Brown & 103 O.R. returned to HdQrs from THIEPVAL all works having been completed. Lieut Gray transferred as M.O. i/c 252 Tunnelling Co R.E. Patients remaining 2.	[illegible]
	20.6.16		Rev Canon King Senior Chaplain attached. Routine. Patients remaining 3	[illegible]
	21.6.16		Routine. Preparations for the reception of large numbers of casualties continue. Patients remaining 3.	[illegible]
	22.6.16		Inspection by D.M.S. 4th Army Surgeon General O'Keefe who expressed himself as highly pleased with the arrangements made to deal with large numbers of wounded. He complimented Corporal Patton M.T. A.S.C. on his ingenious arrangement for carrying 6 lying patients in each motor ambulance car. Patients remaining 2.	[illegible]
	23.6.16		3 O.R. detailed to proceed to assist at a collecting post established at Sheet 57 D. S.E. 1/10000 P.36.d.4.9. for walking cases. Soyer Stove Tarpaulin Kettle & food ~~sent~~ sent. The C.P. to be under Lt Smith RAMC M.O. i/c R.F.A. wagon lines HEDAUVILLE. The Day of the impending operations. Patients remaining 1.	[illegible]

2353 Wt. W2544/1454 700,000 5/15 D. D. & L. A.D.S.S./Forms/C. 2118.

Army Form C. 2118.

WAR DIARY
or
~~INTELLIGENCE SUMMARY.~~

(Erase heading not required.)

Instructions regarding War Diaries and Intelligence Summaries are contained in F. S. Regs., Part II. and the Staff Manual respectively. Title pages will be prepared in manuscript.

Place	Date	Hour	Summary of Events and Information	Remarks and references to Appendices
CLAIRFAYE	24 6 16		9 Huts & 1 other Shelter completed. 600 patients can now be accommodated. Cooking	
			arrangements made for 1000 patients. 3000 lbs Straw supplied by S.S.O. for Paillasses.	[illegible]
			patients remaining 5	
	25 6 16		One private released for Munitions work in Belfast. 2 Horse Ambulance Wagons each	
			with 4 horses in charge of Sergt Walker ASC detailed to proceed to FORCEVILLE to	
			report to OC 108th Field Ambulance. These wagons to assist in the transport of	
			lightly wounded to CLAIRFAYE. One wagon to visit as often as required the	[illegible]
			Collecting post P 36 d 9.9. Patients remaining 4.	[illegible]
	26 6 16		2 men from Salvage Co reported for duty. Patients remaining 2.	
	27 6 16		One Ford Car to report to A.D.M.S. for duty at his office. Patients remaining 4	
		12.30 AM	Lt Lindsay proceed to THIEPVAL WOOD for duty with 9th R Innis Fus. Lt Brown to proceed	[illegible]
			to O C C.P. PAISLEY AVENUE for duty.	
	28.		Capt Johnston with B bearer subdivision and Lt Montgomery with A Bearer Subdivision	
			proceeded by M A Cars to HAMEL and THIEPVAL WOOD respectively. One NCO & 6 OR	
			proceeded to ACHEUX for entraining duty under E.M.O. 2 O.R. proceeded to	
			MARTINSART for Signal duty. Lts Lindsay & Brown returned to HdQrs.	
			2 orderlies detailed to report to VI M.A.C. for telephone duty. Capt Grierson	
			attached temporarily to 110th F.A. to command a bearer Sub Division. Two drivers	[illegible]
			A.S.C. returned from 2 month Course of Farriery at ABBEVILLE. Patients remaining 2.	[illegible]
	29th 6 16		One man sent to Lt Montgomery vice one man returned sick. 3 OR reinforcements arrived. Patients remaining 7	
	30th		2 mounted orderlies attached to A.D.M.S. Two Motor Cyclists to report for duty to D.A.D.M.S. at	
			A.D.S. MARTINSART. Patients remaining 13	[illegible]

15

July 1916

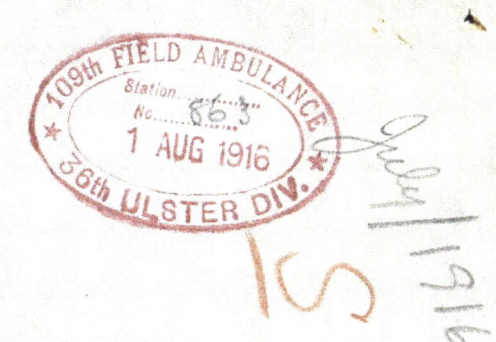

Confidential

War Diary

of

109th Field Ambulance

109 F. Amb.

From 1st July 1916 To 31st July 1916

Volume X

Major Rame
Comdg 109th Fd. Amb.

36
109 F Amb
Vol 10

Army Form C. 2118

Instructions regarding War Diaries and Intelligence Summaries are contained in F. S. Regs., Part II. and the Staff Manual respectively. Title Pages will be prepared in manuscript.

WAR DIARY
or
~~INTELLIGENCE SUMMARY~~
(Erase heading not required.)

109th Field Ambulance 36th Divn

Place	Date	Hour	Summary of Events and Information	Remarks and references to Appendices
CLAIRFAYE	1.7.16	11 AM	Lt Lindsay detailed ~~for~~ report to 9th Royal Innis Fus to take medical charge vice Capt Mulkern Killed. Wire from A.D.M.S.	
		12.30 PM	Wire received from O.C. ~~—~~ Bearer Sub divisions ~~at~~ HAMEL and THIEPVAL asking for reinforcements.	
		1. PM	Capt Russell + 18 O.R proceeded to THIEPVAL & Lt Brown with 18 O.R to HAMEL to reinforce the Bearer sub divisions	
			Six Signallers were posted this morning between MARTINSART and MONMOUTH ROAD to maintain communication between Ambulance PARKS.	[illegible]
			Pte MARKS wounded in SPEYSIDE ST. Patients remaining nil.	
		2 PM	Pte Grainger reported missing	
	2.7.16	8.AM	Wire received from Lt Montgomery asking for 100 Stretchers & blankets required at PAISLEY AVENUE. These were sent immediately.	
		Noon	Pte Grainger yesterday reported missing was ascertained to be Killed. (Wire from A Section B.S.Div.)	
		1 PM	Operation orders received from A.D.M.S — 49th Division is relieving the 36th Division in THIEPVAL. The HAMEL sub sector has been taken over by 87th Bde 29th Div. The following movements will take place tonight :- . . . (2) M.A Car PARK will close (3) Div. Collecting post for walking cases will close at noon tomorrow. (5) B S-Divs of 109 & 110 F.As will be held in readiness to reinforce 49th Div. (11) The 109 F.A will be kept in reserve	[illegible]

1875 Wt. W593/826 1,000,000 4/15 J.B.C. & A. A.D.S.S./Forms/C. 2118.

Instructions regarding War Diaries and Intelligence Summaries are contained in F. S. Regs., Part II. and the Staff Manual respectively. Title Pages will be prepared in manuscript.

WAR DIARY
or
INTELLIGENCE SUMMARY
(Erase heading not required.)

Army Form C. 2118

Place	Date	Hour	Summary of Events and Information	Remarks and references to Appendices
CLAIRFAYE	2.7.16	1.30 PM	Signallers returned from Post.	
		2. PM	A Section B.S Div wires that Pte Daly Killed. Pte Stitt wounded.	
		8. PM	Capt Johnston + Lt. Brown with 56 O.R. rejoined from HAMEL on being relieved by 29 Div.	Rem
			2 mounted orderlies rejoined from duty at ADMS. Remained in Hospl: 1	
	3.7.16	8.30 AM	Capt. Russell + Lt. Montgomery with B.S Div rejoined from THIEPVAL on being relieved by 49th Div: Horse Ambulances + personnel rejoined from FORCEVILLE this evening.	
			Lt. Ian R MacLeod reported his arrival + taken on strength.	
		7.30 PM	Capt. Russell. Lt. Brown + Lt. MacLeod with 23 O.R proceeded for duty with No 3 C.C.S PUCHEVILLERS.	
			M.T. section with 6 ambulance Cars rejoined from M.A PARK having been on duty [illegible] for practically 3 days. Patients remaining 2	Rem
	4.7.16	10 AM.	Operation orders No 13 from ADMS. :- (4) Any sick of 36 Div. held by 110 F.A will be transferred to 109 F.A. which will until further orders deal with daily sick and act as Div. Rest. Station. The Div. Officers Rest Station will be taken over from 110th F.A. by this unit. (5) The F. Ambces of 36 Div. will form a reserve. to move at short notice. (6) The 109 F.A. will collect all sick in Division	

1875 Wt. W593/826 1,000,000 4/15 J.B.C. & A. A.D.S.S./Forms/C. 2118.

Instructions regarding War Diaries and Intelligence Summaries are contained in F. S. Regs., Part II. and the Staff Manual respectively. Title Pages will be prepared in manuscript.

WAR DIARY
or
INTELLIGENCE SUMMARY
(Erase heading not required.)

Army Form C. 2118

Place	Date	Hour	Summary of Events and Information	Remarks and references to Appendices
CLAIRFAYE	4.7.16	10 AM	Catchment Area: FORCEVILLE. HEDAUVILLE. VARENNES. LEALVILLERS. HARPONVILLE	
	..	6 PM	Capt. T. J. Phillips reported his arrival & taken on strength. Patients remaining 1	[illegible]
	5.7.16		Capt Pesel and 23 OR took over D.R.S. from 110 F.A. Capt Grenison & 7 OR took over Div. Officers Rest Station. Lt Chester returned from duty as Town Major at MARTINSART.	
		11 AM	Orders received from A.D.M.S. for Unit to move to VAL de MAISON at 6 P.M. Lt Montgomery by orders from G.H.Q. to proceed to No 1. M.A.C. Struck off strength.	
		6 PM	Unit moved to VAL DE MAISON leaving 80 sick to be transferred tomorrow to new Station.	[illegible]
VAL de MAISON		8.30 PM	Unit arrived, taking up its old Quarters. Sick to be collected from Bdes at RUBEMPRE. PUCHEVILLERS. HERISSART.	
	6.7.16		Patients from CLAIRFAYE brought over by motor ambulances. Remained in Hosp: 78.	[illegible]
		6 PM	Word from A.D.M.S. "Be prepared to move at 3/4 hours notice after 8 tomorrow morning"	
		9 PM	Arrangements made with DADMS [illegible] to leave detachment to look after sick in the event of a move.	
	7.7.16		Capt Phillips relieved Capt Russell at No 3. C.C.S. Patients remaining 61.	[illegible]
		11-16 AM	Unit addressed by A.D.M.S. and thanked for their splendid work during the operations of the Division	
	8.7.16		Routine. Patients remaining 39.	[illegible]

1875 Wt. W593/826 1,000,000 4/15 J.B.C. & A. A.D.S.S./Forms/C. 2118.

Instructions regarding War Diaries and Intelligence Summaries are contained in F. S. Regs., Part II. and the Staff Manual respectively. Title Pages will be prepared in manuscript.

WAR DIARY
or
~~INTELLIGENCE SUMMARY~~
(Erase heading not required.)

Army Form C. 2118

Place	Date	Hour	Summary of Events and Information	Remarks and references to Appendices
VAL DE MAISON	9.7.16	1 PM	Capt Phillips. Lts Brown & MacLeod with 22 OR rejoined from No 3 C.C.S.	Ree
		5 PM	Operation orders No 14 from ADMS with march table. (2) The 37th Amb less D.R.S. will move tomorrow 10th as per attached march table. (4) O.C. 109 F.A. will leave behind 1 officer 1 NCO & 4 OR (one a cook) 1 M.T. Driver and 1 M.A. car. A D.R.S. will be temporarily maintained. A reserve of 7 days rations to be laid in.	
		10 PM	Rations collected from 106 & 109 Bdes (1000)	Ree
	10.7.16	7.30 AM	Unit left (leaving party as above.) in rear of 107 Bde. 50 patients left.	
VACQUERIE	10.7.16	noon	Unit arrived	
		6 PM	Div order with march and entraining table. Unit to march tomorrow evening at 23.0 to AUXI LE CHATEAU to arrive there at 2.15 and entrain ~~..~~ train to leave at 5.22. Motor ambulances to leave tomorrow at 11 AM. for BLAIRINGHEM	
	11.7.16		Lt MacLeod evacuated sick to 4 CCS	Ree
		11 PM	Unit left.	
AUXI LE CHATEAU	12.7	2.15 AM	Unit arrived and entrained.	
		5.22 AM	~~unit~~ Train left.	Ree

1875 Wt. W593/826 1,000,000 4/15 J.B.C. & A. A.D.S.S./Forms/C. 2118.

Instructions regarding War Diaries and Intelligence Summaries are contained in F. S. Regs., Part II. and the Staff Manual respectively. Title Pages will be prepared in manuscript.

WAR DIARY
or
INTELLIGENCE SUMMARY
(Erase heading not required.)

Army Form C. 2118

Place	Date	Hour	Summary of Events and Information	Remarks and references to Appendices
THIENNES	12.7.16	10 AM	Detrained. Fires were lighted and breakfast cooked, the unit marching off at noon and arriving at	R...
COMPAGNE	"	4 P.M.	D.W. order No 46 with march Table. The unit to march tomorrow at 1.30 PM to 109 Bde area.	
"	13.7.16	1.30 PM	Unit left and arrived at	R...
QUELMES	"	4.30 PM	billeted by 109 Bde. On the march a message was received from A.A. & Q.M.G. instructing the 109 F.A. to proceed to CULEM to an empty chateau tomorrow.	
"	14.7.16	10 AM	moved to CULEM	R...
CULEM		12 noon	arrived. Proceeded to open D.R.S. in Empty Chateau. Sick to be collected from 109 Bde area. Patients remaining 27.	R...
	15.7.16		Men employed in cleaning up. Routine. Patients remaining 14.	
	16.7.16		Lt. T.W.G. Johnstone reported his arrival for duty & taken on strength. Patients 33.	R...
	17.7.16		Capt. W. Scott reported his arrival for duty & taken on strength. Patients 33	R...
	18.7.16		Routine. patients 44.	R...
	19.7.16		8 O.R. reinforcements reported for duty. Extract from Div order No 47 received from ADMS with march Table. The 109 F.A. to march to BOLLEZELLE on 21st inst	R...

1875 Wt. W593/826 1,000,000 4/15 J.B.C. & A. A.D.S.S./Forms/C. 2118.

Instructions regarding War Diaries and Intelligence Summaries are contained in F. S. Regs., Part II. and the Staff Manual respectively. Title Pages will be prepared in manuscript.

WAR DIARY

or

~~INTELLIGENCE SUMMARY~~

(Erase heading not required.)

Army Form C. 2118

Place	Date	Hour	Summary of Events and Information	Remarks and references to Appendices
GULEM	19.7.16	Continued.	and to HERZEELE on 22nd leaving one section at BOLLEZEELE to collect sick from 109 Bde in BOLLEZEELE area. Patients 54.	[illegible]
	20.7.16		Routine. Patients evacuated to No 10 Stationary Hosp.	[illegible]
	21.7.16	9 AM	Unit left and arrived at	
BOLLEZEELE		2 PM	billeted by 109 Bde	[illegible]
			Wire received from A.D.M.S to stand fast & await orders.	
	22.7.16		Operation orders No 16 received from A.D.M.S:- (2) 109 F.A will proceed tomorrow to HONDEGHEM AREA and to BAILLEUL on 24th inst when they will relieve 62 F.A at S. 9 d 9 0 Sheet 28 1/40000. For this purpose an advance party will be detailed to proceed to 62 F.A. on 23rd to arrive by noon	[illegible]
	23.7.16	9 AM	Unit left. halted at ZUYTPEENE for 2 hours when fires were lighted and food cooked. arrived at	
HONDEGHEM		5 PM	at U. 6 a. 1. 4 Sheet 27 1/40000 in a farm allotted by Maire. Advanced party left BOLLEZEELE at 9 AM to take over from 62 F.A	[illegible]
	24.7.16	9 AM	Unit left and arrived at	
BAILLEUL		3 PM		
		5	Capt Russell & party reported from VAL de MAISON.	[illegible]

1875 Wt. W593/826 1,000,000 4/15 J.B.C. & A. A.D.S.S./Forms/C. 2118.

Instructions regarding War Diaries and Intelligence Summaries are contained in F. S. Regs., Part II. and the Staff Manual respectively. Title Pages will be prepared in manuscript.

WAR DIARY
or
~~INTELLIGENCE SUMMARY~~
(Erase heading not required.)

Army Form C. 2118.

Place	Date	Hour	Summary of Events and Information	Remarks and references to Appendices
BAILLEUL	25.7.16		Routine. patients 41.	[initials]
"	26.7.16.		Capt Scott proceeded to take temporary charge of 172 Bde R.F.A. Pte Trimble released for munitions. O.C. with D.A.D.M.S. visited A.D.S. ROMARIN + C.P.S. Lt. Brown proceeded to take medical charge of 9th R. Innis. Fus vice Lt. Lindsay sick.	[initials]
	27.7.16.		Capt. Russell to take temporary charge of 14 R. Irish Rifles vice Capt. Gavin on leave. O.C. visited baths at PLOEGSTEERT + reported to A.D.M.S.	
			Operation orders no 17 from A.D.M.S. - (2) The 109 F.A. will take over the evacuation of the trenches ~~[struck out]~~ occupied by 109 BDE today from the 138th F.A. (3) Details of the relief to be arranged by the respective O.s C.	[initials]
		2 P.M.	Capt Johnston + Capt. Pesel with party of 20 O.R. proceeded to take over A.D.S at ROMARIN + C.P.s at HYDE PARK CORNER	
"	28.7.16	10 A.M.	A.D.M.S. with O.C. visited A.D.S + C.P.s and arrangements made for improving C.P.s	[initials]
	29.7.16		Material for erecting ~~[struck out]~~ anti gas curtains at C.P. procured from C.R.E. Capt. Pesel in charge of this work. One N.C.O + 24 O.R. proceeded as a working Party to Ordnance Dump.	[initials]
"	30.7.16		Routine. Patients remaining 9.	[initials]
"	31.7.16		Routine " " 17.	[initials]

1875 Wt. W593/826 1,000,000 4/15 J.B.C. & A. A.D.S.S./Forms/C. 2118.

August 1916

Confidential

War Diary

of

109th Field Ambulance

From 1st Aug 1916 To 31st Aug 1916

Volume XI

36th (Ulster) Div

[signature]
Major RAMC
Comdg 109th F.d Ambce

Instructions regarding War Diaries and Intelligence Summaries are contained in F. S. Regs., Part II. and the Staff Manual respectively. Title pages will be prepared in manuscript.

WAR DIARY
or
INTELLIGENCE SUMMARY.
(Erase heading not required.)

Army Form C. 2118.

Place	Date	Hour	Summary of Events and Information	Remarks and references to Appendices
BAILLEUL	1.8.16		A buzzer telephone having been installed in A.D.S. and connected up with 109th Bde 2 Signallers will proceed to M.O. i/c for duty. Patients remaining 16	[illegible]
	[struck through]		Capt Phillips evacuated to No 2 C.C.S. Struck off strength	
		2 PM	Gas alert. A.D.S. warned by telephone and by 109th Bde	
	2.8.16		Wire from 109 Bde gas alert cancelled wind N.W. Wire from 36 Div. Q 904 begins 109 F.A. at S 9 d 9.0 will supply you with water addressed 36 Div Grouped Schools. Ends. Arrangements made as follows: a water cart to be stationed at the School and a team to go twice a day to refill. Cart to be changed every 4 days for cleaning. Patients remaining 15	[illegible]
	3.8.16		By direction of A.D.M.S. 2 teams H.D. horses with long rein and single horse with horses & drivers to report to Town Major on 4th & daily for sanitary work. Remaining patients 21.	[illegible]
	4.8.16		Routine Patients remaining 26.	[illegible]
	5.8.16	11 AM	Wire A.D.M.S. "Detail an officer to take charge of 11th R Innis Fus for 14 days from 7th inst. Capt Reid detailed. One N.C.O. & 9 O.R. to report to O.C. 150 Fd Co R.E. to work trench tramway at HYDE PARK CORNER	
		6.30PM	O.O. A.D.M.S. re Division to extend its front to left and take over as far as DURHAM ROAD from 50th Division	

Instructions regarding War Diaries and Intelligence Summaries are contained in F. S. Regs., Part II. and the Staff Manual respectively. Title pages will be prepared in manuscript.

WAR DIARY

or

~~INTELLIGENCE SUMMARY.~~

(Erase heading not required.)

Army Form C. 2118.

Place	Date	Hour	Summary of Events and Information	Remarks and references to Appendices
BAILLEUL	5.8.16	6.30PM	ADMS no 33. "Patients may be kept in M.D.S for 7-10 days owing to overcrowding of D.R.S. Patients remaining 19.	
		8.32 PM	36 Div G 91. ADMS 31. Precautions to be taken on the Gas alert being ordered	
	6.8.16		6 O.R. to report to O/c A.D.S. ROMARIN for duty	
		7.10PM.	ADMS 53. 56 57. B. C + D Battys 173 Bde R.F.A. B Batty 154 Bde and D Batty 153 Bde R.F.A will parade their sick at A.D.S. ROMARIN daily	
			Patients remaining 16. Gas Curtains at C.Ps finished.	
	7.8.16		All latrines + Beef stores made fly proof. Routine. O.C. inspected A.D.S + C.P.	
		6.50PM	GAS ALERT. Remaining Patients 17.	
	8.8.16		One O.R evacuated sick. Struck off strength.	
		11.30AM	Capt. Philip Smith ~~[illegible]~~ Rev R.A.M.C. reported his arrival for duty.	
		12.30PM	Wire from A.D.S reporting Pte T. J Patterson Killed by Shell.	
			Pte PATTERSON buried at PLOEGSTEERT. Arrangements made by Revd CLIFFORD 9th R Innis Fus. Patients remaining 23	

2353 Wt. W2544/1454 700,000 5/15 D. D. & L. A.D.S.S./Forms/C. 2118.

Army Form C. 2118.

WAR DIARY
or
~~INTELLIGENCE~~ SUMMARY.

(*Erase heading not required.*)

Instructions regarding War Diaries and Intelligence Summaries are contained in F. S. Regs., Part II. and the Staff Manual respectively. Title pages will be prepared in manuscript.

Place	Date	Hour	Summary of Events and Information	Remarks and references to Appendices
BAILLEUL	9.8.16	11-45 AM	One NCO + 5 OR to report to C.R.E. ALDERSHOT HUTS to work on Hutting Scheme. Party to report at 5 P.M. (A.D.M.S 94).	
		NOON	A reliable N.C.O to proceed to various water tanks to instruct men in charge in the Chlorination of water. (A.D.M.S. 86.) Sergt MORTON detailed for this duty and to proceed mounted tomorrow. Patients remaining 33.	[illegible]
	10.8.16	9.30 AM	Capt Smith proceeded to A.D.S for duty	
		11.45 AM	A.D.M.S 108. "a certain number cases can now be sent to D.R.S.	
			Capt Scott returned from 172 Bde R.F.A	[illegible]
		7. PM	Gas alert off. Patients remaining 36.	
"	11-8.16		Routine	
		5.20 PM.	One N.C.O + 5 men to report tomorrow to O.C. 150 Coy R.E. for work	[illegible]
			Patients remaining 40	
"	12.8.16	3 PM	A.D.M.S 155. "Lt Brown is permanently posted to medical Charge of 5th Battn R Innis Fus." Patients remaining 39	[illegible]
	13.8.16		Capt Russell returned from duty with 14 R Irish Rifles	

Instructions regarding War Diaries and Intelligence Summaries are contained in F. S. Regs., Part II. and the Staff Manual respectively. Title pages will be prepared in manuscript.

WAR DIARY
or
~~INTELLIGENCE~~ SUMMARY.

(*Erase heading not required.*)

Army Form C. 2118.

Place	Date	Hour	Summary of Events and Information	Remarks and references to Appendices
BAILLEUL	13.8.16	10.20PM.	Wire from 36 Div Q. (Q.11) "It is proposed to issue Armstrong huts to units for drying rooms. Experiment with one and report result early on 15th". Patients remaining 33	[illegible]
"	14.8.16		Routine. Armstrong hut fitted up with stove + ropes. 40 dripping garments were dried in 6 hours. This result telephoned to "Q". O.C. met A.D.M.S at SHRINE to select if possible an additional C.P. Ground was found unsuitable. Patients remaining 36.	[illegible]
"	15.8.16	10.30AM	G.O.C 36 Div + A.A.+Q.M.G. inspected drying hut and approved.	[illegible]
		11-AM	O.C visited A.D.S. A.D.M.S wire 36 Division now in IX Corps. Patients remaining 30	
	16.8.16		Lt. Chester granted leave till 21st. Routine Patients remaining 25	[illegible]
	17.8.16	10AM.	O.C visited ROMARIN A.D.S + C.Ps. Patients remaining 22	[illegible]
	18.8.16		Routine Patients remaining 24.	[illegible]
	19.8.16		Routine	
		8.30PM.	A.D.M.S 300 "Submit name of officer to attend course of gas instruction". Lt. T W G Johnson selected. Patients remaining 23.	[illegible]

2353 Wt. W2544/1454 700,000 5/15 D. D. & L. A.D.S.S./Forms/C. 2118.

Instructions regarding War Diaries and Intelligence Summaries are contained in F. S. Regs., Part II. and the Staff Manual respectively. Title pages will be prepared in manuscript.

WAR DIARY
or
INTELLIGENCE SUMMARY.
(Erase heading not required.)

Army Form C. 2118.

Place	Date	Hour	Summary of Events and Information	Remarks and references to Appendices
BAILLEUL	20.8.16	11.30AM	Wire from ADMS 302 "Lt F P MONTGOMERY has been awarded the Military Cross Ptes J Andrews and J E Barr Military Medal" These being immediate rewards for their work during the operations at THIEPVAL. Patients remaining 18.	
	21.8.16		Lt Johnson proceeded to Centre and Left Sectors of Divisional Front today to make himself conversant with the evacuation of those sectors. Patients remaining 17	[signature]
	22.8.16	7.30PM	Capt Davidson arrived for duty.	
		7.50PM	GAS ALERT.	
		9.PM	A DMS "What steps are taken to warn A.D.S. of gas alert?" replied that ADS was warned by telephone, the 105 Inf Bde also warns A.D.S. Patients remaining 31	[signature]
	23.8.16		Routine O C visited ADS & CPS.	
		4.15PM	GAS ALERT Cancelled.	
		8 PM	Lt J FINNEGAN reported his arrival for duty to relieve Capt Scott who is proceeding to South Africa Infantry. Patients remaining 25	[signature]

2353 Wt. W2544/1454 700,000 5/15 D. D. & L. A.D.S.S./Forms/C. 2118.

Instructions regarding War Diaries and Intelligence Summaries are contained in F. S. Regs., Part II. and the Staff Manual respectively. Title pages will be prepared in manuscript.

WAR DIARY

or

~~INTELLIGENCE~~ SUMMARY.

(*Erase heading not required.*)

Army Form C. 2118.

Place	Date	Hour	Summary of Events and Information	Remarks and references to Appendices
BAILLEUL	24.8.16	10 AM	OC proceeded to ROMARIN to meet DDMS IX Corps, who is inspecting the advanced dressing station ~~[illegible]~~ afterwards proceeded to HYDE PARK CORNER & visited C.Ps & R.A.P. Patients remaining 24	
	25.8.16	—	Capt W. W. Scott left to report to 9th South African Infantry.	
		7.PM	Capt Smith detailed to relieve Lt Brown 9th R Innis Fus who is granted 7 days leave. Patients remaining 31.	
	26.8.16		2 NCOs & 18 OR to report daily to Burgomaster PLOEGSTEERT for farm work (Harvesting). Lieut Finnegan sent to ROMARIN to assist Capt Johnston vice Capt Smith posted temporarily to 9 R Innis Fus. Routine work. Soapy water filter almost completed. New Kitchen commenced 6 loads of bricks having been obtained from C.R.E. Arrangements made to commence Horse standings as per plan furnished by A.D.M.S. Patients remaining 29.	
	27.8.16	3.30 PM	ADMS 446 "Detail an officer to take temporary charge of 13th R Ir Rifles from 30th inst for 14 days" Capt Russell detailed. ADMS 447 DR Service between F.As & HdQrs to be instituted to commence on 28th inst. Patients remaining	

Army Form C. 2118.

Instructions regarding War Diaries and Intelligence Summaries are contained in F. S. Regs., Part II. and the Staff Manual respectively. Title pages will be prepared in manuscript.

WAR DIARY
or
~~INTELLIGENCE SUMMARY.~~

(Erase heading not required.)

Place	Date	Hour	Summary of Events and Information	Remarks and references to Appendices
BAILLEUL	28.8.16	–	Routine	[illegible]
		7-PM	Capt. Peel rejoined from duty with 11. R Innis Fus. Patients remaining 24	
	29.8.16	1130AM	GAS ALERT.	[illegible]
			Lt Chester detailed to proceed today to ALDERSHOT HUTS to assist in hutting scheme under "Q". Patients remaining 31	
	30.8.16	9AM	Capt Russel proceeded to 13th R Ir. Rifles.	
		9. AM	One horse ambulance wagon with 2 drivers & 4 horses to proceed to A.D.S. ~~[illegible]~~ to be stationed there and to collect sick in 109th Bde area.	
		12.30PM	GAS ALERT cancelled.	[illegible]
		7.30PM	A.D.M.S. 36th Div. Rest Station overcrowded, arrange to keep proportion of sick for 7 days. Remaining patients 44.	
	31.8.16	10AM	Capt Grierson proceeded to 9 R Innis Fus to relieve Capt Smith who is granted special leave from 1st to 7th Sept.	
		4.30PM	Capt Davidson proceeded to Cassel to 2nd Army Gas school vice Lt Johnson indisposed. Patients remaining 37.	[illegible]

2353 Wt. W2544/1454 700,000 5/15 D. D. & L. A.D.S.S./Forms/C. 2118.

Confidential

War Diary

of

109th Field Ambulance

from 1st Sept 1916 Vol XII To 30th Sept 1916

J. G. Johnston.

Army Form C. 2118

Instructions regarding War Diaries and Intelligence Summaries are contained in F. S. Regs., Part II. and the Staff Manual respectively. Title Pages will be prepared in manuscript.

WAR DIARY
or
~~INTELLIGENCE SUMMARY~~
(Erase heading not required.)

Place	Date	Hour	Summary of Events and Information	Remarks and references to Appendices
BAILLEUL	1-9-16	10 AM	RAMC orders no 17 received notifying that Div. HdQrs will open at St JANS CAPELLE at 5 P.M. A.D.M.S office at BAILLEUL at same hour.	
	"	3 P.M	Gassed cases to be notified to A.D.M.S. if large numbers occur.	[illegible]
			Horse standings. Soapy water filter & other work making satisfactory progress	
			Patients remaining 37.	
"	2-9-16		Capt Russel granted leave of absence from 3rd to 9th inst	
	"	6.56 PM	IX Corps code calls received.	
	"	7 30	A.D.M.S. instructions for a weekly report on Fridays on progress of work undertaken to aid the evacuation of wounded in the event of active operations	[illegible]
		11 10 PM	GAS ALERT. Remaining in Hospital 34.	
	3-9-16	11 AM	A.D.M.S (w 585) ordering A.D.S to be made gas proof at once. This would be practically impossible in the case of ADS at ROMARIN, as the house is nearly entirely composed of windows most of which are without glass.	
	—	3 PM	Capt Grimson reported his arrival on completion of duty with 9th R Inns Fus.	
	"	9 PM	Capt Dowson rejoined from Course of instruction at 2nd Army Gas School.	

Instructions regarding War Diaries and Intelligence Summaries are contained in F. S. Regs., Part II. and the Staff Manual respectively. Title Pages will be prepared in manuscript.

WAR DIARY
or
INTELLIGENCE SUMMARY
(Erase heading not required.)

Army Form C. 2118

Place	Date	Hour	Summary of Events and Information	Remarks and references to Appendices
BAILLEUL	3-9-16	7.30 PM.	A.D.M.S. 595 "Detail an officer to take over Laundry at DRANOUTRE from "an officer of 19th Division at 11 A.M. 4th inst. also arrange to leave one N.C.O. and 2 men in charge."	
		9 PM.	S.O.S. alert. Cancelled.	
		9 PM.	Wire from 150 Coy R.E. "20 men attached to this Coy will be returned to unit tomorrow owing to move of this Coy." Patients remaining 40	[initials]
	4-9-16	9.45 AM	Capt. Grimson proceeded to take over Laundry at DRANOUTRE from 19th Div taking one N.C.O. + 2 men to be left in charge.	
		11 AM	Party returned from duty with 150 Coy R.E.	
		4 PM	A.D.M.S. inspected unit.	
		8.30 PM	A.D.M.S. order no 20 "Divisional move. 109 F.A. will hand over A.D.S. ROMARIN and C.P.s at HYDE PARK CORNER to 59th F.A. and take over A.D.S. DRANOUTRE from 110th F.A. and C.P. LINDENHOEK from 57th F.A."	
		8.30	A.D.M.S. "Collect sick from 109 Bde in new area."	[initials]
			A football match held between 109 F.A. + A.S.C. of 108th F.A. resulted in a draw	
			Patients remaining 46	

1875 Wt. W593/826 1,000,000 4/15 J.B.C. & A. A.D.S.S./Forms/C. 2118.

Instructions regarding War Diaries and Intelligence Summaries are contained in F. S. Regs., Part II. and the Staff Manual respectively. Title Pages will be prepared in manuscript.

WAR DIARY
or
~~INTELLIGENCE SUMMARY~~
(Erase heading not required.)

Army Form C. 2118

Place	Date	Hour	Summary of Events and Information	Remarks and references to Appendices
BAILLEUL	5.9.16	10 AM	Capt Grimson + 12 O.R with one M.A Car + 2 Drivers took over A.D.S DRANOUTRE	
		2.30 PM	C.O. + Lt. T.W.G. Johnston proceeded to LINDENHOEK to reconnoitre C.Ps R.A.Ps and trenches	[illegible]
		9. P.M	Orders received to detail an officer + 15 men to run baths at DRANOUTRE tomorrow. Patients remaining 82. The battalion having moved into new area today a motor cyclist was sent out in the evening to get in touch + inform the M.O of the whereabouts of A.D.S. Wet weather + roads bad for move of Bde	
	6.9.16	9 AM	Lieut Johnson + 21 O.R proceeded to take over C.P. at LINDENHOEK. 15 O.R. proceeded to take over Baths and Laundry at DRANOUTRE no officer being available till tomorrow.	[illegible]
		10 AM	A.D.M.S and C.O. visited A.D.S DRANOUTRE also baths. Capt Johnston + Lt Finnegan rejoined from A.D.S ROMARIN having handed over to 557A. at noon.	
		2 P.M	GAS ALERT	
		8 P.M	Instructions received from A.D.M.S for Capt Davidson to be available to advise Inf Brigadier and to supervise instruction in use of small box respirator	[illegible]
		8 P.M	Second Army Signal Code + Instructions received. Patients remaining 67.	

1875 Wt. W593/826 1,000,000 4/15 J.B.C. & A. A.D.S.S./Forms/C. 2118.

Instructions regarding War Diaries and Intelligence Summaries are contained in F. S. Regs., Part II. and the Staff Manual respectively. Title Pages will be prepared in manuscript.

WAR DIARY
or
INTELLIGENCE SUMMARY
(Erase heading not required.)

Army Form C. 2118

Place	Date	Hour	Summary of Events and Information	Remarks and references to Appendices
BAILLEUL	7.9.16	9.30Am	C.O. & Lt Finnegan proceeded to DRANOUTRE. Lt Finnegan to take charge baths at that place.	
		4.30pm	C.O. & Capt Davidson proceeded to HdQrs 109 Inf Bde to make arrangements for the latters services as Gas officer to be at disposal of Brigade. Patients remaining 60.	AMc
	8.9.16	11AM	C.O. & DADOS visited baths. D.A.D.O.S. agreeing to issue necessary supplies	
		11.30Am	Inspection by D.D.M.S. IX Corps. In the absence of C.O. Capt Johnston conducted D.D.M.S.	
			A great number of sick continuing to be evacuated. A.D.M.S. urges every effort to reduce the wastage. Patients remaining 56	AMc
	9.9.16	noon	Q notifies that harvesting party is to be withdrawn. 35 O.R. to report to Capt Castle ALDERSHOT Huts for work erecting huts.	
		12.30 pm	C.O. visited A.D.S. & C.P.	
		3 PM	C.O. attended meeting of OsC F.As at A.D.M.S. office to consider wastage in Division.	AMc
		4.30PM	A.D.M.S. inspected M.D.S. Patients remaining 59.	

1875 Wt. W593/826 1,000,000 4/15 J.B.C. & A. A.D.S.S./Forms/C. 2118.

Instructions regarding War Diaries and Intelligence Summaries are contained in F. S. Regs., Part II. and the Staff Manual respectively. Title Pages will be prepared in manuscript.

WAR DIARY
or
~~INTELLIGENCE SUMMARY~~
(Erase heading not required.)

Army Form C. 2118

Place	Date	Hour	Summary of Events and Information	Remarks and references to Appendices
BAILLEUL	10.9.16	11 Am	Capt Pesel reports his arrival off leave.	
		4.PM	ADMS "Detail an officer for temporary medical charge of 10th R Irish Rifles from 11th inst". Remaining in hospital 60	[illegible]
	11.9.16	10 am	C.O. with ADMS visited 109 Bde sector of the line	
		11.30 Am	Capt Smith proceeded to take over temporary medical charge of 10th R Irish Rifles.	
			Revd Jackson Wright CF attached vice Rev Canon King CF proceeding to 14 R Ir Rifles	[illegible]
		11 PM	GAS Alert Cancelled. Patients remaining 57	
	12.9.16	10 AM	C.O. visited C.P. and consulted OC 150 Coy RE as to ~~[illegible]~~ best means of improving the dugouts at C.P. That officer advised more sandbags and a layer of concrete slabs as breakers, and agreed to lend a Sapper & provide material. Remaining in Hosp 51.	[illegible]
	13.9.16		Capt Pesel proceeded to relieve Capt Smith who is ordered to report to ADMS 16 Divn for duty: and is struck off strength.	
			C.P.s in future to be known as A.D.S's.	
			Good progress is being made with horse standings at M.D.S.	[illegible]
			A.D.S's fitted with anti gas curtains. Sand bagging of A.D.S at LINDENHOEK progressing.	
			Patients remaining 40	

Instructions regarding War Diaries and Intelligence Summaries are contained in F. S. Regs., Part II. and the Staff Manual respectively. Title Pages will be prepared in manuscript.

WAR DIARY
or
~~INTELLIGENCE SUMMARY~~
(Erase heading not required.)

Army Form C. 2118

Place	Date	Hour	Summary of Events and Information	Remarks and references to Appendices
BAILLEUL	14.9.16	9AM	Capt Davidson proceeded to WAKEFIELD HUTS (109 Bde) to instruct men in adjusting ANTI gas apparatus	
		11AM	MDS inspected by ADMS Instructions from "Q" that all vehicles are in future to be marked with the Red Hand of Ulster. Patients remaining 43.	[illegible]
	15.9.16	11AM	CO visited specimen horse standings at LOCRE. These standings are concrete on top of stone & brick soling. with corrugated iron roofs.	
		7.PM	Capt Russell returned from duty with 13 R. Ir Rifles.	[illegible]
		10.30PM	36 Div "G" notifies that in future GAS ALERT will be known as Wind Dangerous. & Alert off as Wind Safe. Patients remaining 40	
	16.9.16	5PM	Capt Russell detailed to relieve Capt Pusel who has reported sick Routine Patients remaining 34	[illegible]
	17.9.16		Routine. one O.R. transferred from 96 Sanitary section and taken on strength. Patients remaining 28.	[illegible]
	18.9.16		Routine Patients remaining 39.	[illegible]

1875 Wt. W593/826 1,000,000 4/15 J.B.C. & A. A.D.S.S./Forms/C. 2118.

Instructions regarding War Diaries and Intelligence Summaries are contained in F. S. Regs., Part II. and the Staff Manual respectively. Title Pages will be prepared in manuscript.

WAR DIARY
or
~~INTELLIGENCE SUMMARY~~
(Erase heading not required.)

Army Form C. 2118

Place	Date	Hour	Summary of Events and Information	Remarks and references to Appendices
BAILLEUL	19.9.16	6.30 PM	A Gas attack having been arranged for tonight. Capt Davidson with Extra blankets, stretchers etc proceeded to the Line for duty with special regard to anti gas measures.	Rem
		7.10 PM	ADMS 981. "Officers Hospital & Rest Station opened at MONT NOIR" Patients remaining 45	
		11.30 PM	Capt Davidson returned, weather conditions not being favourable, no attack took place.	Rem
	20.9.16		One O.R. detailed to ORS MONT NOIR as cook. Routine. Weather wet, work impeded. Patients remaining 42. CO took over management of Divisional Follies from Major Singleton DSO leaving on promotion	Rem
	21.9.16	10.30 AM	ADMS inspected main Dressing Station.	
		11.30 AM	"Wind Dangerous" Capt Pesel transferred to No 12 CCS HAZEBROUCK.	
		3 PM	C.O. visited ADSs & Sector of Line held by 109 Bde. Patients remaining 41	Rem

1875 Wt. W593/826 1,000,000 4/15 J.B.C. & A. A.D.S.S./Forms/C. 2118.

Instructions regarding War Diaries and Intelligence Summaries are contained in F. S. Regs., Part II. and the Staff Manual respectively. Title Pages will be prepared in manuscript.

WAR DIARY

or

~~INTELLIGENCE SUMMARY~~

(Erase heading not required.)

Army Form C. 2118

Place	Date	Hour	Summary of Events and Information	Remarks and references to Appendices
BAILLEUL	22.9.16	–	Capt Grimson + Lt Johnson changed stations i.e. Capt Grimson to LINDENHOEK, Lt Johnson to DRANOUTRE. Routine. Patients remaining 40	[initials]
	23.9.16	noon	Capt Russell rejoined from duty with 10 R Ir Rifles	
	"	3 PM	Parade took place near KORTEPYP at which the Corps Commander presented ribbons to those Officers + O.R. who had been awarded honours. Ptes ANDRESS and BARR of this unit received the ribbon of the Military Medal. Patients remaining 37	[initials]
	24.9.16		Routine. Patients remaining 49.	
	25.9.16	10 AM	CO + A.D.M.S. visited A.D.S.s + 109 Bde Sector R.A.Ps	
		3 PM	CO proceeded to interview C.R.E. with regard to horse standings + other work. Work at LINDENHOEK progressing satisfactorily. Patients remaining 47	[initials]
	26.9.16	8 AM	Capt Johnston rejoined from leave	
		10 AM	CO visited A.D.S. DRANOUTRE. Routine. Patients remaining 32	[initials]

1875 Wt. W593/826 1,000,000 4/15 J.B.C. & A. A.D.S.S./Forms/C. 2118.

Instructions regarding War Diaries and Intelligence Summaries are contained in F. S. Regs., Part II. and the Staff Manual respectively. Title pages will be prepared in manuscript.

WAR DIARY
or
~~INTELLIGENCE SUMMARY.~~
(Erase heading not required.)

Army Form C. 2118.

Place	Date	Hour	Summary of Events and Information	Remarks and references to Appendices
BAILLEUL	27.9.16		Major Magill granted leave of absence from 28th Sept to 8th Oct: inclusive. Capt Davidson detailed to relieve Lieut Johnson a A.D.S. DRANOUTRE Lt Johnson to proceed as M.O. i/c 10th R. Innis. Fusiliers for 14 days during Capt Pickens absence on leave. Patients remaining 39	J.S.J.
	28.9.16		A.D.M.S. Secret No 1267; 36 Div. G.S. 545 – Code – recd 10.30 a.m. ADMS Secret No 1275 Code calls for IX Corps. – recd at 4 p.m. Patients remaining 44.	J.S.J.
	29.9.16		ADMS Secret No 1287 – 36 Div. G.S No 547 recd at 3 p.m. " Re numbering of Trenches held by the 36th Division with diagram. Patients remaining 38.	J.S.J.
	30.9.16		ADMS. Secret No 1296 recd at 11 a.m. " Alteration of Summer-time to Winter-time 30th Sept.–1st Oct. night. ADMS. Secret No 1299 – GS. 556 – Amendment to 2nd Army Gas Alert and attack instructions. recd at 11 a.m. Patients remaining 30.	J.S.J.

2353 Wt. W2544/1454 700,000 5/15 D. D. & L. A.D.S.S./Forms/C. 2118.

Confidential

War Diary

of

109th Field Ambulance

From 1st Oct 1916

To 31st Oct 1916

Volumn XIII

[illegible]

Major RAMC

Comdg 109 F.A.

Instructions regarding War Diaries and Intelligence Summaries are contained in F. S. Regs., Part II. and the Staff Manual respectively. Title Pages will be prepared in manuscript.

WAR DIARY
or
INTELLIGENCE SUMMARY
(Erase heading not required.)

Army Form C. 2118

Place	Date	Hour	Summary of Events and Information	Remarks and references to Appendices
BAILLEUL	1st Oct. 1916	3 pm	Capt Johnston visited the Advanced Dressing Stations at DRANOUTRE + LINDENHOEK. Patients remaining in Hospital = 29.	JGJ
"	2.10.16	4 pm	Received Wire G.88 from 36th Division — Wind Safe. Patients remaining in Hospital = 35.	JGJ
"	3.10.16		Visited C.R.E with reference to proposed erection of drying-room at LINDENHOEK.	
		6 pm	ADMS. Secret NO 1350 – 36th Divisional G.S. 530 received — Gas Orders. Patients remaining in Hospital = 40.	JGJ
"	4th	2 P.M	ADMS Secret No 1352 received — Sick wastage.	
		"	ADMS Confidential NO 1340 received — Orders by Officers for Chlorination of Water. Patients remaining in Hospital 41.	JGJ
"	5th	10 AM	Capt Johnston visited A.D.S. at DRANOUTRE + LINDENHOEK. Material received + site selected for new drying room at LINDENHOEK. Patients remaining in Hospital. 62.	JGJ
"	6th		Complete Hut received from C.R.E. for use as a waiting-room at DRANOUTRE baths. Capt. H. G. Pesel returned from NO 12 C.C.S. HAZEBRUCK.	
		12 noon	36th Division Secret No. received — Location of Units. Remaining in Hospital - Patients. 54.	JGJ.

Instructions regarding War Diaries and Intelligence Summaries are contained in F. S. Regs., Part II. and the Staff Manual respectively. Title Pages will be prepared in manuscript.

WAR DIARY
or
INTELLIGENCE SUMMARY
(Erase heading not required.)

Army Form C. 2118.

Place	Date	Hour	Summary of Events and Information	Remarks and references to Appendices
BAILLEUL	7.10.16	9.30AM	A.D.M.S. secret number 1390 received — re numbering of List of Code Messages 2nd Army. Our number to be 36/1/128.	
			A.D.M.S. secret number 1395 received — Corrections for list of Code messages.	
			A.D.M.S. secret number 1392 received — Circular A. 33. recommendations for New Year Honours & Awards.	
			Patients remaining in Hospital — 46.	J.G.J.
"	8.10.16		Capt. W. Russell detailed as temporary Medical Officer in Charge 11th R. Innis. Fus. vice Capt D.S. Crosbie on leave.	
			Capt Johnston visited A.D.S.; at DRANOUTRE and LINDENHOEK.	
			Patients remaining in Hospital 56.	J.G.J.
"	9.10.16		Major Magill reported his arrival from leave of absence.	J.G.J.

1875 Wt. W593/826 1,000,000 4/15 J.B.C. & A. A.D.S.S./Forms/C. 2118.

Army Form C. 2118.

WAR DIARY
or
~~INTELLIGENCE SUMMARY.~~
(Erase heading not required.)

Instructions regarding War Diaries and Intelligence Summaries are contained in F. S. Regs., Part II. and the Staff Manual respectively. Title pages will be prepared in manuscript.

Place	Date	Hour	Summary of Events and Information	Remarks and references to Appendices
BAILLEUL	10.10.16	–	Lt Finnegan detailed as Tempory M.O. i/c 41 Heavy Artillery group.	[illegible]
			Routine. Patients remaining 55.	[illegible]
	11.10.16		Routine. Remaining in Hospital 62	
	12.10.16	10.30 AM	Inspection by A.D.M.S of Main Dressing station. Patients remaining 70. This large number for the most part due to an influenzal cold.	[illegible]
	13.10.16		Lt T.W.G. Johnson M.C. reported his arrival from tempory duty with 10th R Innis Fusiliers. Routine. Patients remaining 53	[illegible]
	14.10.16		Capt Johnston visited A.D.S LINDENHOEK and the trenches in the sector prior to relieving Capt Grimson. Patients remaining 41.	[illegible]
	15.10.16	11.30 AM	D.D.M.S IX Corps. inspected Main Dressing Station & expressed himself as very pleased with the condition of the Camp.	
		noon	Capt Johnston relieved Capt Grimson at A.D.S LINDENHOEK. Patients remaining 36.	[illegible]
	16.10.16		One O.R released for munition work	
		6.50 PM	A.D.M.S No 1562 – M.Os of Field Ambulances reduced to 8.	
		9 PM	Capt Grimson proceeded to take tempory medical charge of 153 Bde R.F.A. vice Capt Mercer going on leave. Patients remaining 21.	[illegible]

Instructions regarding War Diaries and Intelligence Summaries are contained in F. S. Regs., Part II. and the Staff Manual respectively. Title pages will be prepared in manuscript.

WAR DIARY
or
INTELLIGENCE SUMMARY.
(Erase heading not required.)

Army Form C. 2118.

Place	Date	Hour	Summary of Events and Information	Remarks and references to Appendices
BAILLEUL	17.10.16		Correspondence re new protected Dugouts at LINDENHOEK received from C.R.E. Routine. Patients remaining 21	[illegible]
"	18.10.16	1030 AM	Inspection by ADMS of A.D.Ss. arrangements made with Engineers to build two new dugouts at Lindenhoek, the Ambulance to supply the labour. Accommodation will thus be provided for 50 casualties. Patients remaining 27	[illegible]
"	19.10.16	7 PM	Wire from 36 Div. "Wind dangerous" all concerned warned. Work on Horse Standings making good progress all horses are now under cover. Patients remaining 21	[illegible]
"	20.10.16	—	24 O.R. detailed for work on new dug outs.	
		11 AM	Visit by AA&QMG who inspected work on standings &c &c.	
		—	Patients remaining 18.	[illegible]
	21.10.16		Routine. Patients remaining 10	
	22.10.16		One O.R. ASC H.T. released for munition work. Div. orders:- Staff Sergt Gillespie Sergt Morton, & Ptes W. McCormick & W.F. Quinn awarded Military Medal. Patients remaining 12.	[illegible]

2353 Wt. W2544/1454 700,000 5/15 D. D. & L. A.D.S.S./Forms/C. 2118.

Instructions regarding War Diaries and Intelligence Summaries are contained in F. S. Regs., Part II. and the Staff Manual respectively. Title pages will be prepared in manuscript.

WAR DIARY
or
INTELLIGENCE SUMMARY.
(Erase heading not required.)

Army Form C. 2118.

Place	Date	Hour	Summary of Events and Information	Remarks and references to Appendices
BAILLEUL	23.10.16	Noon	Parade at 110th F.A. by A.D.M.S. to present ribbons of M.M. to 8 N.C.O.s & men of the Divisional Fd Ambs. Patients remaining 12. One O.R. A.S.C. M.T. transferred Sick to Rest Station.	[illegible]
	24.10.16		One O.R. A.S.C. H.T. taken on Strength, work delayed by bad weather. Patients remaining 12. Capt Russell reported his arrival from temporary duty with 11. R Innis Fus. vice Capt Crosby on leave.	[illegible]
		7.30 P.M.	A.D.M.S. Secret S 114 code message correction	
	25.10.16	9.30 AM	Secret Code words received from A.D.M.S. Routine work. New fire appliances erected for ~~[illegible]~~ camp & Horse Lines. Patients remaining 8.	[illegible]
	26.10.16	12.30 P.M.	Wire from 36 Div "Wind Safe."	
		4 P.M.	CO visited CO 150 Coy R.E. & made arrangements for transport for material to new works in Trenches. Patients remaining 14	[illegible]
	27.10.16	10.30 AM	A.D.M.S. inspected Main Dressing Station	[illegible]
			Wire from 36 Div. "Wind dangerous." Patients remaining 14	

2353 Wt. W2544/1454 700,000 5/15 D. D. & L. A.D.S.S./Forms/C. 2118.

Instructions regarding War Diaries and Intelligence Summaries are contained in F. S. Regs., Part II. and the Staff Manual respectively. Title pages will be prepared in manuscript.

WAR DIARY
or
INTELLIGENCE SUMMARY.
(Erase heading not required.)

Army Form C. 2118.

Place	Date	Hour	Summary of Events and Information	Remarks and references to Appendices
BAILLEUL	28.10.16	9 Am	Request from "Q" through A.D.M.S to make arrangements to provide a ½ pint of cafe au lait to each man using the baths at DRANOUTRE	Rm
		noon	Wire from 36 Div "Wind Safe." Patients remaining 10	
	29.10.16		Capt Russell detailed to relieve Capt Davidson at A.D.S DRANOUTRE	
		8 PM	Copy of Bdg B.Os orders received relative to Raid on enemys trenches. Arrangements made to send extra bearers & cars to A.D.S LINDENHOEK in case of an extraordinary number of casualties. Patients remaining 8	Rm
	30.10.16	10 Am	A.D.M.S & CO inspected A.D.Ss. Capt Davidson granted 14 days leave. (contract)	
		1 PM	Capt Grierson returned from duty with 153 Bde R.F.A. Patients remaining 4. Excessive rain, ground of camps getting very muddy	Rm
	31.10.16	11 Am	Capt Grierson detailed for temporary duty with 11 R. Ir. Rifs	
		2.30 PM	D.M.S 2nd Army & D.D.M.S. IX Corps visited unit. D.M.S ordered Camp to be drained	
		9. PM	Capt Reid proceeded to LINDENHOEK to assist Capt Johnson should a large number of casualties require evacuation. Patients remaining 7	Rm

2353 Wt. W2544/1454 700,000 5/15 D. D. & L. A.D.S.S./Forms/C. 2118.

140/862

36th Div

Confidential

War Diary

of

109th Field Amb

From 1st Nov 1916 To 30th Nov 1916

Vol XIV

R. Maxwell
Lieut Col
Comdg 109 F. Amb

Nov. 16

Vol 14

Instructions regarding War Diaries and Intelligence Summaries are contained in F. S. Regs., Part II. and the Staff Manual respectively. Title pages will be prepared in manuscript.

WAR DIARY
or
~~INTELLIGENCE SUMMARY~~.
(*Erase heading not required.*)

Army Form C. 2118.

Place	Date	Hour	Summary of Events and Information	Remarks and references to Appendices
BAILLEUL	1-11-16	10.15 AM	Inspection of Camp with regard to drainage by D.D.M.S. & A.D.M.S. Good progress of Elephant dug outs at LINDENHOEK. Patients remaining 7	Rm
"	2.11.16		Drainage of Camp and erection of Huts in progress. Patients remaining 5.	Rm
"	3.11.16	10.30 AM	Wind Dangerous. C.O. visited A.D.S.s. Routine. Patients Remaining 11.	Rm
"	4.11.16		Capt Russell detailed to relieve Capt Berry who is in temporary medical charge of 9th Irish Rifles.	Rm
"	5.11.16		Routine. Wind Safe. Patients remaining 8.	Rm
"	6.11.16	4 PM	Pte Stafford detailed to proceed to No 3 Can C.C.S. for temporary duty as dental Mechanic. Patients remaining 12	Rm
	7.11.16		Lieut Johnson granted leave from 7th to 16th inst. C.O. visited A.D.S. & R.A.P. 2 5.9 proof dugouts in progress. Elephants on one. It is intended to connect the dugouts with Regent street by a short trench.	Rm

2353 Wt. W2544/1454 700,000 5/15 D. D. & L. A.D.S.S./Forms/C. 2118.

Army Form C. 2118.

WAR DIARY
or
~~INTELLIGENCE SUMMARY~~.
(Erase heading not required.)

Instructions regarding War Diaries and Intelligence Summaries are contained in F. S. Regs., Part II. and the Staff Manual respectively. Title pages will be prepared in manuscript.

Place	Date	Hour	Summary of Events and Information	Remarks and references to Appendices
BAILLEUL	7.11.16		Continued. Patients remaining 19.	[illegible]
		5 PM	A.D.M.S. visited M.D.S.	
"	8.11.16	3 PM	Visit of D.D.M.S. who inspected the work in progress	[illegible]
			3 O.R. A.S.C. reported arrival for duty vice 3 O.R. evacuated.	
			Patients remaining 20	
	9th		C.O. visited A.D.Ss & made arrangements for stoves in all rooms. Patients remaining 22.	[illegible]
	10th		Use of a convenient field for football obtained. Team entered in Local League. All Hospital huts are being re-roofed with felt. Patients remaining 34.	[illegible]
	11th		Routine. Remaining in hospital 27.	
	12th		Lieut A. G. Rawsthorne reported for temporary duty. Posted to No 2 A.D.S. to relieve Capt Johnston proceeding on 14 days leave. Owing to sick wastage being rather excessive patients are to be kept at Main Dressing Station 7 days before being sent to D.R.S. (A.D.M.S. 1975) Patients remaining 22.	[illegible]

2353 Wt. W2544/1454 700,000 5/15 D. D. & L. A.D.S.S./Forms/C. 2118.

Instructions regarding War Diaries and Intelligence Summaries are contained in F. S. Regs., Part II. and the Staff Manual respectively. Title pages will be prepared in manuscript.

WAR DIARY

or

~~INTELLIGENCE SUMMARY.~~

(Erase heading not required.)

Army Form C. 2118.

Place	Date	Hour	Summary of Events and Information	Remarks and references to Appendices
BAILLEUL	13.11.16	11 AM.	Position & Code Calls received.	
		4.30 PM	ADMS visited Main Dressing Station. Capt Davidson rejoined from leave. New huts for expected increase of patients in process of Erection. Patients remaining 20. Capt Johnston granted leave from 15th to 28th. Capt Pesel granted leave from 15 to 24.	[illegible]
"	14.11.16	10.30 Am.	Wind Dangerous. C.O. visited ADSs and arranged for Concreting of all Cookhouses and latrines. Also arranged with 107 Bde for M.G.C. & T.M.B. personnel to be ~~[illegible]~~ reinoculated. Patients remaining 19.	[illegible]
"	15.11.16		Routine. Plan of Camp showing all buildings drains etc. prepared and forwarded to ADMS. New drains working well. Patients remaining 30.	
"	16.11.16		C.O. visited A.D.S.s. Camp to be named and known as MAGILLIGAN CAMP. (36 NW 4 9 Q). A Gas attack having been arranged for tonight Capt Davidson, Bde Gas Officer detailed to proceed	[illegible]
		8.40 PM	to LINDENHOEK for duty. Patients remaining 30.	

Army Form C. 2118.

Instructions regarding War Diaries and Intelligence Summaries are contained in F. S. Regs., Part II. and the Staff Manual respectively. Title pages will be prepared in manuscript.

WAR DIARY
or
~~INTELLIGENCE SUMMARY.~~
(Erase heading not required.)

Place	Date	Hour	Summary of Events and Information	Remarks and references to Appendices
BAILLEUL	17.11.16		Lieut T.W.G. Johnson returned from leave. Routine. Patients remaining 28.	[illegible]
	18.11.16	10 A.M.	A.D.M.S visited Camp and approved of the work of making increased accommodation. Patients remaining 38.	R
	19.11.16	11.30 A.M.	Wind Safe. Work begun of making Standings for wagons. Great difficulty is experienced in obtaining material. Split pit-props, sand and bricks are being used. Patients remaining 37	[illegible]
	20.11.16	11 A.M.	D.D.M.S visited Camp. C.O. granted acting rank of Lt Col. Patients remaining 41	[illegible]
	21.11.16		Routine Patients remaining 42	
	22.11.16		Capt Russell detailed to relieve Lt Ramsbottom who is proceeding to take temporary charge of 172 Bde R.F.A. On completion of this duty to return to his own unit – 108 F.A. Patients remaining 42	R
	23.11.16		Routine Patients remaining 45.	
	24.11.16		Routine Work at all dressing stations proceeding satisfactorily. Patients remaining 53.	[illegible]
	25.11.16	10 A.M.	Lieut Johnson detailed to take over temporary medical charge of 11th R Rifles vice Capt Grimson who ~~[illegible]~~ took over charge of the Battalion pending Capt Hogg's return from extended leave. Capt Grimson	

2353 Wt. W2544/1454 700,000 5/15 D. D. & L. A.D.S.S./Forms/C. 2118.

Army Form C. 2118.

Instructions regarding War Diaries and Intelligence Summaries are contained in F. S. Regs., Part II. and the Staff Manual respectively. Title pages will be prepared in manuscript.

WAR DIARY
or
~~INTELLIGENCE SUMMARY.~~
(Erase heading not required.)

Place	Date	Hour	Summary of Events and Information	Remarks and references to Appendices
BAILLEUL	25.11.16		proceeding to England on expiration of Contract.	[illegible]
	"	8 PM	Lt. Johnson reported. Capt Hogg having returned from Leave. Patients remaining 52	
	26.11.16		Capt Pesel reported from Leave. 4 wagons can now be accommodated on new standing. A water trough + cistern has been erected at horse lines. Patients remaining 58	[illegible]
	27.11.16		Owing to large numbers of Patients at M.D.S. arrangements have been made to accommodate 30 to 40 patients in A.D.S. DRANOUTRE where there are two large comfortable wards in a good house. Most of the sick are collected in that vicinity transport will be economised and possibly fuel also as a fewer number of stoves will be required. Patients remaining 54.	[illegible]
	28.11.16		Routine. Patients remaining 56	[illegible]
	29.11.16		Capt Pesel detailed to assist Lt Finnegan at No 1 A.D.S where there are already 35 patients. Patients remaining 58	[illegible]
	30.11.16		Routine. Patients remaining 61	[illegible]

2353 Wt. W2544/1454 700,000 5/15 D. D. & L. A.D.S.S./Forms/C. 2118.

Confidential

War Diary

of

109 Field Ambulance

From 1st Dec 1916 To 31st Dec 1916

Vol XV

A. Moore
Lt Col RAMC
Comdg 109 F.A.

Instructions regarding War Diaries and Intelligence Summaries are contained in F. S. Regs., Part II. and the Staff Manual respectively. Title Pages will be prepared in manuscript.

WAR DIARY
or
~~INTELLIGENCE SUMMARY~~
(Erase heading not required.)

Army Form C. 2118

Place	Date	Hour	Summary of Events and Information	Remarks and references to Appendices
BAILLEUL	1.12.16	9 AM	Capt Johnston reported from leave of absence having been married while at home. Capt Davidson reported from duty at Divisional Gas school. Routine. Patients remaining 64.	Rm
"	2.12.16	9 AM	Secret instructions received from ADMS relating to "wind dangerous Periods". Relatively large number of sick in hospital due to, for the most part, an epidemic of mild influenzal colds. Patients remaining 73	Rm
"	3.12.16	"	Capt Davidson detailed for duty at No 1 ADS DRANOUTRE vice Capt Pesel admitted to officers Rest Station MONT NOIR. Lt Finnigan granted leave from 4th to 14th inst	Rm
		3. PM	"Wind Safe". Patients remaining 72	
		8. PM	RAMC operation order No 21. Extract. 109 Fd Amb will take over ADSs at ROMARIN & HYDE PARK CORNER on the move of 109 Inf Bde and will evacuate the sick & wounded of the Bde.	Rm
	4.12.16		In addition to his duty at DRANOUTRE Capt Davidson takes over temporary medical charge of 16th R I Rifles. Routine Patients remaining 66.	Rm
"	5.12.16	1 PM	Consequent on the move of the 109 Inf Bde to the right of the Divisional front as outlined in ADMS Operation Order (see 3rd inst) Capt Johnston took over ADSs at ROMARIN & HYDE PARK CORNER from 75th Fd Amb. and will evacuate sick & wounded of the Bde.	

Instructions regarding War Diaries and Intelligence Summaries are contained in F. S. Regs., Part II. and the Staff Manual respectively. Title Pages will be prepared in manuscript.

WAR DIARY
or
~~INTELLIGENCE SUMMARY~~
(Erase heading not required.)

Army Form C. 2118

Place	Date	Hour	Summary of Events and Information	Remarks and references to Appendices
BAILLEUL	5.12.16	1 P.M.	Capt. Russell handed over No 2 A.D.S. at LINDENHOEK to 16th Division and proceeded to relieve Capt. Davidson in temporary medical charge of 16 R I Rifles	[illegible]
"		4 PM	"Wind Dangerous". Patients remaining 90	
"	6.12.16		Routine. Football match against No 2 CCS Score = 10 of 7.A 2 goals. No 2 CCS nil. Patients remaining 59	[illegible]
"	7.12.16		The dressing station at ROMARIN not recently having been used as such was found in rather a delapidated condition. It is necessary to construct new cook house latrines &c. This work is in progress. accomodation for patients being made more comfortable. a brick fire place is being built in large ward.	[illegible]
			Patients remaining 56	[illegible]
"	8.12.16	11.30 AM	"Wind safe". Routine. Patients remaining 58.	
"	9.12.16	10.30 AM	ADMS accompanied by C.O. inspected ADSs at ROMARIN & HYDE PARK CORNER.	[illegible]
		11 AM	Lt H A Boyle reported his arrival for duty and taken on strength. Capt Pearl evacuated to Base & struck off strength.	

1875 Wt. W593/826 1,000,000 4/15 J.B.C. & A. A.D.S.S./Forms/C. 2118.

Instructions regarding War Diaries and Intelligence Summaries are contained in F. S. Regs., Part II. and the Staff Manual respectively. Title Pages will be prepared in manuscript.

WAR DIARY
or
~~INTELLIGENCE SUMMARY~~
(Erase heading not required.)

Army Form C. 2118

Place	Date	Hour	Summary of Events and Information	Remarks and references to Appendices
BAILLEUL	9.12.16		Capt. Russell rejoined from duty with 16th R I Rifles and proceeded to A.D.S. ~~DR~~ DRANOUTRE for duty	[initials]
		12.30 PM	Wind Dangerous. Patients remaining 62.	[initials]
	10.12.16		Routine. Patients remaining 91	[initials]
	11.12.16	11 AM	2 copies of Trench Code received. Routine. Patients remaining 72	
	12.12.16	7 PM	Wind Safe. Routine. Patients remaining 68. Lt. Boyle detailed for duty at A.D.S. ROMARIN.	[initials]
	13.12.16		Routine. Work continues at Main Dressing Station improving existing accommodation. New latrines are being constructed. Standing for wagons are progressing very slowly owing to difficulty in getting material. Patients remaining 72	[initials]
	14.12.16	10 AM	ADMS visited M.D.S. Lt. Boyle detailed as M.O. 9th R. Innis Fusiliers, struck off strength.	
		2 PM	2 O.R. reinforcements reported for duty. 24 O.R. of the Battalions of 109 Bde reported for a 7 days course of instruction as Stretcher Bearers. Patients remaining 75.	[initials]

1875 Wt. W593/826 1,000,000 4/15 J.B.C. & A. A.D.S.S./Forms/C. 2118.

Instructions regarding War Diaries and Intelligence Summaries are contained in F. S. Regs., Part II. and the Staff Manual respectively. Title Pages will be prepared in manuscript.

WAR DIARY
or
~~INTELLIGENCE SUMMARY~~
(Erase heading not required.)

Army Form C. 2118

Place	Date	Hour	Summary of Events and Information	Remarks and references to Appendices
BAILLEUL	15.12.16	10 AM	Capt. Russell transferred from A.D.S. DRANOUTRE for duty at A.D.S. ROMARIN.	
		8 PM	A.D.M.S. 2476. "Sick of KORTEPYP CAMP to be collected by 110th Fd. Amb." This Camp is occupied by 109 Bde Battalion in Divisional Reserve. Patients remaining 78.	Rm
	16.12.16	1 AM	Lt. Finnegan returned from leave.	Rm
		10 AM	Visited wire saps. Routine. Patients remaining 81	
	17.12.16		Routine. Patients remaining 78	Rm
	18.12.16		Routine " " 80	Rm
	19.12.16		Routine " " 88	Rm
	20.12.16	11 AM	Lt H G Morris reported his arrival for duty and taken on strength.	
		3 30 PM	A.D.M.S visited M.D.S & examined men of 109 Bde undergoing a course of instruction. Remaining in Hosp 79	Rm
	21-12-16		Capt. Russell granted leave from 21st to 31st inst. Patients remaining 66.	
	22.12.16		Lt. Johnson M.C. detailed for duty as M.O. & Sanitary Officer of No 33 Prisoners of War Camp. Patients remaining 92	Rm

1875 Wt. W593/826 1,000,000 4/15 J.B.C. & A. A.D.S.S./Forms/C. 2118.

Instructions regarding War Diaries and Intelligence Summaries are contained in F. S. Regs., Part II. and the Staff Manual respectively. Title Pages will be prepared in manuscript.

WAR DIARY
or
~~INTELLIGENCE SUMMARY~~
(Erase heading not required.)

Army Form C. 2118

Place	Date	Hour	Summary of Events and Information	Remarks and references to Appendices
BAILLEUL	23.12.16		Routine. Sergt Morton proceeded to England on recommendation for commission in infantry. £2-10-0 received from Rev T. Wright towards entertaining patients on Christmas day. Patients remaining 66	[illegible]
"	24.12.16	noon	Lt Finnegan took over temporary charge of 14th R Irish Rifles while Capt Gavin is on leave. Patients remaining 56	[illegible]
"	25.12.16	7 AM	Wind dangerous.	
		11.30 AM	Wind Safe.	
		2.30 PM	Personnel & patients sat down to Xmas dinner which was provided by Officers. Dinner consisted of Soup, Turkey, Ham, Cabbage, Potatoes, Plum pudding, Fruit & nuts and 1 pint beer each man. ADMS was present & spoke a few words of appreciation to the unit. Patients remaining 57.	[illegible]
"	26.12.16	10 AM	Wind dangerous. In the afternoon a football match was played with 110th FA — 110 F.A 2 goals 109 F.A nil. Patients remaining 50	[illegible]
	27.12.16	10.30	Co. with DADMS. IX Corps visited DRANOUTRE and inspected a site for a main dressing station	[illegible]

1875 Wt. W593/826 1,000,000 4/15 J.B.C. & A. A.D.S.S./Forms/C. 2118.

Instructions regarding War Diaries and Intelligence Summaries are contained in F. S. Regs., Part II. and the Staff Manual respectively. Title Pages will be prepared in manuscript.

WAR DIARY
or
INTELLIGENCE SUMMARY
(Erase heading not required.)

Army Form C. 2118

Place	Date	Hour	Summary of Events and Information	Remarks and references to Appendices
BAILLEUL	27.11.16	8.PM.	Operation Order No 22 received from A.D.M.S. "On the 29th inst the front now held by the Division will be reorganised as a two Brigade front. The 108 Bde being withdrawn from the line and its sector will be divided between the 107 + 109th Bdes" "The 108th F.A will clear all casualties from the right Bde except from the left Battalion" Patients remaining 54.	[illegible]
"	28.11.16	2PM	Secret No 2665 from A.D.M.S. a letter from D.D.M.S. IX Corps requesting that C.O of this unit be asked to undertake the construction of a main Dressing Station at DRANOUTRE capable of dealing with 1000 wounded. And also requesting his presence at a conference at D.D.M.S office to consider the scheme, on 29th inst.	
"		2PM	2 copies IX Corps intelligence No I.G. 534/54a. enclosing amendments to B.A.B Code. Patients remaining 56.	
		3PM	C.O. visited DRANOUTRE in connection with proposed Dressing Station.	
"			109 Bde O.O. regarding reorganisation of Front received	
		8.PM	Lowd safe.	

Instructions regarding War Diaries and Intelligence Summaries are contained in F. S. Regs., Part II. and the Staff Manual respectively. Title Pages will be prepared in manuscript.

Army Form C. 2118

WAR DIARY
or
~~INTELLIGENCE SUMMARY~~
(Erase heading not required.)

Place	Date	Hour	Summary of Events and Information	Remarks and references to Appendices
BAILLEUL	29.11.16	11 AM	C.O. attended Conference at D.D.M.S. Office. Map prepared was approved & Lt Col Maxwell instructed to draw up specification of materials required. Same to be drawn from Corps R.E. Park. Patients remaining 57.	[illegible]
"	30.11.		Routine. Specification for material for new Dressing Station forwarded to IX Corps for approval. Patients remaining 59.	[illegible]
"	31.11.		Work at HYDE PARK CORNER progressing. Routine. Patients remaining 55.	[illegible]

1875 Wt. W593/826 1,000,000 4/15 J.B.C. & A. A.D.S.S./Forms/C. 2118.

36

Va 1917

Confidential

War Diary

of

109th Field Ambulance

From 1st Jan 17 To 31st Jan 1917

Vol XVI

36 Div

Vol 16

140/948

31/1/17

J. G. Johnston. Capt RAMC
for O.C. 109 Fd Amb

Instructions regarding War Diaries and Intelligence Summaries are contained in F. S. Regs., Part II. and the Staff Manual respectively. Title pages will be prepared in manuscript.

WAR DIARY
or
~~INTELLIGENCE SUMMARY.~~
(Erase heading not required.)

Army Form C. 2118.

Place	Date	Hour	Summary of Events and Information	Remarks and references to Appendices
BAILLEUL	1·1·17	8 AM	Capt. Russell rejoined from leave of absence	
		3 PM	Capt Russell detailed to proceed to ADS ROMARIN to relieve Capt. J. G. Johnston who reports sick.	
		4 "	Capt Johnston admitted to Officers Rest Station MONT NOIR suffering from enteritis.	[initials]
			New shelves & floor constructed in Pack Store.	
			Patients remaining 50	
	2·1·17		Routine. C.O. visited site of new MDS at DRANOUTRE, and marked out position of huts, cook house etc. Patients remaining 53	[initials]
	3·1·17	11 AM	C.O. visited DRANOUTRE & inspected ADS & new work.	
		3·30 PM	A.D.M.S. inspected M.D.S. a football match was played against IX Corps signals 109 FA 3 goals, signals nil. Patients remaining 49	[initials] [initials]
	4·1·17		Routine. CO visited ROMARIN ADS. Patients remaining 45	[initials]
	5·1·17		Routine. Completion of wagon Park much delayed owing to lack of material. accommodation is now available for 11 vehicles. Patients remaining 43	

2353 Wt. W2544/1454 700,000 5/15 D. D. & L. A.D.S.S./Forms/C. 2118.

Instructions regarding War Diaries and Intelligence Summaries are contained in F. S. Regs., Part II. and the Staff Manual respectively. Title pages will be prepared in manuscript.

WAR DIARY
or
~~INTELLIGENCE~~ SUMMARY.
(Erase heading not required.)

Army Form C. 2118.

Place	Date	Hour	Summary of Events and Information	Remarks and references to Appendices
BAILLEUL	6.1.17		C.O. & Captain T. G. Johnston also Lt & QM Chester mentioned in Despatches. Routine. Football match in the afternoon against 1 (C) C.C.S. 1097.A. 6 goals. C.C.S. 1 goal.	[illegible]
		8 PM	Secret A.D.M.S. S/150. List of Position Calls. Patients remaining 47	
"	7.1.17	3 PM	Lt Morris detailed as Temporary M.O. i/c 9th R. Innis. Fus. while R.M.O. attends Course of Sanitation. Work on new M.D.S. DRANOUTRE in progress. Patients remaining 56.	[illegible]
"	8.1.17		Routine. Lt Dunnigan rejoined from duty with 14th R. Irish Rifles. Patients remaining 46.	[illegible]
	9.1.17	7 AM	Wind "Dangerous"	[illegible]
		11 AM	A.D.M.S. visited M.D.S. Patients remaining 58	

Instructions regarding War Diaries and Intelligence Summaries are contained in F. S. Regs., Part II. and the Staff Manual respectively. Title pages will be prepared in manuscript.

WAR DIARY
or
~~INTELLIGENCE SUMMARY~~.
(Erase heading not required.)

Army Form C. 2118.

Place	Date	Hour	Summary of Events and Information	Remarks and references to Appendices
BAILLEUL	10.1.17		Routine. Lt Col Magill Commanding Officer granted 30 days special leave of absence. Capt. J.G. Johnston takes over duties of C.O. Patients remaining 46	JGJ
"	11.1.17	6 A.M.	36th Div. Wire G 910 received — Wind safe.	
		3 p.m.	Lieut J. Finnegan detailed for duty at A.D.S. ROMARIN to relieve Capt. W. Russell who returns to Headquarters. Patients remaining 47	JGJ
"	12.1.17	12 noon	Capt. J.G. Johnston visited A.D.S. DRANOUTRE on Inspection duty. Patients remaining in Hospital 48	JGJ
"	13.1.17	3 pm.	Secret No S/153 received from A.D.M.S. — Additions to list of Position Calls.	
		6 P.M.	Lieut G. H. Morris rejoined from duty with 9th R. Innis Fusiliers. Patients remaining in Hospital 60.	JGJ
"	14.1.17		Lieut T. W. G. Johnson M.C. granted leave of absence on renewal of contract from 15th to 29th Inst. Lieut G. H. Morris detailed for temporary duty as M.O. i/c. 153rd Brigade R.F.A.	
		11.30 pm	36th Div Wire No G 911 received. — wind dangerous —. Patients remaining 57	JGJ
"	15.1.17		Routine. One N.C.O. & five men detailed to attend course of instruction in Sanitation at No 4 Sanitary Section. Patients remaining 58.	JGJ
"	16.1.17		Routine — Patients remaining in Hospital 68.	JGJ
"	17.1.17		Routine — Patients remaining in Hospital 66	JGJ

Instructions regarding War Diaries and Intelligence Summaries are contained in F. S. Regs., Part II. and the Staff Manual respectively. Title pages will be prepared in manuscript.

WAR DIARY
or
INTELLIGENCE SUMMARY.
(Erase heading not required.)

Army Form C. 2118.

Place	Date	Hour	Summary of Events and Information	Remarks and references to Appendices
BAILLEUL	18.1.17		Routine D.A.D.M.S. visited M.D Stn Patients remaining in Hospital 70	J.G.J.
"	19.1.17	3pm	D.D.M.S & D.A.D.M.S. 9th Corps visited M.D. Stn & expressed approval with the condition of the Camp. Patients remaining in Hospital 59.	J.G.J.
"	20.1.17	5pm	Lieut G.H. Morris rejoined from duty with 153rd Brigade R.F.A. Patients remaining in Hospital 58	J.G.J.
"	21.1.17		Routine Patients remaining in Hospital 52.	J.G.J.
"	22.1.17	11am	Capt J.G. Johnston inspected A.D.S. ROMARIN, and the work at HYDE PARK CORNER	
		3pm	Inspection of Horses by A.D.V.S. for mange, none found – Transport Officer complimented on the hard condition of the Horses. Patients remaining 56	J.G.J.
"	23.1.17		Routine Patients remaining in Hospital 64	J.G.J.
"	24.1.17		O.M. Sergeant attended course of Instruction at IX Corps Cookery School, HAZEBROUCK. Patients remaining in Hospital 49.	J.G.J.
"	25.1.17		Lieut G.H. Morris detailed for temporary duty as M.O. i/c 14th Royal Irish Rifles, to relieve Capt N.G. Gavin sick.	
		7.30pm	109th Brigade Secret Order No 16 received – move of Brigade Headquarters to ENGLISH FARM. Patients remaining in Hospital 50.	J.G.J.
"	26.1.17		Routine. Patients remaining in Hospital 40.	J.G.J.

2353 Wt. W2544/1454 700,000 5/15 D. D. & L. A.D.S.S./Forms/C. 2118.

Instructions regarding War Diaries and Intelligence Summaries are contained in F. S. Regs., Part II. and the Staff Manual respectively. Title pages will be prepared in manuscript.

WAR DIARY
or
INTELLIGENCE SUMMARY.
(Erase heading not required.)

Army Form C. 2118.

Place	Date	Hour	Summary of Events and Information	Remarks and references to Appendices
BAILLEUL	27.1.17	2.p.M.	A.D.M.S's Secret number S155 received — Inspection of valves of Small box respirators twice daily during the frosty weather, & the insertion of a few drops of Glycerine into the valves to prevent this. Patients remaining in Hospital - 48.	J.G.J.
"	28.1.17	3.p.M.	Capt J.G. Johnston visited A.D.S. ROMARIN and HYDE PARK CORNER, on inspection duty. Lieut G.H. Morris reported his arrival from temporary duty with the 14th Royal Irish Rifles. Patients remaining 49.	J.G.J.
"	29.1.17	2.p.M.	Capt J.G. Johnston visited A.D.S. DRANOUTRE, & arranged for carrying on the work at the new Dressing Station.	
		3.p.M.	All Horses washed in Calcium Sulphide solution as a prophylactic against Mange. Patients remaining in Hospital 49.	J.G.J.
"	30.1.17		Routine. Patients remaining in Hospital 55	J.G.J.
	31.1.17	9.A.M.	Lieut G.H. Morris detailed for duty as M.O. i/c 15th Royal Irish Rifles vice Capt I.W. Corkery.	
		3.P.M.	Inspection of the Camp & Hospital by an Italian Officer, with the Staff Captain 109th Brigade; the Italian Major is on a tour of inspection & instruction in our lines. Patients remaining in Hospital 60.	J.G.J.

Vol 17

140/1991

36th Div

Confidential

War Diary

Of

109th Field Ambulance

From 1-2-17

To 28-2-17

Vol XVII

B.E.F.
28-2-17

J.G. Johnston. Capt RAMC
for O.C. 109th Field Amb.

Instructions regarding War Diaries and Intelligence Summaries are contained in F. S. Regs., Part II. and the Staff Manual respectively. Title Pages will be prepared in manuscript.

WAR DIARY
or
~~INTELLIGENCE SUMMARY~~
(Erase heading not required.)

Army Form C. 2118

Place	Date	Hour	Summary of Events and Information	Remarks and references to Appendices
BAILLEUL	1.2.17.		Lieut Y. W. G. Johnson M C. rejoined from leave of absence. Patients remaining in Hospital 64	J.G.J.
"	2.2.17		Capt W. Russell detailed for duty at A. D. S. ROMARIN.	
		2 p.m.	Capt J.G. Johnston visited A.D.S. ROMARIN & HYDE PARK CORNER on inspection duty. Patients remaining in Hospital 56	J.G.J.
"	3.2.17	11 A.M.	A. D. M. S. visited & inspected Headquarters and Main Dressing Station. Patients remaining in Hospital 55.	J.G.J.
"	4.2.17	11 A M	A. D. M. S. visited & inspected A. D. S. DRANOUTRE, and work on New Camp at DRANOUTRE.	
		12 A.M.	Lieut L. S. H. Glanville reported for duty. Patients remaining in Hospital 49.	J.G.J.
"	5.2.17	11 A.M.	A. D. M. S. visited and inspected A.D.S. ROMARIN and HYDE PARK CORNER	
		2 p.m.	Lieut L. S. H. Glanville detailed to take over temporary Medical Charge of 10th Royal Irish Rifles, vice Capt A. Fullerton M. C. on leave of absence. Patients remaining in Hospital 51.	J.G.J.
"	6.2.17	10 A M.	D. D. M. S. IX Corps & Capt J.G. Johnston visited site of new dressing Station at DRANOUTRE, to select positions for the Huts etc, two large Nissen bow Huts have been obtained work of erection to commence tomorrow. Patients remaining in Hospital 59.	J.G.J.

1875 Wt. W593/826 1,000,000 4/15 J.B.C. & A. A.D.S.S./Forms/C. 2118.

Instructions regarding War Diaries and Intelligence Summaries are contained in F. S. Regs., Part II. and the Staff Manual respectively. Title Pages will be prepared in manuscript.

WAR DIARY
or
INTELLIGENCE SUMMARY
(Erase heading not required.)

Army Form C. 2118

Place	Date	Hour	Summary of Events and Information	Remarks and references to Appendices
BAILLEUL	7.2.17	10.30 A.M.	A.D.M.S's Secret No S/159 received —— 2 Copies of IX Corps Intelligence No I.G.77 B.A.B. Code corrections. Work commenced on Huts at new dressing-station DRANOUTRE.	
		3. pm	Capt J.G. Johnston visited this dressing-station. Lieut & Q-Mr. S.C.R. Chester appointed Railhead Disbursing Officer from 7th inst. Patients remaining in Hospital 52.	J.G.J.
"	8.2.17	3 p.m.	Capt. J.G. Johnston visited work on new dressing-station DRANOUTRE. Patients remaining in Hospital 47.	J.G.J.
"	9.2.17	2 p.m.	Capt. J.G. Johnston inspected A.D.S. ROMARIN and HYDE PARK CORNER. Capt. W. Russell detailed for duty at Headquarters, and to take over Medical Charge of 29th Prisoners of War Camp from Lieut. Y.W.G. Johnson. Patients remaining in Hospital 55.	J.G.J.
"	10.2.17		Lieut Y.W.G. Johnson M.C. detailed by A.D.M.S. to take over permanent Medical Charge of 9th Royal Inniskilling Fusiliers from Lieut Boyle relinquishing his Commission on expiration of Contract. All R.A.M.C. personnel attached to the 36th Div. Hutting Co. rejoined their units. Patients remaining in Hospital 58.	J.G.J.

1875 Wt. W593/826 1,000,000 4/15 J.B.C. & A. A.D.S.S./Forms/C. 2118.

Instructions regarding War Diaries and Intelligence Summaries are contained in F. S. Regs., Part II. and the Staff Manual respectively. Title Pages will be prepared in manuscript.

WAR DIARY
or
INTELLIGENCE SUMMARY
(Erase heading not required.)

Army Form C. 2118

Place	Date	Hour	Summary of Events and Information	Remarks and references to Appendices
BAILLEUL	11.2.17		Capt W. Russell visited & inspected work on new dressing station at DRANOUTRE. Patients remaining in Hospital 64.	J.G.J.
"	12.2.17		Lieut G. H. Morris detailed for 5 days Course of instruction in Sanitation at 2nd Army Headquarters at HAZEBROUCK. Capt L. S. H. Glanville detailed to take over temporary Medical charge of 13th Royal Irish Rifles, vice Lieut G. H. Morris who goes on Sanitation course.	
		2 pm	Capt. J. G. Johnston visited new dressing station DRANOUTRE. Patients remaining in Hospital 63.	J.G.J.
"	13.2.17	10 AM	A.D.M.S. secret No 10 received — new Secret Word for Playfair Code. A.D.M.S. Secret No S/160 received — Report on Gas Attack on French & lessons learnt therefrom. Patients remaining in Hospital 46.	J.G.J.
"	14.2.17		Lieut - Colonel R. Magill returned from leave of absence, and resumed Command. Patients remaining in Hospital 48.	J.G.J.

1875 Wt W50/826 1,000,000 4/15 J.B.C. & A. A.D.S.S./Forms/C. 2118.

Army Form C. 2118.

WAR DIARY
or
~~INTELLIGENCE SUMMARY~~.
(Erase heading not required.)

Instructions regarding War Diaries and Intelligence Summaries are contained in F. S. Regs., Part II. and the Staff Manual respectively. Title pages will be prepared in manuscript.

Place	Date	Hour	Summary of Events and Information	Remarks and references to Appendices
BAILLEUL	15.2.17	10.30 AM	Main Dressing Station inspected by A.D.M.S. who expressed himself as very pleased with the condition of the Camp.	
		3 PM	A.D.M.S. met O.C. at DRANOUTRE and inspected A.D.S. and new Camp in construction. The A.D.M.S. was well pleased with the A.D.S. and with the progress of the work at the new Camp.	
			Patients remaining 44.	R.M.
"	16.2.17		Lieut.-Colonel R. Magill sent to Pasteur Institute, Paris, for treatment, having been bitten by a dog suspected of Rabies. Capt J.G. Johnston again takes over the duties of Officer Commanding. Patients remaining in Hospital 53.	J.G.J.
"	17.2.17	2 pm	Capt Johnston visited Dressing Station DRANOUTRE and new Camp in construction	
		4 PM	Lieut G.H. Morris rejoined from course of Sanitation at 2nd Army H.Q. Patients remaining in Hospital 46.	J.G.J.
"	18.2.17		Routine. Patients remaining in Hospital 56	J.G.J.
"	19.2.17		Lieut G.H. Morris detailed for Duty at A.D.S. ROMARIN. –	
		2 p.m.	Capt J.G. Johnston visited A.D.S. ROMARIN on inspection duty.	
		7.15 pm	Secret location of Units (36th Div) d/19.2.17 & Secret Names & Co-ordinates of Camps, Roads & Farms received. Patients remaining in Hospital 53.	J.G.J.

2353 Wt. W2514/1454 700,000 5/15 D. D. & L. A.D.S.S./Forms/C. 2118.

Instructions regarding War Diaries and Intelligence Summaries are contained in F. S. Regs., Part II, and the Staff Manual respectively. Title pages will be prepared in manuscript.

WAR DIARY
or
INTELLIGENCE SUMMARY.
(Erase heading not required.)

Army Form C. 2118.

Place	Date	Hour	Summary of Events and Information	Remarks and references to Appendices
BAILLEUL	20.2.17	2. p.m.	Capt J. G. Johnston visited A. D. S. DRANOUTRE.	
		3 p.m.	Lieut J. Finegan reported for duty at H.Q. from A.D.S. ROMARIN. A.D.M.S. secret number O/O 23/2 d/ 20 2/17 received at noon. Patients remaining in Hospital 38.	J.G.J.
"	21.2.17	2.30 pm	Capt J. G. Johnston visited A. D. S. DRANOUTRE. Patients remaining in Hospital 47.	J.G.J.
"	22.2.17	12. AM.	Captain E. C. Allen Smith reported his arrival for duty & is taken on the strength. Patients remaining in Hospital 45.	J.G.J.
"	23.2.17	10 A.M.	Capt. W. Russell detailed for temporary duty as M.O i/c 11th Royal Innis. Fusiliers. Capt S.C.A. Smith to take over Medical charge of 29th Prisoners of War Camp from Capt Russell. Capt. J. G. Johnston visited A.D.S.s ROMARIN and HYDE PARK CORNER.	
		3 pm.	A.D.M.S. inspected Main Dressing Station. Patients remaining 45.	J.G.J.
"	24.2.17	10 A.M.	109th Brigade Secret number 25 d/ 22.2.17 received.	
		11 AM	Capt. J. G. Johnston visited A.D.Ss ROMARIN and DRANOUTRE, re divisional scheme for growing vegetables on waste land.	
		10 p.m.	36th Divisional Wire No G. 634 received — WIND DANGEROUS. Patients remaining in Hospital 34.	J.G.J.

2353 Wt. W2544/1454 700,000 5/15 D. D. & L. A.D.S.S./Forms/C. 2118.

Instructions regarding War Diaries and Intelligence Summaries are contained in F. S. Regs., Part II. and the Staff Manual respectively. Title pages will be prepared in manuscript.

WAR DIARY
or
INTELLIGENCE SUMMARY.
(Erase heading not required.)

Army Form C. 2118.

Place	Date	Hour	Summary of Events and Information	Remarks and references to Appendices
BAILLEUL	25.2.17		Under the new Divisional scheme for growing vegetables it has been decided to cultivate at Main Dressing Station 1½ acres, at A.D.S. ROMARIN ⅓ acre, and at A.D.S. DRANOUTRE 400 square yards.	
		9 p.m.	36th Divisional Wire No G.645 received — WIND SAFE. Remaining in Hospital 31.	J.G.J.
"	26.2.17	11.30 a.m.	A.D.M.S. and Lt-Col L. J. Comyn A.A. & Q.M.G. visited Main Dressing Station. Patients remaining in Hospital 49	J.G.J.
"	27.2.17		Capt. H. S. Davidson granted leave of absence from 28th February to 10th March. Capt J. Finnegan detailed to relieve Capt Davidson at A.D.S. DRANOUTRE.	
		12.30 p.m.	Capt J.G. Johnston visited A.D.S. DRANOUTRE. Patients remaining in Hospital 63.	J.G.J.
"	28.2.17		Routine. Capt. A [illegible] Chown A.V.C. O.C. 48th Mobile Veterinary Section, inspected all animals for Stomatitis Contagiosa. Patients remaining 54.	J.G.J.

Vol 18

140/2042

Confidential

War Diary

of

109th Field Ambulance

36th Div

From 1st March 1917 To 31st March 1917

Vol XVIII

1st April 1917

J. G. Johnston. Lieut Col
Comdg 109th Field Amb

Army Form C. 2118.

WAR DIARY
or
~~INTELLIGENCE SUMMARY.~~
(Erase heading not required.)

Instructions regarding War Diaries and Intelligence Summaries are contained in F. S. Regs., Part II. and the Staff Manual respectively. Title pages will be prepared in manuscript.

Place	Date	Hour	Summary of Events and Information	Remarks and references to Appendices
BAILLEUL	1.3.17		General Routine Patients remaining in Hospital 43.	J.G.J.
"	2.3.17	10 AM.	A.D.M.S. Secret No S/165 received — 2 copies of B.A.B Code correction.	
		11.30 AM.	Capt J.G. Johnston visited on inspection duty A.D.Stn. ROMARIN.	
		2.30 PM.	Capt J.G. Johnston visited on inspection duty A.D.Stn. DRANOUTRE. Patients remaining in Hospital - 45.	J.G.J.
"	3.3.17	6 am.	36th Divisional Wire received - Wind dangerous.	
			Capt L.S.H. Glanville transferred to 110th Field Ambulance & struck off strength	
		7 p.m.	Capt W. Russell rejoined from temporary duty with 9th Royal Inniskilling Fusiliers. Patients remaining in Hospital 41.	J.G.J.
"	4.3.17		Routine. Patients remaining in Hospital 37.	J.G.J.
"	5.3.17	3 p.m.	A.D.M.S. 36th Division visited and inspected Main Dressing Station & expressed himself well pleased with the arrangements. Patients remaining in Hospital 42.	J.G.J.
"	6.3.17		No 29 Prisoners of War Camp, KEERSEBROM ROAD taken over on departure of the prisoners for STRAAZEELE. One N.C.O. & 3 O.R. to take charge. Patients remaining in Hospital 46.	J.G.J.
"	7.3.17	3 p.m.	Capt. E.C. Allan Smith detailed to attend a lecture and demonstration by Divisional Gas Officer at Divisional H.Q. Patients remaining in Hospital 56.	J.G.J.

Army Form C. 2118.

Instructions regarding War Diaries and Intelligence Summaries are contained in F. S. Regs., Part II. and the Staff Manual respectively. Title pages will be prepared in manuscript.

WAR DIARY
or
INTELLIGENCE SUMMARY.
(*Erase heading not required.*)

Place	Date	Hour	Summary of Events and Information	Remarks and references to Appendices
BAILLEUL	8.3.17	12 noon	Capt. W.H. Hart reported for duty and taken on the strength.	
		2 pm.	Capt J.G. Johnston visited A.D.S. DRANOUTRE. Patients remg in Hospital 59.	J.G.J.
"	9.3.17	2 pm	Capt W. Russell detailed to take over temporary Medical Charge of 11th R. Innis Fus.	
		"	A.D.M.S. Secret No 3666 received – re use of Hydrocyanic Acid in Shells by Germans	
			Patients remaining in Hospital. 59.	J.G.J.
"	10.3.17	10 A.M.	A.D.M.S. New Zealand Division with O.C. No 1 Australian Field Ambulance D.A.D.M.S. 36th Division & Capt J.G. Johnston visited A.D. Stns ROMARIN & HYDE PARK CORNER with a view to taking and handing over same.	
			Patients remaining in Hospital 47.	J.G.J.
"	11.3.17	9 A.M.	A.D.M.S. Secret No 3684 received – One telephone on charge of unit to be removed if Field Ambulance moves.	
		1 p.m.	Secret – Names & Co-ordinates of Camps. Farms & Roads & Location of Units in Divisional Area, received.	
		3 p.m	Capt. J.G. Johnston visited & inspected A.D.S. DRANOUTRE.	
			Patients remaining in Hospital 44.	J.G.J.
"	12.3.17	9 A.M.	Capt. H.S. Davidson rejoined from leave of absence.	
		11 A.M.	A.D.M.S. inspected Main Dressing Station & found all correct.	
		2 pm.	Secret – re continued use of Gas Shells by the enemy, received	
		3 pm.	Capt H.S. Davidson detailed for duty at A.D.S. DRANOUTRE.	
		7.30 pm	A.D.M.S. Secret No O/O No 24 received. Patients remg in Hospital 46.	J.G.J.

2353 Wt. W2544/1454 700,000 5/15 D. D. & L. A.D.S.S./Forms/C. 2118.

Army Form C. 2118.

Instructions regarding War Diaries and Intelligence Summaries are contained in F. S. Regs., Part II. and the Staff Manual respectively. Title pages will be prepared in manuscript.

WAR DIARY
or
INTELLIGENCE SUMMARY.
(Erase heading not required.)

Place	Date	Hour	Summary of Events and Information	Remarks and references to Appendices
BAILLEUL	13.3.17	11.30 AM	36th Divisional Wire No G.956 received — Wind safe.	
		12 noon	Capt. E.C.A. Smith with 19 O.R. detailed to take over the A.D.S. LINDENHOEK from 113th Field Ambulance, 16th Division, this includes personnel for three R.A.P's viz REGENT STREET DUG OUTS, SHAMUS FARM, and S.P.11 in the VIA GELLIA. Patients remaining in Hospital 50.	J.G.J.
"	14.3.17	3 p.m.	Capt. J.G. Johnston visited & inspected A.D. Stn DRANOUTRE.	
		7 p.m.	A.D.M.S. defence scheme for evacuation of wounded necessitated by taking over A.D.S. LINDENHOEK & handing over A.D.S's ROMARIN & HYDE PARK CORNER. O.C. 109th Field Ambulance to proceed to A.D.S. DRANOUTRE to direct the bearers and general evacuation.	
		"	A.D.M.S. Secret No S/172 received — move of D.R.S (108th Field Ambulance) to premises vacated by No 8. C.C.S. in BAILLEUL. Patients remaining in Hospital 47.	J.G.J.
"	15.3.17	9.30 AM	A.D.M.S. Secret No S 173 received — Correction for B.A.B. Code from 6 p.m.	
		2 p.m.	A.D.M.S. No 3734 received — Lt. Col Magill granted 3 weeks sick leave which expires on 4th April 1917.	
		2.30 p.m.	Lieut G.H. Morris and 18 O.R. returned to M.D. Stn. after handing over A.D.S's ROMARIN and HYDE PARK CORNER to No 3. New Zealand Field Ambulance. Staff Sergt. R.S. Gillespie R.A.M.C of this unit awarded the "Italian Bronze Medal for Military Valour" G.R.O. 1565 d/14.3.17	
		8 p.m.	36th Div. Wire G.12 recd — Wind dangerous. Patients remaining in Hospital 54.	J.G.J.

Instructions regarding War Diaries and Intelligence Summaries are contained in F. S. Regs., Part II. and the Staff Manual respectively. Title pages will be prepared in manuscript.

WAR DIARY

or

~~INTELLIGENCE SUMMARY~~

(Erase heading not required.)

Army Form C. 2118.

Place	Date	Hour	Summary of Events and Information	Remarks and references to Appendices
BAILLEUL	16.3.17	10 A.M.	A.D.M.S. and Capt J.G. Johnston visited A.D.S. LINDENHOEK and R.A.P. REGENT St	
		3 p.M.	Capt J.G. Johnston visited A.D.S. DRANOUTRE.	
		4 pM.	A.D.M.S.'s Secret Numbers S/177 + S/178 received = Secret Code + Collection of Sick from new area owing to Brigade moves. Pts remaining <u>in Hospital</u> 61.	J.G.J.
"	17.3.17	11 A.M.	Capt J.G. Johnston attended Court of Enquiry at H.Q. 110th Field Ambce. re damage done to one of our Motor Ambulance Cars and French Civilian Cart in Collision in the Rue de LILLE BAILLEUL.	
		4 pM.	36th Div Wire No G42 received — Wind Safe. Patients remg in Hospital 53.	J.G.J.
"	18.3.17	11 A M	Capt J.G. Johnston visited A.D.S. DRANOUTRE + R.A.P. at S.P. 11 in Via Gellis. also inspecting the A.D.S. in KEMMELL of the 113th Field Ambulance. Patients remaining in Hospital 62.	J.G.J.
"	19.3.17	9.45 AM	A.D.M.S. with D.A.D.M.S. + Capt Johnston visited the trenches and inspected R.A.P. at SHAMUS FARM.	
		8 pm	Secret O/O. No 25 d/ 19/3 received — Section of 110th Field Ambulance to proceed with 109th Brigade into training at St OMER area. Patients remaining in Hospital 53.	J.G.J.
	20.3.17	4-30 pm	Capt J.G. Johnston visited A.D.S. DRANOUTRE on duty. Patients remaining in Hospital 56	J.G.J.
	21.3.17	9.45 AM	A.D.M.S. with Capt Johnston visited A.D.S. LINDENHOEK and R.A.P.s at REGENT St. and S.P. 11. proceeding via LOCRE, La Clytte, and KEMMELL.	
		10 A.M.	Secret Location of Units and Secret Code No 11 received. Patients remaining in Hospital 62.	J.G.J.

Instructions regarding War Diaries and Intelligence Summaries are contained in F. S. Regs., Part II. and the Staff Manual respectively. Title Pages will be prepared in manuscript.

WAR DIARY
or
INTELLIGENCE SUMMARY
(Erase heading not required.)

Army Form C. 2118

Place	Date	Hour	Summary of Events and Information	Remarks and references to Appendices
BAILLEUL	22.3.17	12 noon	36th Division Wire No G 154 received — Wind dangerous.	
			Lieut G. H. Morris transferred to 51st H. A. Group for duty.	
			Capt G. M. Maybury transferred from 110th Field Amb ce & taken on strength.	
			Capt J. G. Johnston visited A. D. S. DRANOUTRE.	
			Patients remaining in Hospital: 66	J.G.J.
"	23.3.17	12 noon	Capt J. G. Johnston visited new work on Main Dressing Station	
			Patients remaining in Hospital = 75.	J.G.J.
"	24.3.17	3 p.m.	O.C. visited on inspection Duty New Main Dressing Stn & A.D.S. DRANOUTRE.	
			Time advanced one hour at 11 p.m. Pts remg in Hosp. 80	J.G.J.
"	25.3.17		Routine Patients remaining in Hospital 84	J.G.J.
"	26.3.17	10 A.M.	Work and Huts at new Main Dressing Stn handed over to 108th Field Amb ce.	
		1 p.m.	A.D.M.S. Secret No S/183 received — Correction for B.A.B. Code.	
			Patients remaining in Hospital 72	J.G.J.
"	27.3.17	9 A.M.	A.D.M.S. Secret No S/184 received — correction for S/183.	
		11 A.M.	A.D.M.S. visited and inspected Main Dressing Station.	
		5 p.m.	Capt. J. G. Johnston visited A.D.S. DRANOUTRE.	
			Patients remaining in Hospital 56	J.G.J.
"	28.3.17	11 A.M.	Capt Johnston visited & inspected A.D.S's & posts in the line.	
			Lieut J Finnegan granted leave from 28/3/17 to 6/4/17.	
			Capt G M Maybury detailed for duty at A.D.S. DRANOUTRE.	
			Patients remaining in Hospital 77.	J.G.J.

1875 Wt. W593/826 1,000,000 4/15 J.B.C. & A. A.D.S.S./Forms/C. 2118.

Instructions regarding War Diaries and Intelligence Summaries are contained in F. S. Regs., Part II. and the Staff Manual respectively. Title Pages will be prepared in manuscript.

WAR DIARY
or
~~INTELLIGENCE SUMMARY~~
(Erase heading not required.)

Army Form C. 2118

Place	Date	Hour	Summary of Events and Information	Remarks and references to Appendices
BAILLEUL	29.3.17	2 pm	A.D.M.S. Secret No S/186 received — 36th Div position Calls & location of Units.	
		3 pm	Capt J.G. Johnston visited A.D.S. DRANOUTRE.	
		7 pm	A.D.M.S. Secret No 3925 received. — Anticipation of gas attacks during April.	
			Patients remaining in Hospital 87.	J.G.J.
"	30.3.17	7.15 pm	A.D.M.S. Secret O/O. No 26 received —— Handing over A.D.Stns & the evacuation of casualties from the line to 108th Field Ambulance & the taking over of KEERSEBROM Camp for a Divisnl Rest Stn.	
			Remaining in Hospital 106.	J.G.J.
"	31.3.17	11 am.	Secret A.D.M.S. No S/188 received — Copy of Code calls for 16th, 19th & 36th Divisions also No S/189 — in event of Gas Shell bombardment wire to be sent to Divisnl Gas Office.	
		2 pm.	Capt J.G. Johnston visited & inspected A.D.S. DRANOUTRE.	
			Patients remaining in Hospital. 68.	J.G.J.

1875 Wt. W593/826 1,000,000 4/15 J.B.C. & A. A.D.S.S./Forms/C. 2118.

Army Form C. 2118

Instructions regarding War Diaries and Intelligence Summaries are contained in F. S. Regs., Part II. and the Staff Manual respectively. Title Pages will be prepared in manuscript.

WAR DIARY
or
INTELLIGENCE SUMMARY
(Erase heading not required.)

Place	Date	Hour	Summary of Events and Information	Remarks and references to Appendices
BAILLEUL	1.4.17	9 A.M.	A.D.M.S. Secret No 3963 received — Officers & O.R. suffering from Shell-Shock to be sent to nearest C.C. Stn and not to No 12 C.C.Stn. as heretofore.	
		12. noon	KEERSEBROM CAMP taken over from No 2 Labour Co. Royal Scots Fusiliers to be opened as a Corps Rest Station.	
		1 p.M.	All R.A.P's and A.D. Stns LINDENHOEK and DRANOUTRE handed over to 108th Field Ambulance.	
		1 p.M.	A.D.M.S. Secret No S/190 received — Collection & evacuation of sick & wounded. Patients remaining in Hospital 51.	J.G.J.
″	2.4.17	12 noon	Divisional Baths at DRANOUTRE handed over to 110th Field Ambulance.	
		8 p.M.	A.D.M.S. Secret No 3995 received — 108th Field Ambce to continue taking patients for a few days until Rest Stn has been painted. 109th & 110th F.Ambs. to retain as many as possible in their M.D. Stns in the meantime. Patients remaining in Hospital 47.	J.G.J.
″	3.4.17	12 noon	Capt E.C.A. Smith detailed as temporary M.O. i/c 8th R. I. Rif. vice Capt Pierce	
		1 p.M.	A.D.M.S. Secret No 4003 received — Dispositions of Infantry Bdes on 6th/7th April.	
		2.30 p.M.	Capt. J.G. Johnston attended a Conference held at Office of D.D.M.S. IX Corps.	
		3 p.M.	A.D.M.S. Secret No S/193 received — Addendum to O.O. No 26 d/ 30.3.17.	
		7 p.M.	A.D.M.S. Secret No 4009 received — Inspection of Valves of Small Box Resp. Patients remaining in Hospital 45.	J.G.J.
″	4.4.17		Routine. Patients remaining in Hospital 43.	J.G.J.

1875 Wt. W593/826 1,000,000 4/15 J.B.C. & A. A.D.S.S./Forms/C. 2118.

Instructions regarding War Diaries and Intelligence Summaries are contained in F. S. Regs., Part II. and the Staff Manual respectively. Title Pages will be prepared in manuscript.

WAR DIARY
or
INTELLIGENCE SUMMARY
(Erase heading not required.)

Army Form C. 2118

Place	Date	Hour	Summary of Events and Information	Remarks and references to Appendices
BAILLEUL	5.4.17	6 AM.	36th Div. Wire No G 446 received — Wind dangerous.	
		11 AM.	Capt. J. G. Johnston visited B. R. C. S. at St. OMER to obtain Comforts for new D.R.S.	
			Patients remaining in Hospital 41.	J.G.J.
"	6.4.17	8 AM.	36th Div. Wire received — Wind Safe.	
			Patients remaining in Hospital 36.	J.G.J.
"	7.4.17	10 AM.	A.D.M.S. Secret No S/195 = Code Calls; S/196 = New addition to B.A.B. Code; S/197 = A.D.M.S. Office closes in BAILLEUL at 4 p.m. & opens at St. JANS CAPPEL same hour	
		6.30 pm.	Capt. W. Russell rejoined from duty with 11th Rs. Innis. Fus.	
		7 pM.	Lieut & Q.M. W. E. Perritt reported his arrival for duty & taken on strength.	
			Patients remaining in Hospital 31.	J.G.J.
"	8.4.17		New Rest Station opened & first Patients received.	
			Remaining in Hospital 34.	J.G.J.
"	9.4.17	6 pM.	Lieut Col R. Magill rejoined from sick leave, & resumed Command.	
		7 pM.	A.D.M.S. Secret No 4086 received — Gold-beaters skin balloons may fall in our lines when easterly wind is blowing. These are to be forwarded intact to Div H.Q.	
			Patients remaining in Hospital 63.	J.G.J.

1875 Wt. W593/826 1,000,000 4/15 J.B.C. & A. A.D.S.S./Forms/C. 2118.

Instructions regarding War Diaries and Intelligence Summaries are contained in F. S. Regs., Part II. and the Staff Manual respectively. Title Pages will be prepared in manuscript.

WAR DIARY
or
~~INTELLIGENCE SUMMARY~~
(Erase heading not required.)

Army Form C. 2118

Place	Date	Hour	Summary of Events and Information	Remarks and references to Appendices
BAILLEUL	10.4.17		Routine work on Rest Station making good progress. accommodation for 650 patients will be available. Patients ~~remaining~~ remaining 112	[illegible]
"	11.4.17	7.30am	Capt H.S. Davison proceeded on 14 days (Contract) leave	[illegible]
		11.30am	ADMS visited M.D.S + D.R.S. Patients remaining 141.	
	12	8am	Lt Finnegan returned from leave.	
		11 am	Secret Correction to B.A.B. Code received.	[illegible]
		4.30	D.M.S. 2nd Army Surgeon General R Porter visited M.D.S + D.R.S + expressed himself as highly pleased with his inspection. Patients remaining 153	
	13"		Capt Mayberry detailed for temporary duty with 15 C.C.S	[illegible]
			Routine. Patients remaining 195.	
	14"		Routine. Owing to continued bad weather very little could be done towards "Spring Cleaning" and Summer preparations. Canteens in the M.D.S. and D.R.S are now in working order. Patients remaining 185	[illegible]
	15"		Continued Rain. Routine. Patients remaining 192.	[illegible]
	16		Physical Drill commenced at 6.30 each morning. before parade each man will receive a cup of cocoa + biscuits. Patients remaining 239.	[illegible]
	17"		Number of patients steadily increasing but very little serious disease. Evacuations from 36 Division comparatively few. attached troops being responsible for majority. Patients remaining 275.	[illegible]

Instructions regarding War Diaries and Intelligence Summaries are contained in F. S. Regs., Part II. and the Staff Manual respectively. Title Pages will be prepared in manuscript.

WAR DIARY
or
INTELLIGENCE SUMMARY
(Erase heading not required.)

Army Form C. 2118

Place	Date	Hour	Summary of Events and Information	Remarks and references to Appendices
BAILLEUL	18.4.17		Routine. Temporary arrangements to bathe patients completed. A sufficient quantity of under clothing obtained to give each man a change, and arrangements made with Divisional Laundry to have the soiled clothing washed.	
		7.PM	Capt. E.C.A. Smith reported from duty with 8 R. Ir. Rifles.	[illegible]
		8.	Secret corrections to B.A.B. Code received	
		11.30	Wind Dangerous. Patients remaining 306	[illegible]
	19.4.17	11.30AM	Wind Safe. Patients remaining 329	
	20.4.17		Lt + QrM. S.C.R. Chester detailed to proceed to C.O.O. CALAIS for probationary duty in the Ordnance Dept. Patients remaining 318.	[illegible]
	21.4.17		Routine Patients remaining 332	[illegible]
	22.4.17		Routine Patients remaining 364	[illegible]
	23.4.17		Routine Patients remaining 351	[illegible]
	24.4.17	11.30AM	Secret B.A.B. corrections received - also instructions re collection of Stores in the event of an advance.	[illegible]
			D.D.M.S. inspected M.D.S + D.R.S. Patients remaining 362.	[illegible]
	25.4.17		Routine. Patients remaining 353	
	26	11 AM	Wind Dangerous. Patients remaining 365	[illegible]
	27	4PM	Wind Safe. Lt Finnegan + 2 NCOs attended a gas lecture at DRANOUTRE Patients remaining 348.	[illegible]

1875 Wt. W593/826 1,000,000 4/15 J.B.C. & A. A.D.S.S./Forms/C. 2118.

Instructions regarding War Diaries and Intelligence Summaries are contained in F. S. Regs., Part II. and the Staff Manual respectively. Title Pages will be prepared in manuscript.

WAR DIARY
or
INTELLIGENCE SUMMARY
(Erase heading not required.)

Army Form C. 2118

Place	Date	Hour	Summary of Events and Information	Remarks and references to Appendices
BAILLEUL	28.4.17		Capt Davidson returned from leave of absence. Improved weather has enabled gardening operations to be carried on, vegetables sown & planted in the D.R.S. and small plot at Officers Quarters. Patients remaining 365	[illegible]
	29.4.17		A.D.M.S. inspected both camps M.D.S. & D.R.S. Capt Mayberry detailed to proceed from 15 C.C.S. to 10 Stationary Hosp for a further tour of duty. Patients remaining 409	[illegible]
	30.4.17		Routine. "Spring cleaning" in progress all huts being whitewashed etc	
		930am	Enemy plane dropped a bomb 150 yds from officers mess no damage resulting although several narrow escapes have occurred from Anti-Aircraft shell fragments. Patients remaining 428	[illegible]

Confidential

War Diary

of

109th. Field Ambulance.

From 1st. May 1917. To 31st May 1917

VOL. XX.

H. Macneill [illegible]
Cmdg 109 F.A.

Instructions re[illegible] War Diaries and Intelligence Summari[illegible] contained in F. S. Regs., Part II. and the [illegible] Manual respectively. Title Pages will be prepared in manuscript.

WAR DIARY
or
~~INTELLIGENCE SUMMARY~~

(Erase heading not required.)

Army Form C. 2118.

Place	Date	Hour	Summary of Events and Information	Remarks and references to Appendices
BAILLEUL	1-5-17	11 AM	Location of 12 & 13 R I Rifles received and arrangements made to collect their sick in the ST JANS CAPPEL area. Routine work, & improvements at Rest-Station. Patients remaining 427.	Ren
..	2 ..	Noon	IX Corps medical arrangements received. Patients remaining 409	Ren
..	3 ..	7.30 AM	Capt. S. G. Johnston proceeded on leave. Capt. E C A Smith ordered to	
		11 AM	take over temporary medical charge of 9th R. Inniskg Fus vice Capt Russell "wind dangerous". Patients remaining 404.	Ren
..	4 ..		Capt Davidson & Lts Finnegan and Gerritt attended 2nd Army Medical Society meeting.	
			Routine work. Patients remaining 383. Apparatus for inhalation of oxygen through Small box respirator submitted to ADMS. Apparatus consists of brass chamber in which is fitted two taps (one with black valve for air the other plain for oxygen) brass chamber is connected to S.B.R by means of a length of inner tubing (motor).	Ren
	5 ..	1 PM	Secret instructions from ADMS relating to the importance of anti gas measures. Flower & vegetable seeds sown in front of M.D.S & R.S. 4 men told off to look after gardens. Patients remaining 410	Ren

Army Form C. 2118.

WAR DIARY
or
~~INTELLIGENCE SUMMARY~~
(Erase heading not required.)

Instructions regarding War Diaries and Intelligence Summaries are contained in F. S. Regs., Part II. and the Staff Manual respectively. Title Pages will be prepared in manuscript.

Place	Date	Hour	Summary of Events and Information	Remarks and references to Appendices
BAILLEUL	6.5.17	–	Pte Glasspool 7 37747 attd IX Corps Water Control taken on strength. Routine. Patients remaining 402	R.M.
	7.5.17		One G.S. Wagon & team with driver to report nightly to 171 Tunnelling Co.	
		1.P.M.	IX Corps orders gas helmets to be worn by all ranks at all times.	
		–	BAB Code correction received.	R.M.
			addition to list of Code calls.	
			Divisional Horse Show took place today.	
			Patients remaining 387	
	8.5.17		Routine. Timber drawn from CRE for construction of superstructure on water carts each to carry 44 petrol tins. Patients remaining 376	R.M.
	9.5.17		Capt Russell relieves Capt Crosbie M.O. i/c 11 R. Innis Fus. for the day. Patients remaining 378	R.M.
	10.5.17	11AM	O.O. No 25 from A.D.M.S. relating to move of 108 F.A. Patients remaining 368	R.M.
	11.5.17		Cookery Inspector report on Cook Houses & diet "very good. Excellent dieting"	R.M.
		7.30PM	A.D.M.S. Secret "108 Bde will relieve 109 Bde on 14th." Arrangements for collection and evacuation as at present. Patients remaining 369	
	12.5.17	10AM	Scheme for evacuation of wounded received from A.D.M.S. S/213. Patients remaining 381	R.M.

2449 Wt. W14957/M90 750,000 1/16 J.B.C. & A. Forms/C.2118/12.

Instructions [illegible]ding War Diaries and Intelligence Summar[illegible]re contained in F. S. Regs., Part II. and the Staff Manual respectively. Title Pages will be prepared in manuscript.

WAR DIARY
or
INTELLIGENCE SUMMARY
(Erase heading not required.)

Army Form C. 2118.

Place	Date	Hour	Summary of Events and Information	Remarks and references to Appendices
BAILLEUL	13.5.17	3.30 PM	S/125 Received from ADMS. Division moves into forward area on 15th. 1097 A to collect sick from II & III Reserve Bdes areas and transport lines. Patients remaining 381.	
	14.5.17		Routine. 1 NCO & nine men detailed for work at new RAP YONGE Street. Patients remaining 397.	
	15.5.17		Capt W Russell granted leave to 29th inst.	
		1 M A	Arrived safe. Patients remaining 418.	
	16.5.17		Routine. White washing of huts. Painting of wagons & general repairs in progress. Patients remaining 429.	
	17.5.17		Capt J.G. Johnston returned off leave.	
		7.45 PM	Secret S/221 from ADMS. Re numbers of Patients in DRS to be gradually reduced also in FAs. Patients remaining 445	
	18.5.17	6 PM	Capt Hart took over temporary medical charge of 9th R Innis Fus vice Capt T.W.G. Johnson proceeding on leave. Patients remaining 450	
	19.5.17	3 PM	C.O. attended conference of Fd Amb Commanders at ADMS. Office. This unit ordered to furnish 3 Bearer Sub divisions if required, arrangements made for evacuation of large numbers of wounded in the event of active operations.	
	"	9 PM	Wind Dangerous. Patients remaining 450	

2449 Wt. W14957/M90 750,000 1/16 J.B.C. & A. Forms/C.2118/12.

Instructions regarding War Diaries and Intelligence Summaries are contained in F. S. Regs., Part II. and the Staff Manual respectively. Title Pages will be prepared in manuscript.

WAR DIARY
or
~~INTELLIGENCE SUMMARY~~
(Erase heading not required.)

Army Form C. 2118.

Place	Date	Hour	Summary of Events and Information	Remarks and references to Appendices
BAILLEUL	20.5.17	11 AM	M.D.S + D.R.S inspected by A.D.M.S. Patients remaining 437	[illegible]
	21.5.17	11 AM	2 copies B.A.B. Code. Remaining Patients. 422	[illegible]
	22.5.17		Lt + QrM Perritt granted leave of absence from 23rd inst to 2nd prox	
		1 PM	Revised instructions re Scabies cases transferred to 50 C.C.S (Secret 465/2.) Patients remaining 396	[illegible] [illegible]
	23.5.17		Routine Patients remaining 343	
	24.5.17		arrangements made to collect sick from new units arriving in the area - 32 Div artillery + 34th Bde R.F.A	[illegible]
		11.30 PM	"wind safe" Patients remaining 342	
	25.5.17		Capt Mayberry reported from duty with No 10 C.C.S.	[illegible]
		10.30 PM	"wind dangerous" Patients remaining 323.	[illegible]
	26.5.17	9.30 AM	ADMS Secret 4615. a list of medical + surgical necessaries to be held for the new R.A.P in YONGE STREET. Patients remaining 282	[illegible]
	27.5.17	11.30 AM	a DMS inspected M.D.S + D.R.S. Patients remaining 282.	[illegible]
		11.9 PM	Heavy shelling of back areas. shells appear to be dropping on our left at CROIX DE POPERINGE and also in the vicinity of Divisional H.Q	[illegible]

2449 Wt. W14957/M90 750,000 1/16 J.B.C. & A. Forms/C.2118/12.

Instructions regarding War Diaries and Intelligence Summaries are contained in F. S. Regs., Part II. and the Staff Manual respectively. Title Pages will be prepared in manuscript.

WAR DIARY
or
INTELLIGENCE SUMMARY
(Erase heading not required.)

Army Form C. 2118.

Place	Date	Hour	Summary of Events and Information	Remarks and references to Appendices
BAILLEUL	28.5.17	8.30 AM	arrangements made for the accommodation of ADMS + ADVS and their Staffs in this Camp (MAGILLIGAN CAMP). Heavy shelling during the night rendered Div. HQ untenable. (ULSTER CAMP)	
		9. AM	ADMS' Office closed at ULSTER CAMP and opens at MAGILLIGAN CAMP.	[illegible]
			Patients remaining 275.	
	29.5.17		During the night Enemy shelled areas on flanks and rear of this camp at intervals	[illegible]
			Routine. Patients remaining 258	
	30.5.17		Routine 281	[illegible]
	31.5.17	10 AM	Capt Russell returned from leave. Patients remaining 278	

2449 Wt. W14957/M90 750,000 1/16 J.B.C. & A. Forms/C.2118/12.

Confidential

War Diary

of

109th Field Ambulance

From 1st June 1917 To 30th June 1917

Vol XXI

[signature]

Lieut Col
Comdg 109 Fld Amb

1st July 1917

Instructions regarding War Diaries and Intelligence Summaries are contained in F. S. Regs., Part II. and the Staff Manual respectively. Title Pages will be prepared in manuscript.

WAR DIARY
or
~~INTELLIGENCE~~ SUMMARY
(Erase heading not required.)

Army Form C. 2118

Place	Date	Hour	Summary of Events and Information	Remarks and references to Appendices
BAILLEUL (MAGILLIGAN CAMP)	1.6.17		The following members of the Unit mentioned in despatches: Lt Col R MAGILL, CAPT. RUSSELL and Cpl MCKAY.	
		2PM.	"COs to select suitable place for men to collect in case camp is shelled, trenches to be dug" S.S. Div. On receipt of these instructions trenches dug in Camp and in Rest Station.	[illegible]
		9PM.	Sufficient trench shelter completed for all personnel and patients. Patients remaining 287.	
"	2.6.17	8 AM	Inspection by A.D.M.S. of the Personnel on Parade. Full marching order.	
		noon	A.D.M.S. 4805, "Detail a medical orderly with dressings etc to report at Prisoners of war Cage on "Z day" at 3 A.M.	[illegible]
		2PM.	2nd Army traffic maps received. Patients remaining 291	
"	3.6.17	10 AM	Lt Perritt returned from leave of absence.	[illegible]
		11 AM	New trench Code received. Routine. Patients remaining 313	
"	4.6.17		Routine. Capt Hart rejoined from temporary duty with 9 R Innis Fus. Patients remaining 305	[illegible]
	5.6.17	8 PM.	While Unit on Parade in Camp field close to Duke of York siding, an Enemy aeroplane dropped bombs on 2 ammunition trains standing in the siding	[illegible]

1875 Wt. W593/826 1,000,000 4/15 J.B.C. & A. A.D.S.S./Forms/C. 2118.

Army Form C. 2118

WAR DIARY
or
~~INTELLIGENCE SUMMARY~~
(Erase heading not required.)

Instructions regarding War Diaries and Intelligence Summaries are contained in F. S. Regs., Part II. and the Staff Manual respectively. Title Pages will be prepared in manuscript.

Place	Date	Hour	Summary of Events and Information	Remarks and references to Appendices
BAILLEUL (MAGILLIGAN CAMP)	5.6.17	8 AM Cont.	a truck immediately took fire and Explosions began to take place as the Siding is situated about 200 yards from the Camp. The parade was dismissed & all the Patients & personnel as well as the horses were hurried out of Camp & sent along the KEERSEBROM ROAD out of danger. No casualties occurred although shells and fragments were falling thickly on the Camp	
		9 AM	Sergt Major T. HARLAND collected a small party and succeeded in saving 8 trucks from the end of one of the burning trains. The members of the party were S/M Harland, Sergt Hall, Cpl Greenwood, Pte Ively all of 10 y D H also Pte Glynn of the 8th R Innis Fusiliers	Alu
		10 AM	Explosions still continuing. One man in Cook House slightly wounded on foot and evacuated	
		2 PM	Explosions almost stopped. Dinners served.	
		4 PM	Patients returned to Camp.	
		6 PM	ADMS Secret S/245 IX Corps arrangements for active Operations received. All the huts in Camp found to be pierced by fragments from Siding. Report of S/M Harland's gallantry furnished to A.D.M.S. Patients remaining 886	Glu

1875 Wt. W593/826 1,000,000 4/15 J.B.C. & A. A.D.S.S./Forms/C. 2118.

Instructions regarding War Diaries and Intelligence Summaries are contained in F. S. Regs., Part II. and the Staff Manual respectively. Title Pages will be prepared in manuscript.

WAR DIARY
or
~~INTELLIGENCE SUMMARY~~
(Erase heading not required.)

Army Form C. 2118

Place	Date	Hour	Summary of Events and Information	Remarks and references to Appendices
BAILLEUL (MAGILLIGAN CAMP)	June 6.17		Routine.	
		noon	Secret information that tomorrow will be "Z" day from A.D.M.S.	
		1 PM	Secret Circ. memo Q63 relating to reorganisation of Divisional trench tramways.	Am
		8 PM	3 Bearer Sub-division under Capts. Davison, Russell & Hart sent to O.C. 110th Field Ambulance for duty tomorrow under that officers orders. 5 Ambulance Cars sent to O.C. 108 Fd Ambulance for duty tomorrow. Patients remaining 312	
..	7.6.17	9 AM	A.D.M.S. Secret 4926 "Documents taken from prisoners who are in F. As should be sent to nearest C.C.S."	Am
			Patients remaining 327	Am
..	8.6.17		Routine. Patients remaining 350	
..	9.6.17		Routine. 360	Am
	10.6.17	3 AM	Secret O.O. No 32 received dealing with relief of 108 & 110 Fd Ambs.	
	..	8. PM	Secret A.D.M.S. 4953 "109th Fd Amb will collect sick of 107 and 108th Inf Bdes"	Am
		10.30 PM	3 Bearer Sub division rejoined from duty with 110 F.A. reporting 2 slight Casualties. Patients remaining 450.	

1875 Wt. W593/826 1,000,000 4/15 J.B.C. & A. A.D.S.S./Forms/C. 2118.

Instructions regarding War Diaries and Intelligence Summaries are contained in F. S. Regs., Part II. and the Staff Manual respectively. Title Pages will be prepared in manuscript.

WAR DIARY

or

~~INTELLIGENCE SUMMARY~~

(Erase heading not required.)

Army Form C. 2118

Place	Date	Hour	Summary of Events and Information	Remarks and references to Appendices
BAILLEUL (MAGILLIGAN CAMP)	11-6-17		Routine Patients remaining 523	[illegible]
"	12-6-17		" " " 521	[illegible]
"	13-6-17	3 PM	ADMS Secret S/252. "109 F.A. will collect sick from 3 Field Coys R.E. The two Battns of this Div. attached to 11th Div. + 16 R I Rifles (P) are on the slopes of KEMMEL. Patients remaining 567	[illegible]
"	14-6-17	2 PM	Capt Mayberry took over temporary charge of 11th R. Innis Fus. 4 O.R. reinforcements received. Remaining in Hosp. 536	[illegible]
"	15-6-17	5 PM	Lt A. F. R. CONDAR reported for duty. Remaining in Hosp 553	[illegible]
"	16-6-17	11 AM	The D.M.S. 2nd Army inspected the ~~[illegible]~~ personnel of 109th and 110th Fd Ambs on parade at MAGILLIGAN CAMP and thanked them for their good work at the Battle of MESSINES	[illegible]
"		2 PM	Secret ADMS 5036. "Units to be in readiness to move to MERRIS Area. Remaining in Hosp 590	[illegible]
"	17-6-17	1 PM	Secret O.O. No 33 from ADMS with instructions for Divisional move.	
"		10.30	O.O. No 33 Cancelled. Patients remaining 575 –	

1875 Wt. W593/826 1,000,000 4/15 J.B.C. & A. A.D.S.S./Forms/C. 2118.

Instructions regarding War Diaries and Intelligence Summaries are contained in F. S. Regs., Part II. and the Staff Manual respectively. Title Pages will be prepared in manuscript.

WAR DIARY

or

~~INTELLIGENCE SUMMARY~~

(Erase heading not required.)

Army Form C. 2118

Place	Date	Hour	Summary of Events and Information	Remarks and references to Appendices
BAILLEUL (MAGILLIGAN CAMP)	18.6.17		Routine	
		7PM	Capt. Hart detailed for temporary duty with 110 F.A. (A.D.M.S.)	
			A.D.M.S. 4907. "Military Medal awarded to Sergt R HALL, Corporal J.E. GREENWOOD and Pte J.H. FEELY." These 3 were members of the party which saved the trucks at Duke of York Siding on the 5th inst.	
			Patients remaining 564.	
	19.6.17	8PM	Capt Russell detailed with one bearer sub-division for temporary duty with 108th Fd Amb. One bearer subdivision also detailed for duty with 110 Fd Amb under Capt Hart. Patients remaining 569.	
	20.6.17	4PM	2 motor ambulance Cars with drivers to report to 110 FA for duty.	
			Patients remaining 613.	
	21.6.17		Routine. Patients remaining 583	
	22.6.17	4PM	A.D.M.S. 4907 "Sergt Major T. Harland awarded the Military Cross for his gallant action on the 5th inst at Duke of York Siding.	
		11PM	Enemy dropped some bombs on the outskirts of the Camp. No damage.	
			Patients remaining 529	

1875 Wt. W593/826 1,000,000 4/15 J.B.C. & A. A.D.S.S./Forms/C. 2118.

Army Form C. 2118.

Instructions regarding War Diaries and Intelligence Summaries are contained in F. S. Regs., Part II. and the Staff Manual respectively. Title Pages will be prepared in manuscript.

WAR DIARY
or
INTELLIGENCE SUMMARY
(Erase heading not required.)

Place	Date	Hour	Summary of Events and Information	Remarks and references to Appendices
BAILLEUL (MAGILLIGAN CAMP)	23.6.17	6 PM	Bearer sub division Con Capt Russell and 5 O.R. rejoined from LINDENHOEK from 108 F^d Amb. Patients remaining 484	[illegible]
	24.6.17	8 Am	One motor ambulance Car returned from duty with 110 F^d Amb.	
		6 P.M.	Capt H.G. Wilson joined for duty and taken on Strength. Patients remaining 422	[illegible]
	25.6.17	2 PM	Capt. H.G. Wilson detailed for temporary duty as M.O. i/c 11 R. Innis Fus. vice Capt ~~[illegible]~~ MAYBERRY proceeding on Report for duty with 11th Division	
		4 PM	A.D.M.S 5184 "on being relieved at 11 R Innis Fus. Capt. Wilson to report for temporary duty with 173 Bde R.F.A. at Report St Duty cuts.	
		7 PM	A.D.M.S 5195 Forward roll of men working directly under (a) IX Corps (b) 2nd Army, so that they may be returned when leaving the area. A.D.M.S 5196 F^d Amblce to hand over to 48th F^d 37 Div on leaving. Patients remaining 413	[illegible]
	26.6.17		Capt G.H. Mayberry proceeded to report for duty with A.D.M.S 11th Division & struck off strength	
		9 PM	O.O. No 35 from A.D.M.S F^d Amb to move to ~~[illegible]~~ MERRIS AREA on 30th inst Patients remaining 399.	[illegible]

2449 Wt. W14957/M90 750,000 1/16 J.B.C. & A. Forms/C.2118/12.

Army Form C. 2118.

Instructions regarding War Diaries and Intelligence Summaries are contained in F. S. Regs., Part II. and the Staff Manual respectively. Title Pages will be prepared in manuscript.

WAR DIARY
or
INTELLIGENCE SUMMARY

(Erase heading not required.)

Place	Date	Hour	Summary of Events and Information	Remarks and references to Appendices
BAILLEUL (MAGILLIGAN CAMP)	27.6.17	3 PM	ADMS. 5210 Tracing of area into which Division moves on 30th	
		4 PM	Capt Russell & 5 O.R. rejoined from duty with 108 Fd Amb at LINDENHOEK	
			OC. 48 Fd Amb visited Camp and reconnoitred the Rest Station & M.D.S.	[initials]
		11.30 PM	"Wind dangerous". Patients remaining 393.	
"	28.6.17		Wire from 109 Bde to meet Bde Billeting Officer at STRAZEELE tomorrow at noon. Capt Johnston detailed.	[initials]
		11 PM	Capt Hart & bearer subdivision rejoined from duty with 110th Fd Amb near WYTSCHAETE. Remaining in hosp. 399.	
	29.6.17	11 am	D.R.S at KEERSEBROM and M.D.S at MAGILLIGAN handed over to 48 Fd Amb. Patients remaining Nil.	
			All Preparations made for move. Capt Johnston proceeded to STRAZEELE to billet.	[initials]
		4.30 PM	O.C. proceeded to reconnoitre the billets & horse lines in new location.	
	30.6.17	6.30 AM	Unit marched to COURT CROIX. Sheet 27. W.B.6.4.6.	[initials]
COURT CROIX		8.30 am	Unit arrived. Good accommodation, march without incident. Roads & weather good.	

2449 Wt. W14957/M90 750,000 1/16 J.B.C. & A. Forms/C.2118/12.

Secret

Confidential

War Diary

of

109th Field Ambulance

Vol XXII

From 1st July 1917 — 31st July 1917

Lieut Col.
Comdg 109 F.A.

WO
95/2498
22

Instructions regarding War Diaries and Intelligence Summaries are contained in F. S. Regs., Part II. and the Staff Manual respectively. Title Pages will be prepared in manuscript.

WAR DIARY
or
~~INTELLIGENCE SUMMARY~~
(Erase heading not required.)

Army Form C. 2118

Place	Date	Hour	Summary of Events and Information	Remarks and references to Appendices
COURT CROIX	1.7.17		Unit closed. Capt Harte detailed to see the sick at D.H.Q daily at 9.30 A.m.	[illegible]
	2.7.17		Capt Davidson detailed for temporary duty with 10 R Innis Fus.	[illegible]
	3.7.17	11 Am	O.O. 36 "Transfer of the Division from IX Corps 2nd Army to XIX Corps 5th Army." "Three Bdes to move on 5th 6.7. 109 Fd Amb to move on 5th to HONDEGHEM area. Move to be completed by 10 A.m one Section to open & collect sick from 109 Inf Bde"	[illegible]
	4.7.17	9 A.m	Lt. A.F. Condar proceeded for temporary duty with 153 Bde R.F.A.	[illegible]
		10 Am	B.O. 51. 3/7/17 "109 Bde moves to TILQUES area on 5.6 & 7."	
		3 PM	Capt Johnston detailed for temporary duty as acting D.A.D.M.S. 36 Ulster Division	[illegible]
	5.7.17	5.30 Am	Unit left COURTE CROIX.	[illegible]
HONDEGHEM	5.7.17	8.15 Am	Unit arrived at billets 200 yds N of HONDEGHEM Church	[illegible]

1875 Wt. W593/826 1,000,000 4/15 J.B.C. & A. A.D.S.S./Forms/C. 2118.

Instructions regarding War Diaries and Intelligence Summaries are contained in F. S. Regs., Part II. and the Staff Manual respectively. Title Pages will be prepared in manuscript.

WAR DIARY
or
~~INTELLIGENCE SUMMARY~~
(Erase heading not required.)

Army Form C. 2118

Place	Date	Hour	Summary of Events and Information	Remarks and references to Appendices
HONDECHEM	5.7.17	4.PM	Bde order List of billets for 109 Fd Amb in ARQUES for night of 6/7th July with march Table	R
	6.7.17	4.15 Am	Unit moved to ARQUES	R
ARQUES	6.7.17	8.30 Am	Unit arrived in ARQUES	R
		11 PM	ADMS 5312 "ADMS office will close at MERRIS 11 AM 7th and open 12 noon at WIZERNES same day. Patients remaining 1 Orders from 109 Bde to move at 3.45 Am 7 to BOUVELINGHEM in rear of 9th R Innis Fus. Lt Finnegan sent to new area to billet.	R
	7.7.17	3.45 Am	Unit marched out: men given tea on march by 9 R Innis Fus from their cookers at 8 A.m.	R
BOUVEL-INGHEM	7.7.17	11.15 Am	Unit arrived. Good billets and accommodation. Long march without incident, road & weather good. Patients remaining 3	R

1875 Wt. W593/826 1,000,000 4/15 J.B.C. & A. A.D.S.S./Forms/C. 2118.

Instructions regarding War Diaries and Intelligence Summaries are contained in F. S. Regs., Part II. and the Staff Manual respectively. Title Pages will be prepared in manuscript.

WAR DIARY
or
~~INTELLIGENCE~~ SUMMARY
(Erase heading not required.)

Army Form C. 2118

Place	Date	Hour	Summary of Events and Information	Remarks and references to Appendices
BOUVELINGHEM	8.7.17	-	Sergt Palmer and Cpl. McCann awarded M.M. for gallantry at WYTSCHAETE.	
			A fairly comfortable little Hospital fitted up in School. accommodation for about 18 patients. Two operating tents erected in addition	[initials]
			Patients remain 4	
..	9.7.17		Routine. 2 hours drill each morning after parade instituted	[initials]
			Lectures in the afternoon. Patients remaining 8.	[initials]
	10.7.17		Routine Patients remaining 12	
	11.7.17		Routine. Arrangements made for Sports on 12th. 100 francs	
			Contribution by Brigadier General Ricardo C.M.G. D.S.O. Comdg 109 Inf Bde	
			Sports to be open to Bde H.Q. Coy. & T.M. Battery. the latter	
			Contributing 50 francs. Patients remaining 16	[initials]
-	12.7.17		Holiday. Sports 11 A.M. to 6 P.M. Patients remaining 17	
	13.7.17	2 PM.	XIX Corps administrative instructions No 8. received	
		..	A.D.M.S. S.079. Lt. Condar to take over temporary medical charge of 36th D.A.C.	[initials]
			from 17th. Patients remaining 16. Personnel marched to LUMBRES & bathed in River	

1875 Wt. W593/826 1,000,000 4/15 J.B.C. & A. A.D.S.S./Forms/C. 2118.

Army Form C. 2118.

Instructions regarding War Diaries and Intelligence Summaries are contained in F. S. Regs., Part II. and the Staff Manual respectively. Title Pages will be prepared in manuscript.

WAR DIARY
or
~~INTELLIGENCE SUMMARY~~
(Erase heading not required.)

Place	Date	Hour	Summary of Events and Information	Remarks and references to Appendices
BOUVELINGHEM	14.7.17		Routine.	
		5 PM	Football Tie in Bde Tournament against 10 R. Innis Fus. Result. Fus 4. Amb 2	R.M.
			Patients remaining 20	
	15.7.17	11.30 Am	Unit marched to ALQUINES and took part in Special Church Parade for 109 Inf Bde after Service Divisional Commander presented medals. Sergts Palmer & Hall. Cpls. Greenwood & McCann & Pte Iseley decorated.	
		2 PM	ADMS S. 419. & S.420. "Importance of anti gas drill. ~~and~~ "Fatal after effects of gas and instructions for action during gas attack"	R.M.
			Patients remaining 21	
	16.7.17	10 Am	36 Div administrative instructions No 1. "Organisation of Pack transport. Field ambulances to furnish 3 mules.	
		3 PM	Capt Johnston resumes from duty as acting DADMS	R.M.
			Patients remaining 17	

2449 Wt. W14957/M90 750,000 1/16 J.B.C. & A. Forms/C.2118/12.

Instructions regarding War Diaries and Intelligence Summaries are contained in F. S. Regs., Part II. and the Staff Manual respectively. Title Pages will be prepared in manuscript.

WAR DIARY
or
~~INTELLIGENCE SUMMARY~~
(Erase heading not required.)

Army Form C. 2118

Place	Date	Hour	Summary of Events and Information	Remarks and references to Appendices
BOUVELINGHEM	17.7.17		Routine. Copy no 11666 of B.A.B. French Code No 3. Patients remaining 16	[illegible]
"	18.7.17		Capt Hart returned from leave. Patients remaining 23	[illegible]
			Lt Col Rhuagill awarded Croix de Chevalier.	
"	19.7.17		Lt Finnegan detailed to report to D.D.M.S. V Corps for duty & to be struck off strength. Patients remaining 21	[illegible]
"	20.7.17		Routine. Patients remaining 20	[illegible]
"	21.7.17		XIX Corps administrative Instructions & medical arrangements received. Patients remaining 23.	[illegible]
	22.7.17		Divisional GYMKHANA held at ACQUIN, the unit took part in the majority of events.	[illegible]
		7.PM	ADMS O.O. No 37 ~~[illegible]~~ "move of F. Ambs to XIX Corps back area	
			17 & 18 S.C. 109 Bde "advanced administrative Instns for move of Bde to WINNEZEELE area. Patients remaining 27	

1875 Wt. W593/826 1,000,000 4/15 J.B.C. & A. A.D.S.S./Forms/C. 2118.

Instructions regarding War Diaries and Intelligence Summaries are contained in F. S. Regs., Part II. and the Staff Manual respectively. Title Pages will be prepared in manuscript.

WAR DIARY
or
~~INTELLIGENCE SUMMARY~~
(Erase heading not required.)

Army Form C. 2118

Place	Date	Hour	Summary of Events and Information	Remarks and references to Appendices
BOUVELINGHEM	23.7.17		Capt Davidson returned from duty with 10 R Innis Fus. Patients remaining 25	[illegible]
		4.PM	108 Bde Billeting orders in WINNEZEELE area. Unit to be billeted in 108 Bde area, and to move by busses on 26th. Transport to go by march route with transport of 109 Bde	
	24.7		Routine arrangements made for move. Patients if any to be brought to new area and handed over to 108 F.A. Patients remaining 19	[illegible]
	25.7	7.30 AM	Capt. Davidson + 4 O.R. proceeded as advance party. Patients remaining 17.	[illegible]
		8.30 PM	Embussing and debussing orders received.	[illegible]
		6.30 AM	Transport moved off.	
	26.7	12.30 PM	Unit moved to embussing point.	
WINNEZEELE		8.30 PM	arrived at WINNEZEELE at J.15b.6.6. 23 Patients transferred to 108 F.A. close by. Patients remaining nil	[illegible]

Instructions regarding War Diaries and Intelligence Summaries are contained in F. S. Regs., Part II. and the Staff Manual respectively. Title Pages will be prepared in manuscript.

WAR DIARY
or
INTELLIGENCE SUMMARY
(Erase heading not required.)

Army Form C. 2118

Place	Date	Hour	Summary of Events and Information	Remarks and references to Appendices
WINNEZEELE	27.7		Routine. Unit to remain packed. Transport arrived at 12 30 P.M.	[initials]
	28.7		"	[initials]
	29.7	11 AM	Capt Davison Capt Hart Capt Russell with 2 N.C.Os & 2 O.R. proceeded to M.D.S. RED FARM, Sheet 28. G 5 d 8.7. for purpose of becoming acquainted with Evacuation from line.	
	"		Bde O.O. from 108 Bde to move to WATOU area No 2 on 30th	[initials]
		6 PM	Capt. Hart detailed for billeting duty with 8. R I Rifles.	
		7 PM	Lt Condor reported from duty with 36 Div Amm. Col.	
		7 30 PM	RAMC O.O. No 38. "109 F.A will collect sick from their Bde during move to WATOU & deliver same to 108 F.A.	[initials]
		11 PM	108 Bde O.O. No 86. "108 F.A will move with 108 Bde.	
	30.7	10.45 AM	Orders from 109 Inf Bde to the effect that 109 Fd Amb will march this evening in rear of Bde to WATOU No 1 area. Unit to be clear of WINNEZEELE by 8.45 P.M.	[initials]
		2.30 PM	Capt Davidson & 2 OR proceeded with Bde Billeting officer to new area	[initials]

1875 Wt. W593/826 1,000,000 4/15 J.B.C. & A. A.D.S.S./Forms/C. 2118.

Army Form C. 2118.

WAR DIARY
or
INTELLIGENCE SUMMARY
(Erase heading not required.)

Instructions regarding War Diaries and Intelligence Summaries are contained in F. S. Regs., Part II. and the Staff Manual respectively. Title Pages will be prepared in manuscript.

Place	Date	Hour	Summary of Events and Information	Remarks and references to Appendices
WINNEZEELE	30.7.	8 PM	Unit moved off	Rw
L 32.b 7.7 (Sheet 27)	31.7.	1 AM	Unit arrived. No accommodation. Tents pitched & tea provided for personnel.	Rw
"		3 PM	Capt Hart rejoined from 8 R I Rifles.	Rw
"		8.30 PM	ADMS S657. "OC. 109 Fd Amb. will detail one officer & 64 bearers to proceed in M. A. Cars to RED FARM M.D.S. G5.d.8.7 Sheet 28. One car to remain at RED FARM for duty."	Rw
		9.30 PM	Capt Davison. Staff Sergt Gillespie & 64 OR proceeded in the Cars of the Unit and in 4 of the 108 F.A.	Rw

2449 Wt. W14957/M90 750,000 1/16 J.B.C. & A. Forms/C.2118/12.

B.E.F.

SUMMARY OF MEDICAL WAR DIARIES OF 109th F.A. 36th Div.

8th Corps. 5th ARMY.

19th Corps from 26th July.

4th Corps III. Army from 23rd August.

Western Front Operations- July-Aug. 1917.

Officer Commanding - Lt.Col. R. MAGILL.

SUMMARISED UNDER THE FOLLOWING HEADINGS:-

Phase "D" 1. - Passchendaele Operations "July-Nov. 1917"

(a) - Operations commencing July 1917.

B.E.F.

109th F.A. 36th Div. — Western Front. July-Aug. 1917.

8th Corps. 5th ARMY.

Officer Commanding - Lt.Col. R.MAGILL.

19th Corps from 26th July.

PHASE "D" 1. - Passchendaele Operations-"July-Nov. 1917"

(a) - Operations commencing July 1917.

Headquarters at BOUVELINGHEM.

July 7th.	Transfer.	Transferred from 2nd Army.
	Decorations.	Sgt. Palmer) awarded M.M. for gallantry Cpl. McCann) at Wytschaete.
	Accommodation.	Hospital for 18 in school and 2 op.tents.
18th.	Decorations.	Lt.Col. R. Magill awarded Croix De Chevalier.
25th.	Ops. R.A.M.C.	7/25th Unit in rest.
26th.	Moves and Transfer.	To Winnizeele 19th Corps Back Area.

B.E.F.

109th F.A. 36th Div. Western Front.

19th Corps 5th ARMY. July-Aug. 1917.

Officer Commanding - Lt.Col.R Magill.

PHASE "D" 1.- Passchendaele Operations-"July-Nov.1917."

(a) - Operations commencing July 1917.

Headquarters at Winnizeele.

July 26th. Moves and Transfer. To Winnizeele 19th Corps Back Area.

30th. Moves. To L. 20. b.7.7. (Sheet 27).

31st. Moves. Detachment. 1 & 64 Bearers to RED FARM M.D.S. G.5.d.8.7. (Sheet 28).

B.E.F.

<u>109th F.A. 36th Div.</u> Western Front.
July-Aug. 1917.

<u>8th Corps. 5th ARMY.</u>

<u>Officer Commanding - Lt.Col. R.MAGILL.</u>

<u>19th Corps from 26th July.</u>

<u>PHASE "D" 1. - Passchendaele Operations-"July-Nov. 1917"</u>

(a) - <u>Operations commencing July 1917.</u>

<u>Headquarters at BOUVELINGHEM.</u>

July 7th.	<u>Transfer.</u>	Transferred from 2nd Army.
	<u>Decorations.</u>	Sgt. Palmer) awarded M.M. for gallantry Cpl. McCann) at Wytschaete.
	<u>Accommodation.</u>	Hospital for 18 in school and 2 op. tents.
18th.	<u>Decorations.</u>	Lt.Col. R. Magill awarded Croix De Chevalier.
25th.	<u>Ops. R.A.M.C.</u>	7th/25th Unit in rest.
26th.	<u>Moves and Transfer.</u>	To Winnizeele 19th Corps Back Area.

B.E.F.

109th F.A. 36th Div. Western Front.

19th Corps 5th ARMY. July-Aug. 1917.

Officer Commanding - Lt.Col.R Magill.

PHASE "D" 1.- Passchendaele Operations-"July-Nov.1917."

(a) - Operations commencing July 1917.

Headquarters at Winnizeele.

July 26th. Moves and Transfer. To Winnizeele 19th Corps Back Area.

30th. Moves. To L. 20. b.7.7. (Sheet 27).

31st. Moves. Detachment. 1 & 64 Bearers to RED FARM M.D.S. G.5.d.8.7. (Sheet 28).

Confidential

War Diary

of

109th Field Ambulance

From 1st Aug 1917 — 31st Aug 1917

Vol XXIII

J.G. Johnston. Capt RAMC
Comdg 109 Fd Amb

Instructions regarding War Diaries and Intelligence Summaries are contained in F. S. Regs., Part II, and the Staff Manual respectively. Title pages will be prepared in manuscript.

WAR DIARY
or
~~INTELLIGENCE SUMMARY.~~
(Erase heading not required.)

Army Form C. 2118.

Place	Date	Hour	Summary of Events and Information	Remarks and references to Appendices
HILLHOEK (L.20.b.7.7. Sheet 27 1:20000)	1.8.17	1.30PM	ADMS 5662 "2 officers. 1 bearer subdivision + 2 tent subdivisions to act as one bearer subdivision to be held in readiness to reinforce bearers of 55 Div."	
"	"	6.30PM	CO. + Capt Johnston attended conference at 109th Bde HQrs. Intended offensive on WIELTJE Front discussed	[initials]
"	2.8.17	6.15	ADMS M1725. "Get in touch with 2/1 Wessex Fd Amb. preparatory to taking over evacuation from line and Corps M.D.S. at RED FARM on 4th inst"	[initials]
"	3.8.17	8AM	Capt Hart + Lieut Conder with 40 ORs proceeded to RED FARM for duty in the line.	[initials]
	"	11.30AM	Capt Davidson + 39 ORs rejoined from duty at WIELTJE reporting 1 killed and 2 wounded.	[initials]
		2 PM	CO + Capt Johnston proceeded to RED FARM to arrange with OC. 2/1 Wessex Fd Amb to take over all A.D.S. Collecting stations + relay posts in the Divisional front on 4th inst.	[initials]
		6.40PM	Divisional administrative instruction No 55 re move of Division into line.	[initials]
		10PM	Capt Hart + 7 OR reported wounded	[initials]
"	4.8.17	9AM	Unit moved to RED FARM. CO. Capt Johnston + Lt + Qm Perritt proceeded in advance to take over RED FARM.	[initials]

D. D. & L., London, E.C.
(A7883) Wt. W809/M1672 350,000 4/17 Sch. 52a Forms/C/2118/14

Army Form C. 2118.

Instructions regarding War Diaries and Intelligence Summaries are contained in F. S. Regs., Part II, and the Staff Manual respectively. Title pages will be prepared in manuscript.

WAR DIARY
or
~~INTELLIGENCE SUMMARY.~~
(Erase heading not required.)

Place	Date	Hour	Summary of Events and Information	Remarks and references to Appendices
RED FARM	4.8.17	Noon	Taking over completed. Capt. Dawson taking over A.D.Ss. at CANAL BANK & WIELTJE Collecting post at St. JEAN. 109th Fd. Amb. have now charge of the ~~[illegible]~~ collection of all sick & wounded from the line & billets & the evacuation. As the M.A. Cars of the unit are on account of the low chassis unsuitable for the bad roads east of YPRES arrangements made with 6 M.A. Convoy to evacuate the wounded from St. JEAN & the CANAL BANK to M.D.S. The Cars of the unit & attached Cars from 108th and 110th Fd. As. to evacuate to C.C.Ss.	
			The following officers are attached for duty:- 108th F.A. Capts. Dunlop, Sowerby, G. Rea & S. Rea. 110th F.A. Capts. Burton & Emerson, also Capt. O'Neill held attached to R.Es. In addition 2 bearer subdivisions each from 108th & 110th Fd. Amb. also 89 O.R. from Tunnelling Coy.	
			The heavy rain of the last week having rendered the ground over which the wounded have to be carried a large number of bearers will be required for the long carries. At present M.A. Cars are unable to proceed further than St. JEAN as ~~[illegible]~~ there is no turning place further forward, and as the road between St. JEAN and WIELTJE is not suitable for wheeled stretchers an additional carry of 800 yards	[illegible]

D. D. & L., London, E.C. (A7883) Wt. W809/M1672 350,000 4/17 Sch. 52a Forms/C/2118/14

Instructions regarding War Diaries and Intelligence Summaries are contained in F. S. Regs., Part II. and the Staff Manual respectively. Title pages will be prepared in manuscript.

WAR DIARY
or
~~INTELLIGENCE SUMMARY.~~
(Erase heading not required.)

Army Form C. 2118.

Place	Date	Hour	Summary of Events and Information	Remarks and references to Appendices
RED FARM	4.8.17	Cont	is imposed on the bearers. For the present 3 officers + 200 bearers are considered necessary for the work at WIELTJE. as there are very few casualties brought to CANAL BANK this ADS will be held by one NCO + 4 OR. the same number will be posted at ST JEAN which will only be used as a loading post: the ADS having been blown in a few days ago. The ADS at WIELTJE is situate in a MINE SHAFT with accommodation for a large number of wounded + bearers.	[illegible]
			Capts Dunlop + G Rea detailed to assist Capt Davidson at ADS. with Lt Conder.	
	5.8.17	Noon	Arrangements made to relieve Bearers in line every 48 hours - this is necessary as the conditions under which the men work are very trying, the ground over which they carry is almost impassable, devoid of shelter + under direct observation of the enemy.	[illegible]
			Lt Conder rejoined from WIELTJE.	
		3 PM	Capt O'Neill detailed to relieve M.O. of 15 R Ir Rifles (sick) with ADMS. one OR wounded.	[illegible]
			Patients admitted 4th - 5th wounded Offs 2. OR 42. Sick 31. P of W wounded 4.	
	6.8.17	10 am	Enemy shelled RED FARM. No casualties or damage	[illegible]

D. D. & L., London, E.C.
(A7883) Wt. W809/M1672 350,000 4/17 Sch. 52a Forms/C/2118/14

Instructions regarding War Diaries and Intelligence Summaries are contained in F. S. Regs., Part II. and the Staff Manual respectively. Title pages will be prepared in manuscript.

WAR DIARY
or
~~INTELLIGENCE~~ SUMMARY.
(*Erase heading not required.*)

Army Form C. 2118.

Place	Date	Hour	Summary of Events and Information	Remarks and references to Appendices
RED FARM	6.8.17	2 PM	Capt G. Rea detailed to relieve temporarily M.O. i/c 10 R Ir Rifles.	
			Major Meredith 108th FA attached for duty.	[initials]
			one bearer wounded. Patients admitted 5–6th. Officers sick 3 wounded 3. OR sick 77. wounded 85 all evacuated.	
	7.8.17	11 AM	Letter received from ADMS 55th Division expressing appreciation of work done by bearers of the unit.	[initials]
		Noon	a Turning place made at WIELTJE for ambulances but owing to the wet & sodden state of the ground this was only successful for a few hours the timber & sand bags etc slipping away under the 5th car to turn. other Efforts are being made and it is hoped to have a permanent place by tomorrow.	[initials]
			arrangements completed for 50 OR from the 108th & 109th Inf Bdes to act as bearers from 4 a m to 4 P M daily. The men being sent up in Cars.	
			Lt Condor to see sick daily at CANAL BANK A.D.S. An officer also detailed to ~~see~~ visit 108 Bde Transport Lines & details. Patients admitted 6–7th. Officers sick 5 wounded 2. OR sick 94. wounded 143. Remaining S. 2. W 3.	[initials]

D. D. & L., London, E.C.
(A7883) Wt. W809/M1672 350,000 4/17 Sch. 52a Forms/C/2118/14

Instructions regarding War Diaries and Intelligence Summaries are contained in F. S. Regs., Part II. and the Staff Manual respectively. Title pages will be prepared in manuscript.

WAR DIARY
or
~~INTELLIGENCE~~ ~~SUMMARY~~.
(Erase heading not required.)

Army Form C. 2118.

Place	Date	Hour	Summary of Events and Information	Remarks and references to Appendices
RED FARM	8.8.17	—	One bearer wounded. Patients admitted 7th–8th. Officers Sick 3 wounded 1. OR Sick 119 wounded 103, P of W wounded 2.	
			To endeavour to lessen the sick wastage, 50 beds provided in the M.D.S. Patients remaining 24	[illegible]
		6PM	~~Turning~~ Turning Place for cars completed at WIELTJE.	
	9.8.17	8PM	Lieuts A.S. Robinson & J. Rice United States Medical Corps reported for duty and taken on Strength. Patients admitted 8–9th. Officers Sick 4. wounded 4. OR Sick 101 wounded 172. Remaining 38.	[illegible]
	10.8.17	5AM	CO & Capt Johnston visited ADSs & RAPs	
		noon	Major Meredith detailed for duty at Corps Rest Station	
			Patients admitted 9th–10th ~~Sick~~ Officers Sick 6 wounded 3. OR Sick 104 wounded 133. Remaining 32.	[illegible]
	11.8.17		Two bearers wounded. Patients admitted 10th–11th Offs Sick 4 wounded 3 OR Sick 130 wounded 248. Remaining ~~[illegible]~~ 41.	[illegible]
	12.8.17		Patients admitted 11th–12th Offs sick 4. wounded 3. OR Sick 134. wounded 147. Remaining 34.	[illegible]

D. D. & L., London, E.C.
(A7883) Wt. W809/M1672 350,000 4/17 Sch. 52a Forms/C/2118/14

Army Form C. 2118.

Instructions regarding War Diaries and Intelligence Summaries are contained in F. S. Regs., Part II. and the Staff Manual respectively. Title pages will be prepared in manuscript.

WAR DIARY
or
~~INTELLIGENCE SUMMARY.~~
(Erase heading not required.)

Place	Date	Hour	Summary of Events and Information	Remarks and references to Appendices
RED FARM	13.8.17	Noon	Sketch & plans for mobile M.D.S. & A.D.S. for use in case of an advance forwarded to A.D.M.S.	[initials]
			One bearer wounded.	[initials]
		6 PM	A.D.M.S. 5856. "Instructions re pack mules for possible advance to carry dressings etc" Patients admitted 12th–13th Offs Sick 2 wounded 4 OR Sick 120 wounded 129. Remaining 26	[initials]
	14.8.17	10 AM	Lieut J Rice U.S.M.C. detailed for duty with No 2 Canadian C.C.S.	
		Noon	To enable O.C. 109 F.A. to proceed to WIELTJE to take charge of evacuation of wounded from front line in the event of offensive operations Lt Col Fawcett DSO 108 F.A. took over charge of M.D.S.	[initials]
		1 PM	XIX Corps medical arrangements received.	
		7 PM	A.D.M.S. 5915 "3 horse drawn Ambulance wagons to be ready to move forward." 2 R.A.M.C. orderlies to be attached to each M.O. in line on 15th inst. Patients admitted 13–14th Offs. Sick 4. wounded 4. O.R. Sick 121. wounded 103. Remaining 28.	[initials]
			Arrangements completed for one officer + 21 O.R. of 16 R. Ir. Rifles (P) 2 officers + 72 O.R. of XIX Salvage Co to report to O.C. 109 F.A. at WIELTJE on the morning of 16th inst to assist in evacuation.	

D. D. & L., London, E.C.
(A7883) Wt W809/M1672 350,000 4/17 Sch. 52a Forms/C/2118/14

Instructions regarding War Diaries and Intelligence Summaries are contained in F. S. Regs., Part II. and the Staff Manual respectively. Title pages will be prepared in manuscript.

WAR DIARY
or
~~INTELLIGENCE SUMMARY.~~
(Erase heading not required.)

Army Form C. 2118.

Place	Date	Hour	Summary of Events and Information	Remarks and references to Appendices
RED FARM	15.8.17		Daily party of 50 O.R. from Inf Bdes as arranged for the 7th and cancelled. 11 O.R. from 108th Bde proceeded this morning.	
		noon	The Horse ambulances of 108 + 109 F.As together with the pack mules (10) of the Divisional F.d Ambs are detailed to report to Div Pack Transport Officer at Pack Camp H.12 b. 7.9 Sheet 28. to be at disposal of O.C. 109 F.A.	
			O.C. with Capts Johnston, Russell + Sowerby proceeded to WIELTJE A.D.S. Lt Conder + 47 O.R. proceeded to CANAL BANK A.D.S. to hold themselves in reserve. Patients admitted Offrs Sick 4. wounded 2. O.R. Sick 148 wounded 72. Remaining 86.	
	16.8.17		5 Officers + 230 O.R. reported to O.C. at MINE SHAFT, WIELTJE to assist in evacuation of the wounded. Casualties in R.A.M.C. 109 F.A. Killed O.R. 3 wounded O.R. 2. Admissions Officers sick 3 wounded 4. O.R. sick 201 wounded 117 Remaining O.R. 40.	
	17.8.17	noon	2 Officers + 73 O.R. of 2/3rd S. Midland F. Ambce reported at the MINE SHAFT WIELTJE for duty in the line.	

D. D. & L., London, E.C.
(A7883) Wt. W809/M1672 350,000 4/17 Sch. 52a Forms/C/2118/14

Instructions regarding War Diaries and Intelligence Summaries are contained in F. S. Regs., Part II. and the Staff Manual respectively. Title pages will be prepared in manuscript.

WAR DIARY

or

~~INTELLIGENCE SUMMARY~~

(*Erase heading not required.*)

Army Form C. 2118.

Place	Date	Hour	Summary of Events and Information	Remarks and references to Appendices
RED. FARM	17-8-17	6 p.m.	1 N.C.O, 10 O.R. A.S.C. 4 OR. RAMC with 3 Horsed Ambulances, 3 Pack Mules & 1 Horse team, rejoined H.Q. from PACK FARM.	
			Casualties O.R. RAMC 109 F Amb. wounded 2.	
			C.O. Capt Russell, Lt. Conder & 95 O.R. rejoined from duty in the line	
			All A.D. Stns & C.Ps. handed over to O.C. 2/3rd S. Mid. Fld Ambce.	
			2 Off + 92 O.R. 110th F. Amb.; 1 Off & 64 O.R. 108. F. Amb. & 75 O.R. Tunnelling Co. rejoined from duty in the line.	
		1 pm.	A.D.M.S. Secret O.O. No 40 received – 109 F. Amb to move to WATOU area.	
			Admissions, Off sick 3 wounded 43, O.R. Sick 86 wounded 839, Rem. 43	J.S.J.
"	18.8.17	2 pm.	A.D.M.S. Secret No 5959 received. – Notes on new Mustard Oil Gas.	
		4 pm	Lieut A.Y.R. Conder detailed as M.O. i/c 11th R. Innis. Fus. vice Capt Moir wounded. Admissions Off sick nil wounded 12.	
			O.R. sick 32, wounded 45. Remaining 40.	J.S.J.
"	19.8.17	9.30 am	Unit moved from RED. FARM (G 5. d 8 5) to HILLHOEK (L. 20. b. 7. 7).	
HILLHOEK	"	1 p.m.	Unit arrived here, to remain packed, no sick collected or admitted.	
		4 pm	Capt W.B.G. Angus reported his arrival for duty, taken on the strength.	J.S.J.

D. D. & L., London, E.C.
(A7883) Wt. W809/M1672 350,000 4/17 Sch. 52a Forms/C/2118/14

Army Form C. 2118.

Instructions regarding War Diaries and Intelligence Summaries are contained in F. S. Regs., Part II. and the Staff Manual respectively. Title pages will be prepared in manuscript.

WAR DIARY
or
~~INTELLIGENCE SUMMARY.~~
(Erase heading not required.)

Place	Date	Hour	Summary of Events and Information	Remarks and references to Appendices
HILLHOEK	20.8.17	12.15pm	36th Div. Secret Location of Units d/- 19. 8. 17 received.	
		4 pm	Urgent order from A.D.M.S. to move forthwith to WINNEZEELE Area; received.	
		5.30pm	109th Bde. S.C 12/764 received. - Instructions for advance party of the Brigade.	
		5.45pm	Unit moved from HILLHOEK. (L 20. L. 7. 7).	
WINNEZEELE	"	9.30pm	Unit arrived in WINNEZEELE Area (J. 8. c. central).	JSf
"	21.8.17	7.30am	One N.C.O. detailed to proceed with 109th Bde. advance party to new area.	
		7pm.	109th Bde Secret - Administrative Instructions for move of Brigade - recd.	
		8pm.	ADMS. Secret. O.O. No 41 rec'd. - Instructions for move from XIX Corps.	
			V Army to IV Corps. III Army; 109. F.Amb. train at 2.30 pm from CAESTRE	JSf
"	22.8.17	4.45am	Capt H.S. Davidson detailed as billeting Officer to proceed to new area.	
		11. am.	Lieut. J. Rice. U.S.M.C. rejoined from duty at No 2 (Can) C.C.S. taken on strength.	
		2.pm.	Capt. W.B.G. Angus detailed to take over Medical charge of 108th Army Bde. F.A.	
			from Capt. S.R.B. Campbell, who will rejoin 108th Field Ambce.	
		2pm.	ADMS Secret No 6032 rec'd. Sick evacuation to CCS's in new Area.	
			Medical Cases to 21 & 48. CCS YTRES. Surgical Cases to 55 CCS. TINCOURT.	
		3pm	ADMS Secret No 6031 rec'd. Route for Lorries - M.A. Con to BAPAUME.	JSf

Instructions regarding War Diaries and Intelligence Summaries are contained in F. S. Regs., Part II, and the Staff Manual respectively. Title pages will be prepared in manuscript.

WAR DIARY

or

~~INTELLIGENCE SUMMARY.~~

(Erase heading not required.)

Army Form C. 2118.

Place	Date	Hour	Summary of Events and Information	Remarks and references to Appendices
WINNEZEELE	23.8.17	11.30am	A.D.M.S. Secret No 6039 received — 109th Fld Ambce to proceed by No 23	
			train from CAESTRE at 2 pm on 24th inst.	JGJ
"	24.8.17	7. am	Lt Col Magill proceeded on leave to 4th Sept 1917. Capt J. G. Johnston	
		~~7.30am~~	to take over Command.	
		7.30 am	The Unit, less M.T. Section which is to proceed by Road, moved from	
			WINNEZEELE area to entrain at CAESTRE.	
CAESTRE.		11 am	Arrived here, men had dinner, Horses & Wagons entrained & ready to move	
			at 1 pm. train left 2 p.m.	
BAPAUME		10 pm	Train arrived in BAPAUME. Unit detrained & marched to BARASTRE.	JGJ
BARASTRE	25.8.17	2 am	Unit arrived in Camp at. O. 10. a. 5. 2.	
		10. am	A.D.M.S. No 6057 received — Sick of 107th & 109th Bdes to be collected by	
			109th F. Ambce & taken to 110th Fld Ambce.	
		10 am	A.D.M.S. No 6053. received — Location of Units of 36th Div.	
		11 am	" " 6063 " — IV Corps Medical arrangements.	
		noon.	Lieut J. Rice. U.S.M.C. to report to No 4 C.C.S. for duty. struck off strength.	
		10 pm	A.D.M.S. Secret No 6072 recd. — Scheme for collection & evacuation of sick	JGJ

D. D. & L., London, E.C.
(A7883) Wt. W809/M1672 350,000 4/17 Sch. 52a Forms/C/2118/14

Instructions regarding War Diaries and Intelligence Summaries are contained in F. S. Regs., Part II. and the Staff Manual respectively. Title pages will be prepared in manuscript.

WAR DIARY
or
~~INTELLIGENCE SUMMARY.~~
(Erase heading not required.)

Army Form C. 2118.

Place	Date	Hour	Summary of Events and Information	Remarks and references to Appendices
BARASTRE	26.8.17	10.30am	ADMS. Secret O.O. No 42 received — Move of Field Ambulance.	
			109th Fld Ambce to move to MARICOURT, an advance party of 2 Officers & 20 OR	
			to take over on 28th inst. the Corps Rest Stn at this place.	
		noon.	D.D.M.S. IV Corps visited the Camp.	
		10pm.	107th Bde. Secret Order No 170 received — Move of Brigade on 27th inst.	JJ
"	27.8.17	11 am.	D.D.M.S. IV Corps visited & inspected the Camp.	
		1.20pm	ADMS secret No S/290 received — Code Calls. 36th Div.	JJ
"	28.8.17	11 am.	ADMS. Secret No 6113 received — the 8th & 9th R.I.R. are to be amalgamated &	
			known as the 8/9th R.I. Rifles. — the 1st R. Ir. Fus posted to 107th Bde.	
			Capt Davidson Lt. G. R. Pettitt & 20 OR's proceeded as advance party	
			to IV Corps Rest Stn at MARICOURT.	
			ADMS Secret No S/291 received — Correction No for B.A.B Code No 3.	JJ
	29.8.17	8 am.	Unit moved from BARASTRE (O.10.a.5.2) via ROCQUIGNY. COMBLES	
			& GUILLEMONT to MARICOURT arriving 1 p.m.	
MARICOURT		4 pm	Diploma awarded to Sergt R. McKay of this unit by French Government	
			for agricultural work received.	JJ

D. D. & L., London, E.C.
(A7883) Wt. W809/M1672 350,000 4/17 Sch. 52a Forms/C/2118/14

Army Form C. 2118.

Instructions regarding War Diaries and Intelligence Summaries are contained in F. S. Regs., Part II. and the Staff Manual respectively. Title pages will be prepared in manuscript.

WAR DIARY
or
~~INTELLIGENCE SUMMARY.~~
(Erase heading not required.)

Place	Date	Hour	Summary of Events and Information	Remarks and references to Appendices
MARICOURT.	29.8.17	7 pm	ADMS. Secret No 6145 received — Copy of report on the treatment of Traumatic Shock & Gas infection.	
		7 pm.	Lieut H. J. C Churchill reported his arrival for duty taken on strength.	JSJ
"	30.8.17	9 am	Lieut J. Robinson U.S.M.C. detailed for temporary duty as MO i/c 8th Pontoon Park at BELLEVUE FARM.	
		noon	Administration of IV Corps Rest Stn taken over from 28th Fd Amb (9th Div)	
		2 pm.	Lieut Churchill & 18 O.Rs detailed for temporary duty at 38th C.C.S BRAY-sur SOMME. Patients remaining 502	JSJ
"	31.8.17	9 am	28th Field Ambulance marched out. Patients remaining 499.	JSJ

B.E.F.

SUMMARY OF MEDICAL WAR DIARIES OF 109th F.A. 36th Div.

8th Corps. 5th ARMY.

19th Corps from 26th July.

4th Corps III. Army from 23rd August.

Western Front Operations- July-Aug. 1917.

Officer Commanding - Lt.Col. R. MAGILL.

SUMMARISED UNDER THE FOLLOWING HEADINGS:-

Phase "D" 1. - Passchendaele Operations "July-Nov. 1917"

(a) - Operations commencing July 1917.

Aug. 3rd.	<u>Moves. Detachment.</u> 2& 40 Bearers to RED FARM for duty in line.	
		1 & 59 rejoined.
	<u>Casualties R.A.M.C.</u> 0 & 1 killed. 0 & 2 wounded.	
4th.	<u>Moves.</u> To RED FARM.	
	<u>Medical Arrangements.</u> Following posts taken over and evacuation of front line .	
		C.M.D.S. RED FARM.
		A.D.S's. CANAL BANK & WIELTJE.
		Col.P. St. JEAN.
		4 & 2 Br. S.D's 108th F.A.) attached for duty. 2 & 2 Br. S.D's 110th F.A.)
	<u>Casualties R.A.M.C.</u> Capt. Hart wounded.	
		0& 7 wounded.
5th.	<u>Casualties.</u> 2 & 42 wounded admitted. Ps.of W. wounded 4	

B.E.F.

109th F.A. 36th Div. Western Front.

19th Corps. 5th ARMY. August 1917.

Officer Commanding - Lt.Col. R. Magill.

PHASE "D" 1. - Passchendaele Operations-"July-Nov.1917"

(a) - Operations commencing July 1917.

Headquarters at Red Farm.

Aug.6th.	Operations Enemy. RED FARM shelled - no casualties or damage.
	Casualties R.A.M.C. 0 & 1 wounded.
	Casualties. 3 & 85 wounded admitted.
7th.	" 2 & 143 wounded "
8th.	Casualties R.A.M.C. 0 & 1 wounded.
	Medical Arrangements. 50 beds provided in M.D.S. in order to lessen sick wastage.
	Casualties. 1 & 103 wounded admitted.
9th.	" 4 & 172 wounded admitted.
10th.	3 & 133 wounded admitted.
11th.	Casualties R.A.M.C. 0 & 2 wounded.
	Casualties. 3 & 248 wounded admitted.
12th.	3 & 147 " "
13th.	Casualties R.A.M.C. 0 & 1 wounded.
	Casualties. 4 & 129 wounded admitted.
14th.	Medical Arrangements. Command of M.D.S. taken over by Officer Commanding 108th Field Ambulance.
	Casualties. 4 & 103 wounded admitted.

109th F.A. 36th Div. Western Front.

19th Corps. 5th Army. August 1917.

Officer Commanding - Lt.Col. R. MAGILL.

4th Corps III. Army from 23rd August.

PHASE "D" 1. - Passchendaele Operations - "July-Nov. 1917.

(a) - Operations commencing July 1917.

Headquarters at Red Farm.

Aug. 15th. Casualties. 2 & 72 wounded, admitted.

16th. Medical Arrangements. 3 & 230 Bearers reported at Mine Shaft Wieltje for evacuation of wounded.

Casualties R.A.M.C. 0 & 3 killed, 0 & 2 wounded.

Casualties. 4 & 117 wounded admitted.

17th. Casualties R.A.M.C. 0 & 2 wounded.

Moves. Detachment. 3 & 95 rejoined Headquarters from line.

Medical Arrangements. A.D.S's and forward posts. handed over to 2/3rd S.M.F.A.

Casualties. 43 and 839 wounded admitted.

18th. " 12 and 45 wounded admitted.

19th. Moves. To Hillhoek L.20 b.7.7. (Sheet 27).

20th. " To Winnizeele. J8.c. central (Sheet 27).

23rd. Moves and Transfer. To 4th Corps, 3rd Army and commenced move to New Area.

Aug. 3rd. **Moves. Detachment.** 2& 40 Bearers to RED FARM for duty in line.

1 & 59 rejoined.

Casualties R.A.M.C. 0 & 1 killed. 0 & 2 wounded.

4th. **Moves.** To RED FARM.

Medical Arrangements. Following posts taken over and evacuation of front line .

C.M.D.S. RED FARM.

A.D.S's. CANAL BANK & WIELTJE.

Col.P. St. JEAN.

4 & 2 Br. S.D's 108th F.A.) attached for duty.
2 & 2 Br. S.D's 110th F.A.)

Casualties R.A.M.C. Capt. Hart wounded.

0& 7 wounded.

5th. **Casualties.** 2 & 42 wounded admitted. Ps.of W. wounded 4.

B.E.F.

109th F.A. 36th Div. Western Front.

19th Corps. 5th ARMY. August 1917.

Officer Commanding - Lt.Col. R. Magill.

PHASE "D" 1. - Passchendaele Operations-"July-Nov.1917"

(a) - Operations commencing July 1917.

Headquarters at Red Farm.

Aug.6th.	Operations Enemy. RED FARM shelled - no casualties or damage.
	Casualties R.A.M.C. 0 & 1 wounded.
	Casualties. 3 & 85 wounded admitted.
7th.	" 2 & 143 wounded "
8th.	Casualties R.A.M.C. 0 & 1 wounded.
	Medical Arrangements. 50 b[illegible] provided in M.D.S. in order to lessen sick wastage.
	Casualties. 1 & 103 wounded admitted.
9th.	" 4 & 172 wounded admitted.
10th.	3 & 133 wounded admitted.
11th.	Casualties R.A.M.C. 0 & 2 wounded.
	Casualties. 3 & 248 wounded admitted.
12th.	3 & 147 " "
13th.	Casualties R.A.M.C. 0 & 1 wounded.
	Casualties. 4 & 129 wounded admitted.
14th.	Medical Arrangements. Command of M.D.S. taken over by Officer Commanding 108th Field Ambulance.
	Casualties. 4 & 103 wounded admitted.

109th F.A. 36th Div. Western Front.
19th Corps. 5th Army. August 1917.
Officer Commanding - Lt.Col. R. MAGILL.
4th Corps III. Army from 23rd August.

PHASE "D" 1. - Passchendaele Operations - "July-Nov. 1917
(a) - Operations commencing July 1917.

Headquarters at Red Farm.

Aug. 15th. Casualties. 2 & 72 wounded, admitted.

16th. Medical Arrangements. 5 & 230 Bearers reported at Mine Shaft Wieltje for evacuation of wounded.

Casualties R.A.M.C. 0 & 3 killed. 0 & 2 wounded.

Casualties. 4 & 117 wounded admitted.

17th. Casualties R.A.M.C. 0 & 2 wounded.

Moves. Detachment. 3 & 95 rejoined Headquarters from line.

Medical Arrangements. A.D.S's and forward posts handed over to 2/3rd S.M.F.A.

Casualties. 43 and 839 wounded admitted.

18th. " 12 and 45 wounded admitted.

19th. Moves. To Hillhoek L.20 b.7.7. (Sheet 27).

20th. " To Winnizeele. J8.c. central (Sheet 27).

23rd. Moves and Transfer. To 4th Corps 3rd. Army and commenced move to New Area.

WO 95/2443

Confidential

War Diary

of

109th Field Ambulance

From 1st Sept 1917

To 30th Sept 1917

Vol XXIV

[signature] Lieut Col
Comdg 109 F.A.

30. 9. 17

Instructions regarding War Diaries and Intelligence Summaries are contained in F. S. Regs., Part II. and the Staff Manual respectively. Title pages will be prepared in manuscript.

WAR DIARY
or
~~INTELLIGENCE SUMMARY.~~
(Erase heading not required.)

Army Form C. 2118.

Place	Date	Hour	Summary of Events and Information	Remarks and references to Appendices
MARICOURT	1.9.17		Capt Underhill E. taken on the strength, but attached for temporary duty to 108th Field Ambce.	
		11. am	D.D.M.S. IV Corps visited & inspected the Rest Station.	
		3 pm	36th Division Secret Location of Units received from A.D.M.S.	
			Remaining in Rest Stn. Sick Officers 7. OR 404. Scabies Officers 3 OR 67.	JGJ
"	2.9.17		Capt J.G. Johnston visited BELLEVUE FARM to inspect Medical equipment there.	
			Remg in Hosp. Sick Officers 6, OR 342. Scabies Officers 3 OR 68.	JGJ
"	3.9.17	2 pm	Capt Johnston visited Divisional Headquarters to see A.D.M.S.	
			Two O.R. attached to 37 Sanitary Section at YTRES for temporary duty.	
		3.30 pm	A.D.M.S. Secret No 17 recd — new Playfair Code word.	
			Remg in Hosp. Sick Off 6, OR 324, Scabies Off 3. OR 66	JGJ
"	4.9.17	3.30 pm	A.D.M.S. Secret Location of Units 36th Division received.	
		6 pm	Football match played with R.O.D. R.E. Score 109 F.A. 2. R.O.D. RE - nil.	
			Remg in Hospital Sick Officers 6 OR 309. Scabies Officers 3 OR 67.	JGJ
	5.9.17	10 am	The D.M.S. III Army accompanied by D.D.M.S. IV Corps & A.D.M.S. 36th Division inspected the C. Rest Stn Scabies Hospital + Officers Hospital	

D. D. & L., London, E.C. (A7883) Wt. W809/M1672 350,000 4/17 Sch. 52a Forms/C/2118/14

Army Form C. 2118.

Instructions regarding War Diaries and Intelligence Summaries are contained in F. S. Regs., Part II, and the Staff Manual respectively. Title pages will be prepared in manuscript.

WAR DIARY
or
INTELLIGENCE SUMMARY.
(Erase heading not required.)

Place	Date	Hour	Summary of Events and Information	Remarks and references to Appendices
MARICOURT	5.9.17	3pm	ADMS Secret No S/293 received — Correction for B.A.B Trench Code No 3	
			to be taken into use from midnight 6/7th September.	
		3pm	Secret Location of Units of 36th Division received.	
		3.30pm	ADMS Wire No M 1992 received — Wind dangerous.	
		6pm	Football Match played with 38 CCS at BRAY. Score 38 CCS 1. 109th No	
			Remg in Hospital Sick Off 6. OR 314. Scabies Off 4 OR 56.	JGJ
"	6.9.17	4pm	ADMS Secret No 6269 received — Amendments to Location of Units of 4th	
		6.30pm	Concert held for the patients in Church Army Hut by the men of the Ambulance	
			Remg in Hospital Sick Off 6 OR 315 Scabies Off 4 OR 64.	JGJ
"	7.9.17	4pm	Lt. Col R. Magill D.S.O. rejoined from leave of absence.	
		4.15pm	The Corps Commander accompanied by D.D.M.S. visited & inspected the	
			IV Corps Rest Stn & expressed his approval of all the arrangements.	
			Remg in Hospital Sick Off 6. OR 305 Scabies Off 4 OR 75	JGJ
"	8.9.17	3PM	Location of Units received.	
		6PM	Concert in Church Army Hut given by Divisional Pierrot Troupe for Patients	
			Remng in Hosp. Sick Off 6. OR 317 Scabies Offs 4. OR 76	RM

D. D. & L., London, E.C.
(A7883) Wt. W809/M1672 350,000 4/17 Sch. 52a Forms/C/2118/14.

Instructions regarding War Diaries and Intelligence Summaries are contained in F. S. Regs., Part II. and the Staff Manual respectively. Title pages will be prepared in manuscript.

WAR DIARY
or
~~INTELLIGENCE SUMMARY.~~
(Erase heading not required.)

Army Form C. 2118.

Place	Date	Hour	Summary of Events and Information	Remarks and references to Appendices
			Routine.	
MARICOURT	9.9.17	4 PM	Football match against 68 aux Petrol Co ASC.	
			Remaining in Hosp. Offs sick 6 OR 300. Scabies Offs. 4 OR 79.	AM
	10.9.17		Routine.	
"	10.9.17	4 PM	AA & QMG 36 Div visited C.O. and inspected Camp.	
			Remaining in Hosp. Sick Offs 6 OR 293 Scabies Off 4. OR 82	AM
"	11.9.17	noon	Capt. CC Gibson RAMC reported his arrival for duty.	
		7 PM	Lt A.S Robinson USAR rejoined from temporary duty with 8th Balloon PK.	
			Remaining in Hosp. Offs sick 6 OR. 293. Scabies Offs. 5 OR 84.	AM
"	12.9.17	8 AM	Capt Russell proceeded to Amiens to purchase scythes etc. It is proposed to cut & save clover for winter forage.	
			Routine, Remaining in Hosp. Sick Offs 6. OR 278 Scabies Offs 5 OR. 87	AM
"	13.9.17	6 PM	"[Bird?] Safe" Concert held in CA Hut by troupe of the [?] Amb. for patients.	
			Remaining in Hosp. Sick Offs 7. OR 279. Scabies Offs 5. OR 89	AM
"	14.9.17		Transport engaged in collecting materials to repair & roof stables & other buildings in Camp.	
			Routine Remaining in Hosp. Sick Offs 7. OR. 266. Scabies Offs 5. OR 86	AM

D. D. & L., London, E.C.
(A7883) Wt W809/M1672 350,000 4/17 Sch. 52a Forms/C/2118/14

Instructions regarding War Diaries and Intelligence Summaries are contained in F. S. Regs., Part II, and the Staff Manual respectively. Title pages will be prepared in manuscript.

WAR DIARY
or
~~INTELLIGENCE~~ SUMMARY.
(Erase heading not required.)

Army Form C. 2118.

Place	Date	Hour	Summary of Events and Information	Remarks and references to Appendices
MARICOURT	15.9.17	11 AM	Lt A Robinson U.S.A.R detailed by ADMS to take over medical charge of 11th R Innis Fus.	
			Capt. Johnston visited ADMS. Pte Cameron sent to A.P.M to undergo 56 days F.P. No1 awarded by F.G.C.M for absence without leave.	
			Remaining in Hosp. Sick Offs 7. OR 278. Scabies Offs 5 OR 83.	✓
	16.9.17	10 AM	O.C 36 D.S.C. inspected motor ambulances of unit.	
			Remaining in Hosp Sick Offs 7. OR 281. Scabies Offs 6. OR 76	✓
	17.9.17	Noon	ADMS 36 Division inspected Camp.	
			Lt Phillips detailed to report to 142 Fd Amb LECHELLE for duty.	
			Remaining in Hosp. Sick Offs 10 OR 279. Scabies Offs 5 OR 73.	✓
	18.9.17		Routine. Remaining in Hosp Sick Offs 9 OR 349. Scabies Offs 5 OR 87	✓
	19.9.17	Noon	G.O.C 36 Div Major General O.S.W. Nugent CB DSO visited the Fd Amb. The personnel were drawn up on Parade & received the General with the general salute. The G.O.C having addressed the parade presented the insignia of the Croix de Chevalier to the O.C. & afterwards inspected the parade. The Divisional band attended. The G.O.C then inspected the Rest Station	

D. D. & L., London, E.C. (A7883) Wt W809/M1672 350,000 4/17 Sch. 52a Forms/C/2118/14

Instructions regarding War Diaries and Intelligence Summaries are contained in F. S. Regs., Part II. and the Staff Manual respectively. Title pages will be prepared in manuscript.

WAR DIARY

or

~~INTELLIGENCE SUMMARY.~~

(Erase heading not required.)

Army Form C. 2118.

Place	Date	Hour	Summary of Events and Information	Remarks and references to Appendices
MARICOURT	19.9.17	Cont.	and Expressed himself highly pleased with the Unit –	
"	"		Remaining in Hosp Sick Offs 8. OR 342. Scabies Offs 4. OR 82.	[illegible]
"	20.9.17		Capt. Johnston proceeded to HdQrs IV Corps for temporary duty in DDMS Office.	
		10 am	Capt Underhill reported his arrival for duty.	
			Remaining in Hosp. Sick Offs 8. OR. 341. Scabies Offs. 4. OR 86	[illegible]
"	21.9.17		ADMS Secret German circular on Gas Gangrene prophylactic serum.	
			Routine Remaining in Hosp. Sick Offs. 9. OR 357. Scabies Offs 4 OR 81	[illegible]
"	22.9.17		Routine. Work on fencing in duck board paths in progress, draining and general preparations for winter.	
		6 PM	Concert by 7 A Troupe to patients. Remaining in Hosp. Sick Offs. 7 OR 388. Scabies Offs 4 OR 89	[illegible]
"	23.9.17		Routine. Remaining in Hosp Sick Offs. 7. OR 383. Scabies Offs 4. OR 94.	[illegible]
"	24.9.17		" " " Sick Offs 7 OR 379. Scabies Offs. 4 OR 87	[illegible]
"	25.9.17	10 am	Names Submitted for New Years Honours.	
		"	Sentence of 1 Year I.H.L. promulgated on Pte Mitchell convicted by F.G.C.M. on 21.9.17 for absence without leave. Remaining in Hosp. Sick Offs. 6 OR. 287. Scabies 4 OR 86	[illegible]

D. D. & L., London, E.C.
(A7883) Wt. W809/M1672 350,000 4/17 Sch. 52a Forms/C/2118/14

Army Form C. 2118.

WAR DIARY
or
~~INTELLIGENCE SUMMARY.~~
(Erase heading not required.)

Instructions regarding War Diaries and Intelligence Summaries are contained in F. S. Regs., Part II, and the Staff Manual respectively. Title pages will be prepared in manuscript.

Place	Date	Hour	Summary of Events and Information	Remarks and references to Appendices
MARICOURT	26.9.17		Routine. Patients Remaining Sick Offs. 7 OR. 279. Scabies 5 OR. 88	Rm
"	27.9.17	10 AM	Pte Phillips W tried by F.G.C.M for absence without leave	
			Remaining in Hosp Sick Offs 7 OR 299 Scabies Offs 5 OR 87	Rm
"	28.9.17		Routine. Remaining Sick Offs 8. OR 284. Scabies Offs 5. OR 85	Rm
	29.9.17		" " " " 8. " 285. " " 5 " 81	Rm
"	30.9.17		Capt. Johnston returned from duty at Office of D.D.M.S. IV Corps	
			Remaining in Hosp. Sick Offs 9. OR 303. Scabies Offs 5. OR 76	Rm

D. D. & L., London, E.C.
(A7883) Wt W809/M1672 350,000 4/17 Sch. 52a Forms/C/2118/14

Vol 25

140/2477.

Confidential

War Diary

of

109th Field Ambulance

From 1st Oct 1917

Vol XXV

To 31st Oct 1917

[signature] Lt Col
Comdg 109 F.A.

11

Oct. 1917

Instructions regarding War Diaries and Intelligence Summaries are contained in F. S. Regs., Part II. and the Staff Manual respectively. Title pages will be prepared in manuscript.

WAR DIARY
or
~~INTELLIGENCE~~ SUMMARY.
(Erase heading not required.)

Army Form C. 2118.

Place	Date	Hour	Summary of Events and Information	Remarks and references to Appendices
MARICOURT	1.10.17	3 PM	D.D.M.S. 14 Corps inspected Camp.	
"		4 PM	F.G.C.M. sentence of 6 months I.H.L. on Pte Phillips W. for overstaying leave promulgated. Remaining in Hosp. Off. 8. OR. 292. Scabies Off. 4 OR 80.	[signature]
"	2.10.17		Capt Johnston granted leave 3rd to 17 inst.	
	"	5 PM	Location of Units received from A.D.M.S. Remaining in Hosp:– Offs 7 OR 332. Scabies Offs 6. OR 67.	[signature]
	3 "		Routine. Afternoon football match versus R.Es. Patients remaining. Off 9. OR 291. Scabies Offs 7. OR 77.	[signature]
"	4 "		Work on Stables, Hut for personnel, and new dining room and Kitchen in progress.	
		5 PM	Divisional Band visited Rest Station and played from 5–7. Patients remaining Off 9. OR 274. Scabies Offs 7. OR 72.	[signature]
"	5 "		Rewards for gallantry published in Divisional R.O. 3.10.17. Military Cross Capt Russell. D.C.M. Pte W.F. Quinn. Military Medals:– Sgt. McKay. Cpl. Service & Millar. Ptes. Cook and Neill.	[signature]

D. D. & L., London, E.C.
(A7883) Wt. W809/M1672 350,000 4/17 Sch. 52a Forms/C/2118/14

Instructions regarding War Diaries and Intelligence Summaries are contained in F. S. Regs., Part II. and the Staff Manual respectively. Title pages will be prepared in manuscript.

WAR DIARY
or
~~INTELLIGENCE SUMMARY.~~
(Erase heading not required.)

Army Form C. 2118.

Place	Date	Hour	Summary of Events and Information	Remarks and references to Appendices
MARICOURT	5.10.17	6 PM	Concert by FA Troupe for Patients in C.A Hut.	Rem
			Patients remaining. Offs 13 OR 296 Scabies Offs 6 OR 83	
"	6.10.17		Routine. Patients remaining Offs 14. OR 292. Scabies Offs 5 OR 100	Rem
		4 PM	B A B Code correction received.	
"	7.10.17		Routine Rem in Hosp. Offs 14. OR 265 Scabies Offs 6 OR 98.	Rem
"	8.10.17	4 PM	Secret medical arrangements No 1 & Scheme for evacuation from line received from ADMS	
		"	3rd Army CM 9175 received suspending sentence on Pte Mitchell	
			Rem in Hosp. Offs 14 OR 268. Scabies Offs 6 OR 97.	Rem
"	9.10.17		Routine. Rem in Hosp Offs 15 OR 265 Scabies Offs 5 OR 100	Rem
"	10.10.17		Routine. All heating apparatus at Scabies Hospital enclosed & roofed over thus saving fuel. Rem in Hosp. Offs 15 OR 253. Scabies Offs 5 OR 106	Rem
"	11.10.17	11 AM	DDMS IV Corps inspected Camp. Rem in Hosp. Offs 6 OR 253. Scabies Offs 5 OR 110	Rem
	12.10.17		Routine Rem in Hosp. Offs 13 OR 304. Scabies Offs 5 OR 118.	Rem
			Concert by FA Troupe	
	13.10.17		CO visited School of Sanitation PERONNE. Rem in Hosp. Offs 14 OR 298. Scabies Offs 5 OR 120	Rem

D. D. & L., London, E.C.
(A7883) Wt. W809/M1672 350,000 4/17 **Sch. 52a** Forms/C/2118/14

Instructions regarding War Diaries and Intelligence Summaries are contained in F. S. Regs., Part II. and the Staff Manual respectively. Title pages will be prepared in manuscript.

WAR DIARY
or
~~INTELLIGENCE~~ SUMMARY.
(*Erase heading not required.*)

Army Form C. 2118.

Place	Date	Hour	~~Summary of Events~~ and Information	Remarks and references to Appendices
MARICOURT	14.10.17	3.30 PM	Football match Versus Signals. 1–1.	
		6 PM	F.A. Troupe gave a performance to Labour Coy BRAY. Rem in Hosp Off 14 OR 320 Scabies Off 5 OR 131.	[illegible]
	15.10.17		Capt [illegible] proceeded on leave to 26th inst. Rem in Hosp Off 16 OR 301. Scabies Off 5 OR 135	[illegible]
	16.10.17		Football match Sergeants v Corporals. 9–3. Rem in Hosp Off 15 OR 300 Scabies Off 5 OR 124	[illegible]
	17.10.17		Routine Rem in Hosp. Off 14. OR 322. Scabies Off 5. OR 132.	[illegible]
	18.10.17		Routine Rem in Hosp Off 14 OR 318. Scabies Off 4. OR 135	[illegible]
	19.10.17		Routine Pte Scar taken on Strength from 38 CCS vice Pte McCalman transferred to 38 CCS. Rem in Hosp Off 14 OR 312 Scabies Off 4 OR 131	[illegible]
	20.10.17		Capt Johnston returned from leave. 5 OR reinforcements taken on strength. Rem in Hosp. Off 12 OR 331. Scabies Off 2. OR 158	[illegible]
		4.30 PM	Football match RAMC V. ASC. 7–nil.	[illegible]
		6.30 PM	Concert to patients by F.A. Troupe.	
	21.10.17		Capt Johnston detailed to report at office of DDMS IV Corps for temporary duty as DADMS.	
		3 PM	Football match 109 FA V 108 FA at ROYAUCOURT. 109 FA 2 goals 108 FA nil	[illegible]

D. D. & L., London, E.C.
(A7883) Wt. W809/M1672 350,000 4/17 Sch. 52a. Forms/C/2118/14

Instructions regarding War Diaries and Intelligence Summaries are contained in F. S. Regs., Part II, and the Staff Manual respectively. Title pages will be prepared in manuscript.

WAR DIARY
or
INTELLIGENCE SUMMARY.
(Erase heading not required.)

Army Form C. 2118.

Place	Date	Hour	Summary of Events and Information	Remarks and references to Appendices
MARICOURT	21.10.17		"Contd" Rem in Hosp. Off 12 OR. 328. Scabies Off 2 OR 149	[illegible]
"	22.10.17		Routine Remain Hosp Off 12 OR 326 Scabies Off 2 OR 150	
"	23.10.17	4 PM	3rd Army CM 9318 received suspending sentence of 6 months I.H.L. on Pte	[illegible]
			Phillips. Routine. Rem in Hosp, Off 14 OR. 326. Scabies Off 2 OR 152	[illegible]
"	24.10.17		Routine Remaining in Hosp Off 14 OR 385 Scabies Off 2 OR 133	[illegible]
"	25.10.17		Routine Rem in Hosp Off 12 OR 387 Scabies Off 2 OR 125	[illegible]
"	26.10.17		C.O. proceeded to Army H.Qrs to see D.D.R. with regard to remounts	
			Rem in Hosp Off 12 OR 406 Scabies Off 3 OR 128	[illegible]
"	27.10.17	12 noon	~~[illegible]~~ D.D.M.S. - IV Corps inspected Camp.	[illegible]
		"	2 U.S.A. medical officers visited the Unit and were greatly interested	
			in the routine of the Hospital. Remaining in Hospital Off 14 OR 411	
			Scabies Off 3. OR 129.	[illegible]
	28.10.17		Q.M. Sgt. Hill reported for duty having been in hospital in Ireland.	
			Hut for personnel finished. Rem in Hosp. Off 14 OR 359 Scabies Off 3 OR 121	[illegible]
	29.10.17	8 AM	2 Off & 10 OR proceeded to AMIENS on one day pass.	
			Capt Davidson returned from leave of absence. Rem. Off 14 OR 402 Scabies Off 2 OR 126	[illegible]

Army Form C. 2118.

Instructions regarding War Diaries and Intelligence Summaries are contained in F. S. Regs., Part II. and the Staff Manual respectively. Title pages will be prepared in manuscript.

WAR DIARY
or
INTELLIGENCE SUMMARY.
(*Erase heading not required.*)

Place	Date	Hour	Summary of Events and Information	Remarks and references to Appendices
MARICOURT	30.10.17	11AM	A.D.M.S inspected Camp with Lt. Forres 15.0 Co R.E. and made enquiries as to method of fumigating clothing by Clayton Machine. They saw the apparatus at work. Rem in Hosp off. 13 OR 437. Scabies off 3 OR 115	[illegible]
	31.10.17	4PM	CO attended Conference at A.D.M.S Office. Rem in Hosp off 13 OR 413 Scabies off 3 OR 114	[illegible]

Vol 26

140/2578

Confidential

War Diary

of

109th Field Ambulance

From 1st Nov 1917 To 30th Nov 1917

Vol XXVI

[signature]
Lieut Col

19

Nov 1917

Army Form C. 2118.

Instructions regarding War Diaries and Intelligence Summaries are contained in F. S. Regs., Part II, and the Staff Manual respectively. Title pages will be prepared in manuscript.

WAR DIARY
or
~~INTELLIGENCE~~ SUMMARY.

(Erase heading not required.)

Place	Date	Hour	Summary of Events and Information	Remarks and references to Appendices
MARICOURT	1.11.17		Routine. Patients remaining Offs 14 OR 509	Rh
	2.11.17		Capt. J G Johnston rejoined from duty with D.D.M.S. IV Corps.	Rh
			Patients remaining Off 14 OR 548.	
	3.11.17	3 PM	Capt C C S Gibson ordered to proceed to 108th Fd Amb for temporary duty (ADMS)	Rh
			~~Capt~~ Lt H J C Churchill transferred to 38 CCS. Struck off strength from 31.10.17	Rh
			authority D.M.S 3rd Army 1326/543/31/10/17.	
			Patients remaining Offs 15 OR 494.	
	4.11.17		Routine. League Football match V 110 Fd Amb. 109 FA 5 goals 110 FA 1 goal.	
			Patients remaining Offs 13 OR 454.	Rh
	5.11.17		Routine Patients remaining Off 13 OR438.	Rh
	6.11.17	2.30 PM	ADMS No 20 6/11/17 New Code Word. Patients remaining Off 12 OR416	Rh
	7.11.17		Routine Patients remaining Off 13 OR 444	Rh
	8.11.17	4. PM	ADMS 7030 Code word cancelled	
			Location of Units received. Patients remaining Off 12 OR 448	Rh
	9.11.17	3am	Lt & QM Perritt proceeded on leave till 24 inst	
		6.30 PM	Field Amb. troupe Concert for patients. Patients remaining Off 14 OR433.	Rh

D. D. & L., London, E.C. (A7883) Wt. W809/M1672 350,000 4/17 **Sch. 52a** Forms/C/2118/14

Instructions regarding War Diaries and Intelligence Summaries are contained in F. S. Regs., Part II. and the Staff Manual respectively. Title pages will be prepared in manuscript.

WAR DIARY
or
INTELLIGENCE SUMMARY.
(Erase heading not required.)

Army Form C. 2118.

Place	Date	Hour	Summary of Events and Information	Remarks and references to Appendices
MARICOURT	10.11.17		Routine. Patients remaining Offs 14. OR 341	[illegible]
	11.11.17		" " " Offs 14. OR 355	[illegible]
	12.11.17	6 PM	9 A Troupe gave a Concert to patients of 41 Stationary Hosp.	
			Routine Patients remaining Offs 14. OR 427.	[illegible]
	13.11.17		Routine Patients remaining Offs 18. OR 426	
	14.11.17	1 PM	S/307 from ADMS medical arrangements in event of active operations.	
		4 PM	OC & Capt Johnston attended at Office of ADMS & discussed medical arrangements. 109 Fd Amb to provide 2 Offs + 108 Bearers. 6 MA Cars 6 GS wagons one motor cycle to be under command of 110 Fd Amb. Each ambulance personnel to wear a distinctive badge. 109 FA a black rectangle on each shoulder	[illegible]
			Patients remaining Offs 17 OR 415	
	15.11.17	4 PM	S.308 from ADMS secret Playtair Lord	
			S 311 correction to S.307 received on 14.11.17.	
			Patients remaining Offs 19 OR 383	[illegible]
	16.11.17	4.15 PM	S.307/1 received from ADMS. Medical arrangements.	[illegible]

D. D. & L., London, E.C.
(A7883) Wt W809/M1672 350,000 4/17 Sch. 52a Forms/C/2118/14

Instructions regarding War Diaries and Intelligence Summaries are contained in F. S. Regs., Part II. and the Staff Manual respectively. Title pages will be prepared in manuscript.

WAR DIARY

or

~~INTELLIGENCE~~ SUMMARY.

(*Erase heading not required.*)

Army Form C. 2118.

Place	Date	Hour	Summary of Events and Information	Remarks and references to Appendices
		Contd		
MARICOURT	16.11.17	4.15 PM	Operation Order No 43 from ADMS	[illegible]
			Patients remaining Off 18 OR 347.	[illegible]
	17.11.17	5.30 PM	Station Code calls 36 [illegible] received	
			Routine Patients remaining Off 17 OR 354.	[illegible]
	18.11.17		Routine " " Off 17 OR 344	[illegible]
	19.11.17		2 Off 188 OR 5 M A Con 6 G S wagons proceeded to report for duty with 110	[illegible]
			Fd Amb Patients remaining Off 14 OR 437.	[illegible]
	20.11.17		Routine 300 Stretchers & 3000 blankets sent to ADS ROYAULCOURT (ADMS)	
			Patients remaining Off 16 OR 366	[illegible]
	21.11.17		Routine Patients remaining Off 14 OR 490	
	22.11.17		" " " " 12 " 543	[illegible]
	23.11.17	5 PM	ADMS 7292 Capt Gibson to take over medical charge of 2 R Ir Rifles &	
			to be struck off strength Patients remaining Off 14 OR 598	[illegible]
	24.11.17		Routine Patients remaining Off 18 OR 629	[illegible]
	25.11.17	11.30 PM	Lt & QM Perrott returned from leave, Patients remaining Off 19 OR 699	[illegible]
	26.11.17		Routine patients remaining Off 13 OR 640	[illegible]

D. D. & L., London, E.C.
(A7883) Wt. W809/M1672 350,000 4/17 Sch. 52a Forms/C/2118/14

Instructions regarding War Diaries and Intelligence Summaries are contained in F. S. Regs., Part II, and the Staff Manual respectively. Title pages will be prepared in manuscript.

WAR DIARY
or
~~INTELLIGENCE SUMMARY.~~
(Erase heading not required.)

Army Form C. 2118.

Place	Date	Hour	Summary of Events and Information	Remarks and references to Appendices
		Cont		
MARICOURT	26.11.17		300 Stretchers sent to MDS RUYAULCOURT ~~[illegible]~~ (DDMS.) Patients in Rest Station provided with straw paillasses.	[illegible]
"	27.11.17	4.30 PM	~~[illegible]~~ Operation Orders received from ADMS.	
		"	2 Offs + bearers + transport rejoined from duty with 110 Fd Amb during operations. 2 slight Casualties	[illegible]
			Patients remaining Off 16 OR 684	[illegible]
	28.11.17		Routine Patients remaining Off 18 OR 736	[illegible]
	29.11.17		Routine Off 21 OR 755	
		7.15 PM	Wire from ADMS Division will move to 17 Corps area on 29th	[illegible]
		10 PM	Wire from 36 Div Q 109 FA will arrive in new area on 2nd and will be billeted at SOMBRIN.	
			2 Off + 60 OR arrived as advance party from 2/1 North Midland to relieve 109 FA [illegible]	[illegible]
	30.11.17	5 PM	DDMS wires proceed to rejoin Division on relief.	
		6.30 PM	DDMS wires relief of your Fd Amb by FA of 59 Division cancelled.	
		"	~~FA~~ 2/1 North Midland FA 59 Div arrived to take over.	
			Patients remaining Off 19. OR 672	[illegible]

D. D. & L., London, E.C. (A7883) Wt. W809/M1672 350,000 4/17 Sch. 52a Forms/C/2118/14

Vol 27

Confidential

War Diary

of

109th. Field Ambulance.

from 1st. Dec. 1917. to 31 st. Dec. 1917.

VOL.

XXVII.

19

Lt. Colonel
R. A. M. C.

Instructions regarding War Diaries and Intelligence Summaries are contained in F. S. Regs., Part II. and the Staff Manual respectively. Title pages will be prepared in manuscript.

WAR DIARY
or
~~INTELLIGENCE SUMMARY.~~
(Erase heading not required.)

Army Form C. 2118.

Place	Date	Hour	Summary of Events and Information	Remarks and references to Appendices
MARICOURT	1-12-17	11AM	36 Div 'G' wire:- 109 F.A. will move today to ROCQUINEY via COMBLES starting 1 PM. To report on arrival to 108 Bde.	[initials]
"	"	12.10PM	36 Div 'G' wire:- Cancel my wire today ref. move of 109 F.A.	[initials]
"	"	2 PM	2/1 N. Mid F.A. moved out. Taking over from 109 F.A. cancelled.	[initials]
"	"	7.15PM	A.D.M.S. No 7338:- Lt. G. Adams + Lt. J Scott. posted to 109 F.A. 28/11/17. Lt. Adams detailed to to report to C.R.E. to take over medical charge of R.Es 25/11/17. Patients remaining Offs 12. O.R. 601. Scabies Offs 3. O.R. 114.	[initials]
"	2-12-17	4PM	Lt Scott reported his arrival. Patients remaining Offs 12 O.R. 616 Scabies Offs 3 O.R. 100	[initials]
"	3-12-17	4.30PM	Advance party of 112 F.A. 16 Div. arrived to take over	
"		4.40	A.D.M.S. wire:- Prepare to hand over. Orders following.	[initials]
		5.10PM	A.D.M.S. wire:- Hand over C.R.S. to F.A. of 16th Division. Report completion & wire. Patients remaining Offs. 11 O.R. 711. Scabies Offs 3 O.R. 105.	[initials]
	4-12-17	3.45PM	Completion of handing over. Patients handed over Offs. 17. O.R. 903.	[initials]
		"	Orders from A.D.M.S. to send advance party to C.M.D.S. at FINS.	
		4-30PM	Advance party proceeded.	[initials]
		"	Order received from A.D.M.S. to move out tomorrow.	[initials]

Instructions regarding War Diaries and Intelligence Summaries are contained in F. S. Regs., Part II. and the Staff Manual respectively. Title pages will be prepared in manuscript.

WAR DIARY
or
~~INTELLIGENCE SUMMARY~~.
(Erase heading not required.)

Army Form C. 2118.

Place	Date	Hour	Summary of Events and Information	Remarks and references to Appendices
MARICOURT	5.12.17	6AM	Unit moved out	
FINS.	" "	noon	Arrived at III Corps C.M.D.S no accommodation available. Marched back to	
NURLU	"	2PM	Unit arrived. poor accommodation. Men in billets & tents. Horses in the open. Weather cold. Keen frost.	
	"	10AM	Captains Davidson & Russell who had formed part of advance party proceeded to A.D.S + R.A.Ps in line taken over by 36 Div	
		6.45PM	Wire from ADMS received:- Send as soon as possible 2 MOs & 50 OR 12 stretchers 4 wheeled stretchers + 2 Ford cars to report to ADS 61st Div in large dugout on road between TRESCAULT and VILLERS PLUICH at R 13 a 2.8, to assist in evacuation of 61st Div + Right Bde of 36 Division. The following proceeded Capt. Underhill + Lt Scott + 48 OR with Equipment as ordered.	
			ADMS wires to collect sick of Transport Lines W 13 a.	
			Instructions from ADMS:- no patients to be retained all sick to be transferred to C.M.D.S.	
			C.O visited ADMS + discussed evacuation, 1OS 3A to clear from RAPs to ADS the latter under 61st Div.	

Instructions regarding War Diaries and Intelligence Summaries are contained in F. S. Regs., Part II. and the Staff Manual respectively. Title pages will be prepared in manuscript.

WAR DIARY
or
~~INTELLIGENCE~~ ~~SUMMARY~~.
(Erase heading not required.)

Army Form C. 2118.

Place	Date	Hour	Summary of Events and Information	Remarks and references to Appendices
NURLU	6.12.17	10 AM	Arrangements made with O.C. 204 Coy A.S.C. to have the transport accommodated in his Camp.	[initials]
		4.50 pm	A.D.M.S. wires:- Detail 50 additional bearers to report forthwith to Capt. Underhill to assist in clearing the line. Party proceeded at 5.20 PM by M.A. Cars.	[initials]
		"	A.D.M.S. wires: 2 Ford cars will be detailed by 108 F.A. ~~[illegible]~~ to report to you for duty in line.	
			4 Cars from 21 M.A.C. reported for duty.	
			Rations for party in line to be sent to 2/3 S. Mid F.A. at V.11.b.4.4. each day for transmission.	[initials]
		8.30 AM	2 Ford cars reported from 108 F.A. proceeded to report to Capt Underhill	
	7.12.17	10 AM	Under orders of A.D.M.S. Capt G.G. Johnston proceeded to METZ to take over from 17 F.A.	[initials]
		noon	Capt Johnston returned & reported that 17 F.A. were not moving	[initials]
		2.45 PM	A.D.M.S. visited Camp and arranged with C.O. to send a party to METZ to endeavour to obtain accommodation for the ~~[illegible]~~ personnel, transport to be left	[initials]

Instructions regarding War Diaries and Intelligence Summaries are contained in F. S. Regs., Part II. and the Staff Manual respectively. Title pages will be prepared in manuscript.

WAR DIARY
or
~~INTELLIGENCE SUMMARY.~~
(*Erase heading not required.*)

Army Form C. 2118.

Place	Date	Hour	Summary of Events and Information	Remarks and references to Appendices
NURLU	7.12.17	Cont.	at A.S.C Camp NURLU less 3 Horse Ambulance wagons + 1 limber, Motor Ambulances to accompany unit.	JR
	"	~~4 PM~~ 4 PM	Capt Davidson + 21 O.R. with one horse ambulance proceeded on this duty.	JR
		[illegible] 5 PM	2 Offs + 64 O.R. of 110 F.A. already in left sector of line attached for duty + rations. C.O. of F.A. assuming responsibility of evacuating Divisional Front to A.D.S. The latter under 61st Div. Capt Underhill to be in charge at Bearer Post R.8.b.3.7 Sheet 57 C.	JR
	8.12.17	11.15 AM	"Thaw precautions."	
		1 PM	Personnel moved to METZ	JR
METZ EN COUTURE		3 "	Arrived, men accommodated in one Nissen Hut + tents.	
		3.15	Under ADMS 7433. 2 clerks proceeded to 21 CCS to record transfers of 36 Div.	JR
		7.15 PM	ADMS instructions for collection of sick of 36 Divisional units in line and vicinity of METZ.	JR
	9.12.17	10 AM	One officer + 20 bearers proceeded to Bearer Post to relieve similar number.	JR
	10.12.17	9 AM	Capt J. G. Johnston detailed as D.A.D.M.S. 36 Division proceeded to D.H.Q to take over duty.	JR

Instructions regarding War Diaries and Intelligence Summaries are contained in F. S. Regs., Part II. and the Staff Manual respectively. Title pages will be prepared in manuscript.

WAR DIARY
or
~~INTELLIGENCE~~ SUMMARY.
(Erase heading not required.)

Army Form C. 2118.

Place	Date	Hour	Summary of Events and Information	Remarks and references to Appendices
METZ	11-12-17	6PM	Capt. Russell + 8 O.R. proceeded to relieve similar party at W. W. Post of ~~[illegible]~~ 47th Div. at TRESCAULT.	[initials]
			Staff Sergeant Gillespie evacuated sick.	
	12-12-17	11 AM	1 N.C.O. + 6 O.R. detailed for duty with 306 Bde R.F.A.	
		Noon	1 Sergeant + 20 O.R. reported from 110 F.A. for duty. Total number from that unit now amounting to 2 Offs. + 85 O.R.	[initials]
		2.45 PM	A.D.M.S. 7497 orders to build splinter proof shelters at TRESCAULT with issue note for materials to be drawn from R.E. Dump FINS.	[initials]
	13.12.17	6 AM	6 G.S. Wagons proceeded to R.E. Dump at FINS from transport lines NURLU and drew material dumping same at TRESCAULT.	[initials]
		10.30 AM	1 N.C.O. + 6 O.R. returned from 306 Bde R.F.A. their services not being required.	[initials]
		Noon	30 O.R. relieved in line, by similar number.	[initials]
		7. P.M.	2 Offs + 51 O.R. of 149 F.A. R.N. Div arrived as advance party for instruction in evacuation of line	
			A.D.M.S. orders re relief of F.A. by R.N.D. F.A.	[initials]

2353 Wt. W2541/1454 700,000 5/15 D. D. & L. A.D.S.S./Forms/C. 2118.

Army Form C. 2118.

WAR DIARY
or
~~INTELLIGENCE SUMMARY.~~
(Erase heading not required.)

Instructions regarding War Diaries and Intelligence Summaries are contained in F. S. Regs., Part II. and the Staff Manual respectively. Title pages will be prepared in manuscript.

Place	Date	Hour	Summary of Events and Information	Remarks and references to Appendices
METZ	14.11.17	9AM	1 off & 41 OR. of 149 F.A. proceeded with Capt Christie to Line to relieve a equal party of 109 F.A. and learn scheme of evacuation. 2 bearers of 109 to remain at each R.A.P. to instruct.	[initials]
		noon	1 off & 45 OR returned from line.	
		9.30PM	109 Inf Bde orders re move of Bde to ROCQUIGNY on 15th	[initials]
		10PM	orders issued to Capts Underhill & Russell ~~Lef~~ re move of F.A. with Brigade. Capt Russell to rejoin on Relief by 149 F.A. Capt Underhill & 50 bearers to remain in line under O.C. 149 F.A. until 36 Div relieved.	[initials]
	15.11.17	9AM	Capt Davison proceeded to ROCQUIGNY to billet with S.C. 109 Bde.	
		noon	~~Capt~~ Lt Morgan 110 F.A. proceeded to take temporary charge of 9. R Irish Fus.	[initials]
		2PM	all personnel of 110 F.A. proceeded to join their unit.	
			Unit moved from METZ to ROCQUIGNY. transport from NURLU to join unit at destination	
ROCQUIGNY		6PM	Unit arrived.	[initials]
		9PM	O.O. from A.D.M.S. move of 36 Division to LUCHEUX.	[initials]
	16.11.	7AM	109 Bde order. Bde to move to MONDICOURT. Personnel by train. transport	[initials]

Instructions regarding War Diaries and Intelligence Summaries are contained in F. S. Regs., Part II. and the Staff Manual respectively. Title pages will be prepared in manuscript.

WAR DIARY
or
~~INTELLIGENCE SUMMARY.~~
(Erase heading not required.)

Army Form C. 2118.

Place	Date	Hour	Summary of Events and Information	Remarks and references to Appendices
ROCQUIGNY	16.12.17		Cont. by road. Staging 16/17th in COURCELLES-LE-COMTE. Unit to be located in MILLY	[illegible]
..	..	Noon	Personnel moved to ETRICOURT and entrained to MONDICOURT.	[illegible]
MILLY	..	9.45PM	Unit arrived. Billets found by Lt & Qm Perritt	
..	17.12	6PM	Capt Russell + transport arrived.	[illegible]
			Capt Underhill + 5 O.R. arrived having travelled with 107 Bde	
			Unit collecting sick from Bde + transferring to 3 C.C.S. DOULLENS	[illegible]
..	18.12		Refitting. Parades + setting up drill	[illegible]
	19.12		Routine	[illegible]
..	20.17		"	[illegible]
..	21.12		Routine.	[illegible]
	22.12	7PM	appointment of Capt Johnston as DADMS confirmed struck off strength.	[illegible]
	23.12.17		Hospital for Sick and Scabies opened. Poor accommodation.	[illegible]
			preparations for Christmas entertainment of personnel of unit	
..	24.12	7 Noon	ADMS + Col Rock RMS who is relieving Col Bray as ADMS visited unit	
		2.45PM	ADMS 76th. Private J 2 Mitchell awarded military medal	[illegible]

Instructions regarding War Diaries and Intelligence Summaries are contained in F. S. Regs., Part II, and the Staff Manual respectively. Title pages will be prepared in manuscript.

WAR DIARY
or
~~INTELLIGENCE SUMMARY.~~

(*Erase heading not required.*)

Army Form C. 2118.

Place	Date	Hour	Summary of Events and Information	Remarks and references to Appendices
MILLY	24.12.17	7PM	ADMS 7618. "one officer to proceed with 109 Bde billeting party to new area on 26th inst to report to DAAG. 18 Corps at QUERRIEUX at 12 noon," ~~[illegible]~~ ~~[illegible]~~	[illegible]
..	25.12.17	8AM	Warning order from ADMS for move of Bde ~~[illegible]~~	[illegible]
	"	12.30PM	Men of Unit Entertained to dinner	
	"	6PM	ADMS "Administrative Instruction No 6. 36 Div move of Division & time tables	
"	26.12.17	9AM	Capt Underhill proceeded as advance officer with Bde billeting party to new area	
		"	Capt Russell proceeded on leave	
		2.36 PM	Bde order No 99. received re move of Bde on 29th	
..	27.12	10.30 AM	ADMS visited unit	
		7 PM	March Tables received from Bde	
	28.12.17	8.30AM	Lt Scott with transport less 10 axles proceeded by road. Staying night of 28/29th in CONTAY area	
	29.12.17	7.30 AM	Personnel & 10 axles proceeded by march route to MONDICOURT to	

D. D. & L., London, E.C.
(A7883) Wt. W809/M1672 350,000 4/17 Sch. 52a Forms/C/2118/14

Instructions regarding War Diaries and Intelligence Summaries are contained in F. S. Regs., Part II. and the Staff Manual respectively. Title pages will be prepared in manuscript.

WAR DIARY
or
~~INTELLIGENCE~~ SUMMARY.
(*Erase heading not required.*)

Army Form C. 2118.

Place	Date	Hour	Summary of Events and Information	Remarks and references to Appendices
MILLY	29.12.17	am	Entrain for MOREUIL. Roads blocked by snow. Sick unable to be moved by motors. O.C. with QM & 30 OR remained behind with	Rn
			sick. O.C. visited HALLOY to ensure no sick left by Battalions	Rn
DOMART sur LA LUCE	"	10.30 pm	Unit arrived.	
		midnight	Transport arrived.	
"	30.12	noon	O.C. & Rear party with 14 sick arrived by rail from DOULLENS.	Rn
			Hospital opened for sick of Bde	
		4 PM	Lt SCOTT detailed to see sick of Div. Machine Gun Corps at HANGARD	Rn
			DMS 5th Army "Light cases to be retained in FA for 14 days."	
			Patients remaining 25	Rn
"	31st		~~[illegible]~~, Routine. Equipment gone over & checked.	
			patients 54.	Rn

D. D. & L., London, E.C. (A7883) Wt. W809/M1672 350,000 4/17 Sch. 52a Forms/C/2118/14

Confidential.

36
Vol 28

War Diary

of

109th. Field Ambulance.

From 1st. January 1918 To 31st. January 1918.

VOL. XXVIII.

[signature]
Lt. Colonel
R.A.M.C.

17

Instructions regarding War Diaries and Intelligence Summaries are contained in F. S. Regs., Part II. and the Staff Manual respectively. Title pages will be prepared in manuscript.

WAR DIARY
or
INTELLIGENCE SUMMARY.
(Erase heading not required.)

Army Form C. 2118.

Place	Date	Hour	Summary of Events and Information	Remarks and references to Appendices
DOMART SUR LA LUCE	1-1-18	10.30 AM	A.D.M.S. inspected Unit and Hospital.	[illegible]
			Baths & ironing arrangements completed for Scabies patients. Patients remaining 38.	[illegible]
"	2-1-18		Routine. Patients remaining 57	[illegible]
"	3.1.18	7 PM	3 ORs reinforcements reported for duty. Patients remaining 68.	[illegible]
"	4-1-18	6 PM	Confidential letter from A.D.M.S. calling for recommendations for higher appointments	[illegible]
			Patients remaining 75.	[illegible]
	5.1.18	3 PM	Secret No 7744 from A.D.M.S. containing locations in PROYART area to which Division will move on 7th. 104 F.A. to move to MEZIERES	
	"		Secret 7745 re assumption of stables in French area. Patients remaining 78	[illegible]
"	6-1-18	8 AM	25 Patients likely to be well within 14 days transferred to 42 Stationary Hospital by rail	[illegible]
	"	10 AM	Lt Perrit proceeded to MEZIERES to billet.	[illegible]
		2 PM	O.C. proceeded to MEZIERES to inspect billets	
		"	109 Inf Bde order 100 received also March Table. 109 F.A. to move off at 11 AM to MEZIERES on 7th.	[illegible]
		4. PM	Received Adm. instructions 36 Division No 8, re new area to be taken over from French by the Division. Patients remaining 56	[illegible]
"	7-1-18	11 AM	Unit moved off for MEZIERES a distance of 8 kilometres. Road frozen and very difficult for transport.	[illegible]
MEZIERES	"	12.15 PM	Unit arrived. 65 Patients transported to MEZIERES good accommodation.	[illegible]

A5834 Wt. W4973/M687 750,000 8/16 D. D. & L. Ltd. Forms/C.2118/13.

Instructions regarding War Diaries and Intelligence Summaries are contained in F. S. Regs., Part II. and the Staff Manual respectively. Title pages will be prepared in manuscript.

WAR DIARY

or

~~INTELLIGENCE SUMMARY.~~

(Erase heading not required.)

Army Form C. 2118.

Place	Date	Hour	Summary of Events and Information	Remarks and references to Appendices
MEZIERES	7-1-18	6.50 PM	Wire from A.D.M.S. "O.C. to attend conference tomorrow at A.D.M.S.' office at 2.30 P.M."	
		"	" " " " Detail M.O. to report forthwith for temporary duty with 11th Batn. R. Innis. Fus.	[illegible]
		8.0 PM	Lt. Scott proceeded for duty with 11th R. Innis. Fus.	[illegible]
			Patients remaining 65	
	8-1-18	[illegible]	Orders from 109 Inf Bde to send an officer with Bde Billeting Party to billet in NESLE area. Captain [illegible] proceeded.	[illegible]
		"	Secret 109 Bde order No B.M. 11/884 containing probable moves of Bde in the next few days. 109 F.A. to move to MARCHE – ALLOLARD [illegible]	[illegible]
		2.30 PM	C.O. attended conference at A.D.M.S. office. Evacuation of Sector to be taken over from French discussed. 109 F.A. to be responsible for. H.Q. of Ambulance to be at ARTEMPS. M.D.S. at GRAND SERAUCOURT. Existing French A.D.S. to be taken over.	[illegible]
			C.O. arranged with 36 Div Q for busses to move patients tomorrow.	[illegible]
		3 PM	[illegible] arrangements for sector of line to be taken over from French received	[illegible]
		3.45 PM	March Table for 9th inst received from 109 Bde. 109 F.A. to move off at 9.40 A.M. instead of 14 R [illegible]. Patients remaining 64.	[illegible]
	9-1-18	9.40 AM	Unit moved off [illegible] to be taken at MOON.	[illegible]

A7092 Wt. W128 9/M1293 750,000. 1/17. D. D & L. Ltd. Forms/C2118/14.

Instructions regarding War Diaries and Intelligence Summaries are contained in F. S. Regs., Part II. and the Staff Manual respectively. Title pages will be prepared in manuscript.

WAR DIARY
or
~~INTELLIGENCE~~ SUMMARY.
(Erase heading not required.)

Army Form C. 2118.

Place	Date	Hour	Summary of Events and Information	Remarks and references to Appendices
MARCHE-ALLOUARD	9-1-18	5.15 P.M.	Unit arrived. 72 Patients transported by busses. Good billets for the Sick. Road very Slippery. Snowing latter part of march.	[initials]
			Captain Underhill & 7 O.R. detailed to remain with sick Patients remaining 72. at MARCHE ALLOUARD until unit is settled in new area.	[initials]
	10-1-18	4. PM	Secret 109 Bde Order No 2 – Bde to move to ARTEMPS area on 11th inst. 109 F.A to OLLEZY. Patients remaining 79	[initials]
	11-1-18	8.30 AM	Unit moved off. Lt Perritt going in advance to arrange billets in OLLEZY. 15 Scabies patient marching with unit. Capt Underhill remaining behind with 8 O.R and one motor ambulance Car. ~~[illegible]~~ 71 Patients left in his charge.	[initials]
OLLEZY	11-1-18	4.30 PM	Unit arrived, billeted in French Hospital where all ranks were most hospitably received.	[initials]
	12-1-18	10 AM	O.C. with Capt Davidson visited M. le Medecin Divisionaire at 6me Div HdQrs. when the French arrangements ~~for~~ Evacuation were explained, the O.C. presenting a letter of introduction from A.D.M.S. O.C. & Capt Davidson with M. le Medecin Divisionaire proceeded to ~~A.D.S~~ at JEANNE D'ARC Sheet 66 C A25a.7.3 This A.D.S. serving the sector south of The River SOMME.	[initials]
		4. PM	C.O. saw M.Os of 104 Bde Battns and arranged to attach 4 bearers & 1 runner to each Battn in front line, also a similar party with 107 Bde Battns holding that Bde Sector South of SOMME CANAL at GRUGIES. Arrangements made with French G.B.D. & American Ambulance section to cooperate until ~~[illegible]~~ completion of relief by the 36 Division.	[initials]

A7092 Wt. W128.9/M1293 750,000. 1/17. D. D & L. Ltd. Forms/C2118/14.

Army Form C. 2118.

Instructions regarding War Diaries and Intelligence Summaries are contained in F. S. Regs., Part II. and the Staff Manual respectively. Title pages will be prepared in manuscript.

WAR DIARY
or
~~INTELLIGENCE~~ SUMMARY.

(Erase heading not required.)

Place	Date	Hour	Summary of Events and Information	Remarks and references to Appendices
OLLEZY	12-1-18	5 PM	5 O.R proceeded to R.A.P. A.18.c.1.5. to join 8/9. R I Rifles 107 Bde. Evacuation from this R.A.P. by wheeled stretcher to Car Post. Sheet 66c A 17. d. 6.5. The A.D.S. at JEANNE D'ARC will be administered by the G.B.D. until the 109th Bde goes in tomorrow night. 10 O.Rs proceeded to A.D.S. to learn line.	[initials]
		7 PM	Capt. A H Sewing. Lts S W Tipston & M.A. O'Brien all of U.S. army reported for duty. Patients remaining 87.	[initials]
				[initials]
"	13-1-18	9 AM	Unit moved off.	[initials]
ARTEMPS	"	10 AM	Unit arrived taking over French G.B.D. Quarters.	
		noon	Capt. Davidson. Lt Tipton & 26 O.R proceeded to A.D.S. JEANNE D'ARC to take over from French. 5 O.R. attached to 9th R Innis Fus. & 5 O.R to 10 R Innis Fus. these Battns taking over front of 109 Bde tonight.	[initials]
			Patients remaining 2 offs & 90 O.R.	
"	14-1-18		Taking over of line from French completed midnight 13/14th.	[initials]
"		11 AM	Capt Russell rejoined from leave.	
			3 cars from 31 M.A.C. & 2 from 110 F.A. reported for duty.	
			Relief of French completed without a casualty. Patients remaining Offs 2 O.R 64	[initials]
	15-1-18	11 AM	A.D.M.S. Co. & D.A.D.M.S. visited A.D.S. & R.A.Ps.	
		noon	Capt Underhill & party rejoined from MARCHE ALLOUARD. all patients under his charge having either been returned to duty or transferred.	[initials]

Instructions regarding War Diaries and Intelligence Summaries are contained in F. S. Regs., Part II. and the Staff Manual respectively. Title pages will be prepared in manuscript.

WAR DIARY
or
~~INTELLIGENCE~~ SUMMARY.
(*Erase heading not required.*)

Army Form C. 2118.

Place	Date	Hour	Summary of Events and Information	Remarks and references to Appendices
ARTEMPS	15.1.18	3 PM	Dental Surgeon attended to all patients of Division.	
		4. PM	Capt Russell with 4 O.R. proceeded to take over premises in GRAND SERAUCOURT (at present occupied by Section of American Ambulance) to establish a Main Dressing Station. All wounded from the Division to be evacuated through this M.D.S. ~~[illegible]~~ + to pass through books of 109 F.A. The Collection of wounded from the 109 Bde Sector North of SOMME CANAL to be under the direction of 110 F.A. who have an A.D.S. near DALLON.	
			Patients remaining Offs 2. OR 45.	
	16.1.18	2 PM	Lt. O'Brien + 4 O.R. proceeded to Gd. SERAUCOURT to assist Capt Russell much work being necessary there.	
		3.45 PM	A.D.M.S. 7867. 109 F.A. to collect all sick in Div. area South of SOMME CANAL + East of St. SIMON + AVESNE	
			All sick transferred or discharged to duty. None remaining	
	17.1.18	3.30 PM	A.D.M.S. wires. M.O. from ADS JEANNE D'ARC to see sick of 173 Bde R.F.A. during absence of Capt Blair on leave	

A7092 Wt. W128 9/M1293 750,000. 1/17. D. D & L. Ltd. Forms/C2118/14.

Instructions regarding War Diaries and Intelligence Summaries are contained in F. S. Regs., Part II. and the Staff Manual respectively. Title pages will be prepared in manuscript.

WAR DIARY
or
~~INTELLIGENCE~~ SUMMARY.
(Erase heading not required.)

Army Form C. 2118.

Place	Date	Hour	Summary of Events and Information	Remarks and references to Appendices
ARTEMPS	17-1-18	4PM	ADMS here. Sent sub division to be held in reserve to be placed at disposal of D.M.S. 5th Army.	
			3 G.S. wagons to report to S.S.O. for duty.	
	18-1-18	noon	3 G.S. wagons to report to French representative, DURY.	
			ADMS 7899. "Lt Scott posted to medical charge of 11 R Innis Fus." Struck off strength from 8-1-18	
		4PM	6 OR proceed to report to M.O. R.A.P. GRUGIES for work on R.A.P.	
			Motor Ambulance Cars not to ~~[illegible]~~ leave Car Post GRUGIES or JEANNE D'ARC during daylight ~~[illegible]~~ except for cases of urgency.	
	19-1-18	10.30 AM	ADMS inspected M.D.S.	
	20-1-18		Work at A.D.S. M.D.S. & HQrs proceeding.	
			3 limbered wagons detailed for 3 days duty at advanced D.H.Q. G.D. SERAUCOURT	
			3 G.S. wagons for duty with 109 Bde HQ Res.	
	21-1-18	10AM	Capt Underhill proceeded for temporary duty with 14 R.I. Rifles	
			2 limbered wagons to report to C.R.E.	
		11AM	Dental Surgeon attended.	

Instructions regarding War Diaries and Intelligence Summaries are contained in F. S. Regs., Part II. and the Staff Manual respectively. Title pages will be prepared in manuscript.

Army Form C. 2118.

WAR DIARY
or
INTELLIGENCE SUMMARY.
(Erase heading not required.)

Place	Date	Hour	Summary of Events and Information	Remarks and references to Appendices
ARTEMPS	21-1-18	11 AM	CO visited M.D.S. + line	[illegible]
		4.30 PM	Sand bags, duck boards + felt drawn from R.E. Dump + sent to A.D.S.	
		5 PM	a large room at M.D.S being rendered useless on account of a supposed German booby trap Capt Russell consulted an R.E. Officer as to the advisability of clearing out the room which was full of rubbish + he decided to risk the trap. He cleared out everything in the room + found nothing of any interest. This room had lain unused since the German evacuation although room was wanted by the French and American occupiers.	[illegible]
	22-1-18	Noon	12 O.R. proceeded to A.D.S. to relieve a similar number	[illegible]
		4 PM	CO visited M.D.S.	[illegible]
	23-1-18	8 PM	Lt. J. W. Ripton U.S.A. detailed to relieve Lt Adams M.C. 9th R. Innis Fus who is proceeding on leave.	
			Lt M. A. O'Brien detailed to relieve Lt Ripton at A.D.S. JEANNE D'ARC.	[illegible]
	24-1-18	[redacted]	Routine.	
	25-1-18		12 O.R. proceeded to relieve others at GRUGIES Car post and R.A.P.	[illegible]

A7092 Wt. W128 9/M1293 750,000. 1/17. D. D & L. Ltd. Forms/C2118/14.

Army Form C. 2118.

Instructions regarding War Diaries and Intelligence Summaries are contained in F. S. Regs., Part II. and the Staff Manual respectively. Title pages will be prepared in manuscript.

WAR DIARY
or
~~INTELLIGENCE SUMMARY.~~
(Erase heading not required.)

Place	Date	Hour	Summary of Events and Information	Remarks and references to Appendices
ARTEMPS	26.1.18	2. PM	CO attended Conference at Office of A.D.M.S. arrangements for proposed gas Centre discussed, afterwards C.O visited French Hospital at CUGNY and was shewn Gas Centre and arrangements for treatment of gas cases both "mustard" and lethal.	[initials]
	27.1.18	1.30 PM	Secret 109 Bde order with instructions of regarding relief of 109 Bde by 108 Bde on 28th & 29th.	[initials]
	28.1.18	9am	2 G.S. wagons proceeded for duty at Clothing dump OLLEZY	[initials]
		11AM	C.O. visited M.D.S	[initials]
			1 N.C.O + 19 O.R. proceeded to 172 Tunnelling Coy for work in line	
	29.1.18	11 AM	C.O visited M.D.S. arrangements for treatment of gassed cases complete. Alkaline baths. oxygen, Clothing. protection for attendants &c	[initials]
	30.1.18	7am	1 G.S. + 2 limbered wagons proceeded for duty with C.R.E. for two days	[initials]
		3 PM	Capt. Sewing detailed to take temporary medical charge of 11 R Innis Fus during Lt Scott's absence on leave	
	31.1.18	10 AM	O.C. with A.A + Q.M.G. visited M.D.S. A.D.S + line. arrangements made for Soup Kitchen at JEANNE D'ARC Units to supply material	[initials]

A7092 Wt. W128 9/M1293 750,000. 1/17. D. D & L. Ltd. Forms/C2118/14.

Confidential

Vol 29

War Diary

of

109th. Field Ambulance.

from 1st. Feby. 1918. to 28th. Feby. 1918.

VOL. XXIX

H. S. Davidson Capt. R.A.M.C.

14

Army Form C. 2118.

Instructions regarding War Diaries and Intelligence Summaries are contained in F. S. Regs., Part II. and the Staff Manual respectively. Title pages will be prepared in manuscript.

WAR DIARY
or
~~INTELLIGENCE SUMMARY.~~
(Erase heading not required.)

Place	Date	Hour	Summary of Events and Information	Remarks and references to Appendices
ARTEMPS	1.2.18	11.30 AM	3 M.A.C. Cars relieve 3 others at M.D.S.	[initials]
	2.2.18		Capt W Russell detailed to see sick of 16 R Ir Rif (P) during absence of M.O.	[initials]
		2.30 PM	C.O. visits M.D.S.	
	3.2.18	4 PM	D.D.M.S. XVIII Corps visited H^d Qrs of unit and M.D.S.	[initials]
	4.2.18	7 AM	3 G.S. wagons proceeded to VILLESELVE to assist in move of 2nd R Innis Fus	[initials]
		5 PM	Capt Dawson returned to H^d Qrs from duty at A.D.S. leaving Lt O'Brien in charge	
	5.2.18	9 AM	One G.S. wagon proceeded to Clothing Dump OLLEZY for duty.	[initials]
			6 O.R. relieved a similar number at A.D.S.	[initials]
"	6.2.18	8.30 AM	One G.S. wagon proceeded for duty to Canteen Stores HAM	
		10.30 AM	C.O. attended Conference at Office of D.D.M.S. & received orders to withdraw M.O. & Equipment from A.D.S. The M.D.S. to become A.D.S.	[initials]
		3.30 PM	A.D.M.S. 8/71. Medical Situation 18 Corps 4.2.18	[initials]
	7.2.18	11 AM	C.O. visited A.D.S. & line	
			Capt Tweedie reported from duty with 14 R Ir Rifles.	[initials]

D. D. & L., London, E.C.
(A7883) Wt W809/M1672 350,000 4/17 Sch. 52a Forms/C/2118/14

Instructions regarding War Diaries and Intelligence Summaries are contained in F. S. Regs., Part II, and the Staff Manual respectively. Title pages will be prepared in manuscript.

Army Form C. 2118.

WAR DIARY
or
~~INTELLIGENCE SUMMARY.~~
(Erase heading not required.)

Place	Date	Hour	Summary of Events and Information	Remarks and references to Appendices
ARTEMPS	7.2.18	3PM	Location of Div Units received	[initials]
	8.2.18		Capt Underhill granted leave from 10th to 24th inst	[initials]
	do		CO visited M.D.S. and arranged with Capt Russell O i/c for extra racks in cellars.	
	9.2.18		Work progressing at Hd Qrs & A.D.S. an Elephant dug out at Hd Qrs started by the French as protection against E.A bombs nearing completion.	[initials]
			Additional accommodation at Gd SERAUCOURT taken over	
	9.2.18	1.30PM	Code names for 36 Division received. also Station Code Calls	[initials]
	10.2.18	2PM	Secret marks of Vehicles received. This Unit marks to remain as before.	[initials]
		4.PM	Capt Sewring M.O.R.C. U.S.A. proceeded to report to DDMS to attend 18 Corps R.A.M.C. School from 11th to 17th inst.	[initials]
	11.2.18	2.15PM	Secret location of units of Div received	[initials]
		2.15 PM	Secret A.D.M.S. No 8240 received.	[initials]
		2.15 PM	Secret ADMS No 8254 received.	[initials]
		8PM	Lt. M. A. O'Brien rejoined Hd. Qrs from A.D.S. Jeanne d'Arc under orders A.D.M.S. A.D.S. to become merely a bearer post.	[initials]

D. D. & L., London, E.C.
(A7883) Wt. W809/M1672 350,000 4/17 Sch. 52a Forms/C/2118/14

Instructions regarding War Diaries and Intelligence Summaries are contained in F. S. Regs., Part II. and the Staff Manual respectively. Title pages will be prepared in manuscript.

WAR DIARY
or
~~INTELLIGENCE SUMMARY.~~
(Erase heading not required.)

Army Form C. 2118.

Place	Date	Hour	Summary of Events and Information	Remarks and references to Appendices
ARTEMPS.	12.2.18	10.30AM	D.A.D.M.S visited A.D.S, GD SERAUCOURT.	H.H.B.
		2 P.M.	Secret Medical Situation 18th Corps received.	H.H.B.
			Work begun on cellars at A.D.S. GD SERAUCOURT. To be racked for patients (stretcher cases).	H.H.B.
		6 P.M.	Lt J.W TIPTON M.O.R.C. rejoined from temporary duty with 9th R. Innis. Fus.	H.H.B.
	13.2.18	3 PM	Lt M.A O'BRIEN. M.O.R.C. detailed to report for duty to A.D.M.S. 30th Div. Struck off strength.	H.H.B.
		3.30 PM	Secret Loc of Units received from A.D.M.S.	H.H.B.
	14.2.18		Nothing to note	H.H.B.
	15.2.18	10.30AM	Lt Col MAGILL attended conference at D.D.M.S.' office re medical arrangements of 18th Corps	H.H.B.
		4 PM	2 G.S. wagons detailed for duty at Transport Lines of 9th R. Innis. Fus	H.H.B.
	16.2.18.	10 AM.	~~Lt~~ Lt J.W. TIPTON detailed for duty temporarily as M.O. to 16th R.I. Rifles and resume occupation of A.D.S. JEANNE D'ARC. under orders A.D.M.S.	H.H.B.
		2.15 PM	Secret location of units 60/16th received	H.H.B.

D. D. & L., London, E.C.
(A7883) Wt W809/M1672 350,000 4/17 Sch. 52a Forms/C/2118/14

Instructions regarding War Diaries and Intelligence Summaries are contained in F. S. Regs., Part II. and the Staff Manual respectively. Title pages will be prepared in manuscript.

WAR DIARY
or
~~INTELLIGENCE SUMMARY~~.
(*Erase heading not required.*)

Army Form C. 2118.

Place	Date	Hour	Summary of Events and Information	Remarks and references to Appendices
ARTEMPS	17.2.18.	5PM.	Capt A.H. SEWING rejoined from 18th Corps School of Instruction. Detailed to relieve Lt. J.W. TIPTON at A.D.S. JEANNE D'ARC.	H.S.D.
		8P.M.	Lt J.W. TIPTON detailed to attend course of instruction of III Army at 61 C.C.S and subsequently course in sanitation: courses to last from 18th to 28th.	H.S.D.
	18.2.18	8AM	Lt Col MAGILL proceeded on leave granted from 19/2/18 to 12/3/18. Capt. H.S DAVIDSON acting in command during his absence. Capt. S.P. RAE taken on strength for rations.	H.S.D.
		NOON.	C.O. visited Right sub-sector of line with A.D.M.S and inspected R.A.P. of subsector also A.D.S for that portion of line. Re-arrangement of medical arrangements for Right sector considered.	H.S.D.
		2P.M.	Dug-out at A 17.b. used as relay post handed over to H.Q of 9th R. Innis. Fus. and all bearers withdrawn (two remaining attached to M.O. of that unit)	H.S.D.
	19.2.18	NOON.	Lt J SCOTT. RAM.C (S.R) reported for duty under orders A.D.M.S. and taken on strength	H.S.D.
			C.O. visited Right sub-sector of Left section of line with A.D.M.S.	H.S.D.
		5PM.	Lt J SCOTT detailed for duty at A.D.S. JEANNE D'ARC to relieve Capt. A.H. SEWING M.O.R.C., U.S.A.	H.S.D.

D. D. & L., London, E.C.
(A7883) Wt. W80/M1672 350,000 4/17 Sch. 52a Forms/C/2118/14

Army Form C. 2118.

Instructions regarding War Diaries and Intelligence Summaries are contained in F. S. Regs., Part II, and the Staff Manual respectively. Title pages will be prepared in manuscript.

WAR DIARY
or
~~INTELLIGENCE SUMMARY.~~
(Erase heading not required.)

Place	Date	Hour	Summary of Events and Information	Remarks and references to Appendices
ARTEMPS	19.2.18	9 PM.	Capt A.H. Sewing M.O.R.C. U.S.A. reported Amb. Hd. Qrs from A.D.S. on relief by Lt J. Scott	A.H.
	20.2.18	5 PM.	A.D.M.S. visited Amb. H.Q. and held conference with Q Masters of Div^n	A.H.
	21.2.18	2 PM.	Capt Lindsay RAMC. reported for transport to 2nd R. I. Rifles to take up duties R.M.O. to that Batt^n.	A.H.
		5 PM.	Capt. C.C.G. Gibson RAMC, on relief by Capt Lindsay reported for duty and taken on strength. Capt. A.H. Sewing M.O.R.C. U.S.A. detailed for duty with 50th Div^n and struck off strength	A.H.
	22.2.18	2 PM	A.D.M.S. [illegible] In accordance this unit is responsible for the sick of units in HAPPENCOURT and HAMEL.	A.H.
			A.D.M.S. [illegible] received	A.H.
			10 O.R. reinforcements arrived and taken on strength.	A.H.
	23.2.18	2.30 PM	Medical board on Capt. Mulholland [illegible] M.S.C. for a permanent commission. Capt. [illegible] President, members Capt W. Russell, Capt S.P. [illegible]	A.H.
		3 PM	Capt. C.C.G. Gibson [illegible] by Chemical Adviser V^th Army at HAM on Gas [illegible].	A.H.
		3.15 PM.	Secret directions [illegible] to 36th Div^n received	A.H.

D. D. & L., London, E.C.
(A7853) Wt. W203/M1672 350,000 4/17 Sch. 52a Forms/C/2118/14

Instructions regarding War Diaries and Intelligence Summaries are contained in F. S. Regs., Part II. and the Staff Manual respectively. Title pages will be prepared in manuscript.

WAR ~~DIARY~~
or
INTELLIGENCE SUMMARY.
(Erase heading not required.)

Army Form C. 2118.

Place	Date	Hour	Summary of Events and Information	Remarks and references to Appendices
ARTEMPS	24.2.18	11 AM	O.C. visited M.D.S. and R.M.Os at HAMEL to arrange for collecting of sick.	H.J.D.
		2 PM	Lt. J. Scott detailed to report for duty at Hd Qrs on relief of A.D.S. by R.M. Os of Centre and Right sector in the line.	H.J.D.
		3 PM	Secret location of units of 36th Divn received.	H.J.D.
	25.2.18	2 PM	Secret. Location of units of 36th Divn received.	H.J.D.
		2.30 PM	O.C. visited projected R.A.P. at A17 d 7.2. (Sheet 66C.1.) and M.D.S.	H.J.D.
		3.40 PM	A.D.M.S. visited M.D.S.	H.J.D.
	26.2.18	2.30 PM	Board on Major Keating 2nd R. Irish Rifles, President Col H.S. Roch ADMS, members Capt W. Russell, and Capt C.C.G. Gibson.	H.J.D.
		6 A.M.	A water cart detailed to carry water for use of Divn Soda Water Factory each day.	H.J.D.
		3.30 PM	A.D.M.S. visited Hd Qrs to classify Hope O.R. in the village.	H.J.D.
			Lt J. Scott Rtnd detailed for duty A.D.S.	
		3 PM	King's Birthday Honours. Names submitted by O.C.	H.J.D.

D. D. & L., London, E.C.
(A7883) Wt. W803/M1672 350,000 4/17 Sch. 52a Forms/C/2118/14

Army Form C. 2118.

Instructions regarding War Diaries and Intelligence Summaries are contained in F. S. Regs., Part II, and the Staff Manual respectively. Title pages will be prepared in manuscript.

WAR DIARY
or
~~INTELLIGENCE SUMMARY.~~
(Erase heading not required.)

Place	Date	Hour	Summary of Events and Information	Remarks and references to Appendices
ARTEMPS.	27.2.18.	11 AM	O.C. visited A.D.S. and advanced post on Left Sector.	[illegible]
	28.2.18.	10.30 AM	O.C. attended conference at A.D.M.S. Office re medical arrangements.	[illegible]
		2.30 PM	A.D.M.S. and O.C. visited advanced post on Left Sector. Inspected dug-outs.	[illegible]
		2.30 PM	Summary A.D.M.S. 5498 received.	[illegible]
		3 PM	D.M.S. V Army Circ. Memo No. 59 received.	[illegible]

D. D. & L., London, E.C.
(A7883) Wt. W8o1/M1672 350,000 4/17 **Sch. 52a** Forms/C/2118/14

Mar. 1918

Confidential

War Diary

of

109th. Field Ambulance.

6

from 1st. March 1918. to 31st. March 1918.

VOL. XXX.

[signature] Lt. Colonel R.A.M.C.
Commanding.

140/2900

Vol 30

Instructions regarding War Diaries and Intelligence Summaries are contained in F. S. Regs., Part II. and the Staff Manual respectively. Title pages will be prepared in manuscript.

WAR DIARY
or
~~INTELLIGENCE~~ SUMMARY.
(Erase heading not required.)

Army Form C. 2118.

Place	Date	Hour	Summary of Events and Information	Remarks and references to Appendices
ARTEMPS.	[illegible].3.18	2PM.	Sgt Crellin 1 N.C.O. 12 O.R. detailed for work on dug-out at Grugies.	[illegible]
		2.30 PM.	10 Reinforcement O.R. reported for duty and taken on strength.	[illegible]
		3.45 PM.	Secret No 0/5/8 received from A.D.M.S.	[illegible]
	2.3.18	2 PM.	Secret A.D.M.S. No 8520 received.	[illegible]
		2 PM.	Secret A.D.M.S. No 8522 received.	[illegible]
	3.3.18	10 AM.	Lt J. W. Tipton detailed to report for duty as Temp. M.O. with 23rd Entrenching Batn in place of Lt. Unger M.O.R.C.	[illegible]
		Noon.	Sgt Gordon detailed to attend course with V. Army School of Sanitation.	[illegible]
	4.3.18	Noon.	Capt E. Underhill rejoined from leave.	[illegible]
		4 PM.	Secret A.D.M.S. No 8522 addendum received.	[illegible]
	5.3.18	2.30 PM.	Conference of M.O.s at M.D.S. with A.D.M.S. on the evacuation of sick and wounded from the battle line.	[illegible]
	6.3.18	11 AM.	O.C. visited R.A.P. Jeanne d'Arc and the Left Sector of the line with A.D.M.S.	[illegible]
		2 PM.	Lt A.F.R. Conder reported for duty and taken on the strength.	[illegible]
	7.3.18		Routine. Capt S. P. Rae taken off strength on completion of Sanitation course.	[illegible]

D. D. & L., London, E.C.
(A7883) Wt. W809/M1672 350,000 1/17 Sch. 52a. Forms/C/2118/14

Instructions regarding War Diaries and Intelligence Summaries are contained in F. S. Regs., Part II. and the Staff Manual respectively. Title pages will be prepared in manuscript.

WAR DIARY
or
~~INTELLIGENCE SUMMARY.~~
(Erase heading not required.)

Army Form C. 2118.

Place	Date	Hour	Summary of Events and Information	Remarks and references to Appendices
ARTEMPS	8.3.18	3 PM	Secret location of units A.D.M.S. received.	~~[illegible]~~
		3 PM	Secret B.A.B. code No 4 received.	~~[illegible]~~
		3 PM	Report received that E.A. had bombed R.A.P. B 26 a 1.6 and inflicted some damage to M. Ambulances stationed there.	~~[illegible]~~
	9.3.18	11 PM	Clocks advanced one hour for Summer Time	~~[illegible]~~
	10.3.18	11 AM	Capt E Underhill detached for duty at M.D.S. in place of Lt J. Scott who is detailed for duty with 108th Fd. Amb.	~~[illegible]~~
		2 PM	Lt Lockridge taken on strength for rations during course of ~~equitation~~	~~[illegible]~~
		2 PM	Secret location of units received from A.D.M.S.	~~[illegible]~~
	11.3.18	10 AM	Capt W Russell attended Conference at D.D.M.S. Office on 1. Reduction of mobilisation Equipment 2. Establishment of Corps Central Records Bureau.	~~[illegible]~~
		6 PM	Lt A.F.R. Conder, detailed to relieve Lt Tyte (sick) as M.O. i/c 23rd Entrenching Battⁿ.	~~[illegible]~~

D. D. & L., London, E.C.
(A7883) Wt. W803/M1672 350,000 1/17 Sch. 52a Forms/C/2118/14

Instructions regarding War Diaries and Intelligence Summaries are contained in F. S. Regs., Part II. and the Staff Manual respectively. Title pages will be prepared in manuscript.

WAR DIARY
or
~~INTELLIGENCE SUMMARY.~~
(Erase heading not required.)

Army Form C. 2118.

Place	Date	Hour	Summary of Events and Information	Remarks and references to Appendices
ARTEMPS.	12.3.18	—	Routine	
	13.3.18	12 noon	OC visited the R.A.Ps and "strong points" in the line with A.D.M.S and	
			D.A.D.M.S. Arrangements made with Battn Commanders for R.A.P.	
			dugouts to be reserved or constructed within these redoubts.	
		6 P.M.	Lt A.F.R. Conder returned from duty as M.O. i/c 23rd Entrenching	
			Battn.	
		7 P.M.	Lt Col [illegible] returned from leave.	
	14.3.18	11 am	Co visited A.D.S. Co SERAUCOURT.	
			One Sergt reinforcement reported for duty	
	15.3.18	9 am	D.D.M.S + A.D.M.S visited R.A.Ps + A.D.S. afterwards inspected Hd Qrs	
			of Unit at ARTEMPS	
	16.3.18		Pte Quinn W.J. D.C.M. promoted corporal with effect from 2.4.18.	
	17.3.18		Divisional holiday	
			Capt [illegible] proceeded on leave to U.K. till 7.4.18	
			CO visited line	
	18.3.18		Lt + Qr Mr [illegible] proceeded on leave to U.K. till 2.4.18	

D. D. & L., London, E.C.
(A7853) Wt. W6o7/M1672 350,000 4/17 Sch. 52a Forms/C/2118/14

Instructions regarding War Diaries and Intelligence Summaries are contained in F. S. Regs., Part II. and the Staff Manual respectively. Title pages will be prepared in manuscript.

WAR DIARY
or
INTELLIGENCE SUMMARY.
(Erase heading not required.)

Army Form C. 2118.

Place	Date	Hour	Summary of Events and Information	Remarks and references to Appendices
ARTEMPS	19.3.18	10AM	CO visited the D.S.	[illegible]
		3PM	ADMS inspected transport of Unit.	
			10R transferred to 108 FA	
			Reserve rations, medical comforts ~~and~~ dressings, splints & water supplies	[illegible]
			to RAPs in Strong Points supplied.	✓
	20.3.18		CO visited MDS. Capt Underhill detailed to take charge of bearers at	
			CRUCIFIX in event of enemy attack. Capt Gibson to take party	[illegible]
			of bearers to JEANNE D'ARC & direct evacuation from right sector.	✓
	21.3.18	4.30am	Enemy commenced intense bombardment. Capt Underhill proceeded	[illegible]
		6AM	to CRUCIFIX with ADMS. on receipt of order to "man Battle Stations" and	
			Capt Gibson proceeded with bearer party to JEANNE D'ARC.	
			Lt Condor proceeded to MDS to assist Capt Hassell who was in charge.	
			Wounded men from batteries in the vicinity of ARTEMPS were brought in	
			to 9th Ambce HQ in odd numbers.	[illegible]
		7AM	First wounded arrived at MDS. These cases were brought from HAPPENCOURT	✓
			by FA Cars. These cases were sent to 61 CCS. a wire from DDMS saying	

D. D. & L., London, E.C. (A7883) Wt. W803/M1672 350,000 4/17 Sch. 52a Forms/C/2118/14

Army Form C. 2118.

Instructions regarding War Diaries and Intelligence Summaries are contained in F. S. Regs., Part II. and the Staff Manual respectively. Title pages will be prepared in manuscript.

WAR DIARY
or
~~INTELLIGENCE SUMMARY.~~
(Erase heading not required.)

Place	Date	Hour	Summary of Events and Information	Remarks and references to Appendices
ARTEMPS	21.3.18		that no cases were to be sent to 41 CCS at CUGNY	[illegible]
		7.30 am	first car load of wounded from line arrived; these cases came from Left Sector	
		8.30 am	second car load arrived from Left Sector. After the arrival of this car wounded	
			were wheeled to QUARRIES North of Gd SERAUCOURT. Cars not being able to	
			proceed north of this point owing to road having been broken up by shell fire.	
			No cases or communications arrived from Right Sector front. At	
		9 AM	a Ford car with runner was sent to JEANNE D'ARC to endeavour to get	
			information + restore communication. This car + runner did not come back	
			and no news of situation on Right could be obtained. Meantime cases	
			came in a steady stream from units in the Battle Zone to M.D.S. these	
			being brought in by F.A. Cars. In addition cases were brought in to ARTEMPS	
			from TUGNY and the various Battery Positions in the neighbourhood.	
			In spite of a good deal of shelling in ARTEMPS + Gd SERAUCOURT no casualties	
			occurred in these villages.	
		10 AM	orders received from [illegible] for Transport to march to ANNOIS to Lines of	[illegible]
			11th Fd Ambce and await further orders. By this time ARTEMPS was empty	

Instructions regarding War Diaries and Intelligence Summaries are contained in F. S. Regs., Part II. and the Staff Manual respectively. Title pages will be prepared in manuscript.

WAR DIARY
or
~~INTELLIGENCE SUMMARY.~~
(Erase heading not required.)

Army Form C. 2118.

Place	Date	Hour	Summary of Events and Information	Remarks and references to Appendices
ARTEMPS	21.3.18		of troops with the exception of Batteries in action, and a Kite Balloon section packing up their balloon.	
		1 PM	Orders received to send all Equipment of M D S to New Dressing Station formed by 110 Fd Ambce at St SIMON. This was carried out by means of M A Cars and lorries. The latter not being required for the walking wounded who were sent down by train from Gd SERAUCOURT.	[initials]
			An officer & Bearer Party from 108 FA were of great assistance during the morning in and around M.D.S.	[initials]
		2 PM	Gd SERAUCOURT evacuated by Fd Ambce with the exception of a small party and a few blankets & stretchers.	
			ARTEMPS clear of Fd Ambce. The unit less transport rendezvoused at St SIMON. Capts Gibson & Underhill & 73 O.R. missing, also 2 M A Cars.	
		5 PM	Unit marched to ANNOIS leaving Lt Corder to act as liason between 110 & 109 Fd As. During the day 100 wounded were collected & evacuated. The Rear party at Gd SERAUCOURT coming under the order of 110th Fd Ambce.	
			Surplus stretchers were conveyed from St SIMON to D.R.S at OLLEZY	[initials]

D. D. & L., London, E.C. (A7883) Wt. W803/M1672 350,000 4/17 Sch. 52a Forms/C/2118/14

Instructions regarding War Diaries and Intelligence Summaries are contained in F. S. Regs., Part II. and the Staff Manual respectively. Title pages will be prepared in manuscript.

WAR DIARY
or
~~INTELLIGENCE~~ SUMMARY.
(Erase heading not required.)

Army Form C. 2118.

Place	Date	Hour	Summary of Events and Information	Remarks and references to Appendices
ANNOIS	21-3-18	6 PM	Unit arrived. Wagons repacked.	
"	[illegible]	11 PM	Under orders from ADMS Unit plus transport of 110th Fd Amb marched to Billets in	[initials]
BROUCHY	22-3-18		BROUCHY arriving at 3 AM. Much delay on road owing to road being blocked	
			by heavy gun ditched near VILLESELVE. Met remainder of 110th F.A. at BROUCHY	[initials]
	"	10 AM	Unit marched to ESMERY HALLON.	
ESMERY HALLON	"	1 PM	Unit arrived and remained until 11 PM when all troops having left the Village it was	
			thought adviseable to move to LIBERMONT. During the day a number of	
			walking wounded from C.C.S at HAM were picked up and conveyed to C.C.S at	[initials]
			ROYE.	
LIBERMONT	23-3-18	12.30 AM	Unit arrived	
"		9 AM	Unit moved to a point 1000 yards East of BEAULIEU on FRETOY Road and	
			bivouacked. On the march the M.A. Cars were detached & ordered to report for duty	[initials]
			to 110th Fd Amb. who were evacuating the line at BROUCHY.	
BEAULIEU	24-3-18	9 AM	O.C. & Captain Russell proceeded with ADMS to BERLANCOURT to reconnoitre	
			the line before relieving 110th F.A. Arrangements made to ~~[illegible]~~ work with a	[initials]
			Field Ambulance of ~~[illegible]~~ 14th Div at TIRLANCOURT CHATEAU as a M.D.S.	

D. D. & L., London, E.C. (A7883) Wt. W803/M1672 350,000 4/17 Sch. 52a. Forms/C/2118/14

Instructions regarding War Diaries and Intelligence Summaries are contained in F. S. Regs., Part II. and the Staff Manual respectively. Title pages will be prepared in manuscript.

Army Form C. 2118.

WAR DIARY
or
~~INTELLIGENCE SUMMARY.~~
(Erase heading not required.)

Place	Date	Hour	Summary of Events and Information	Remarks and references to Appendices
BEAULIEU	24.3.18		On the above party arriving at BERLANCOURT where 110 FA had established an A.D.S.	
			Capt Russell proceeded to VILLESELVE the CO ~~drove~~ to COLANCOURT to	
			reconnoitre at this time the Division were holding the line approximately from	
			a point ~~one mile~~ north of FRENICHES to FLAVY LE MELDEUX – S end of	Sheet 66 D
			COLANCOURT to a point a few hundred yds E of VILLESELVE. The left	
			of this line FRENICHES – FLAVY LE MELDEUX was held by an Entrenching Battalion	
			The wounded from this point were evacuated through FRENICHES. Wounded from	
			COLANCOURT were brought down by Stretcher & wheeled stretcher to a car post at	
			V 18 d 2.9 thence to Dressing Station at TIRLANCOURT V 22 a 3.8.	
			Wounded from VILLESELVE front by cars from an aid post in the village	
			to BERLANCOURT thence by M.A.C. cars to TIRLANCOURT. Shortly	
			after taking over the evacuation the Aid Post at VILLESELVE was vacated	
			by the R.M.Os and wounded were collected by cars under officers in and	
		4 PM	around the village. At about 4 o'clock P.M. the Division retired from	
			the VILLESELVE line & cars were no longer able to reach the village.	
			Before the retirement all wounded had been brought away.	[initials]

(A7883) Wt. W593/M1672 350,000 4/17 Sch. 52a Forms/C/2118/14
D. D. & L., London, E.C.

Instructions regarding War Diaries and Intelligence Summaries are contained in F. S. Regs., Part II. and the Staff Manual respectively. Title pages will be prepared in manuscript.

WAR DIARY
or
INTELLIGENCE SUMMARY.
(Erase heading not required.)

Army Form C. 2118.

Place	Date	Hour	Summary of Events and Information	Remarks and references to Appendices
BEAULIEU	24.3.18	4.30 PM	At this time the enemy began to shell BERLANCOURT very heavily. The post became untenable and at about 5.30 PM Capt Russell with his party retired to TIRLANCOURT CHATEAU	
			In the meantime the C.O. had returned to TIRLANCOURT & sent to the unit for Lt Coudes & party of bearers with some equipment to receive & dress wounded at the Chateau. This party with the addition of Capt Sowerby arrived at about 7 PM. Capt Sowerby with a party of 12 bearers proceeded to BERLANCOURT to assist Capt Russell & relieve 110th F.A. The remainder set to work dressing & recording cases. Hot drinks were provided for wounded.	
			On the return from BERLANCOURT of the C.O. he found that all the M.A.C. cars had been sent away by the officer of the F.A. who was in occupation. A few of these cars were recovered. This action coupled with the fact that some of the divisional cars were commandeered by other units at NOYON greatly handicapped the evacuation later on in the day.	[initials]
		6 PM	At this time the enemy began to shell heavily the village and road North	

D. D. & L., London, E.C.
(A7883) Wt. W803/M1672 350,000 4/17 Sch. 52a Forms/C/2118/14

Instructions regarding War Diaries and Intelligence Summaries are contained in F. S. Regs., Part II. and the Staff Manual respectively. Title pages will be prepared in manuscript.

WAR DIARY
or
INTELLIGENCE SUMMARY.
(Erase heading not required.)

Army Form C. 2118.

Place	Date	Hour	Summary of Events and Information	Remarks and references to Appendices
BEAULIEU	24.3.18		of GUISCARD. the troops were retiring in a S W direction towards	
			MUIRANCOURT and no more wounded coming in it was thought	
			expedient to withdraw from the CHATEAU to MUIRANCOURT one	
			car being left. this was sufficient to evacuate the remaining stretcher cases.	
			the walking wounded being sent under Capt Sowerby by road to MUIRAN	
			COURT where an empty ADS hut was made use of. During the night	
			17 stretcher cases were collected & brought in as well as about 20 walking	
			wounded. These cases were all fed and dressed. Blankets & food being	
			brought from the Chateau. The village was clear of troops by	
	25.3.18		4 a.m. on 25th at 5 A.M. there being no cars available the walking	
			cases were marched off under Capt Sowerby to BUSSY. Previously	
			a R.F.C. tender was made use of and conveyed 4 stretcher cases to	
			C.C.S. shortly after 5 A.M. 4 cars of 105 F.A. arrived and also 2	
			lorries brought by A.D.M.S. The lorries were sent after the walking	
			party & having picked them up the wounded were all evacuated none	
			being left. The bearers proceeding in other cars which then arrived	

Army Form C. 2118.

WAR DIARY
or
INTELLIGENCE SUMMARY.
(Erase heading not required.)

Instructions regarding War Diaries and Intelligence Summaries are contained in F. S. Regs., Part II. and the Staff Manual respectively. Title pages will be prepared in manuscript.

Place	Date	Hour	Summary of Events and Information	Remarks and references to Appendices
AMY	25.3.18	9AM	The cars + bearers arrived at AMY to which place the transport had already marched. The O.C. rejoined later having remained at MURANCOURT to pick up Lt. Coulter who had been sent to NOYON to ascertain why the cars had not returned. Over 200 wounded were collected + evacuated	[initials]
	"	4PM	The unit marched to GUERBIGNY + billeted in the CHATEAU at WARSY.	[initials]
WARSEY	26.3.18	10AM	Unit marched out with orders to proceed to HARGICOURT. The motor ambulances detached with orders to report to 108 F.A. who were going to evacuate from the Division who had taken up a line from ERCHES southwards. On the march I received orders from DA+QMG to march to GRIVESNES.	[initials]
GRIVESNES	26.3.18	3PM	Unit arrived and billeted.	
	27.3.18	10AM	Unit marched to AUBVILLERS + bivouacked. In this village 108 F.A. had established an A.D.S.	[initials]
		6PM	Unit marched to CHIRMONT + billeted.	
CHIRMONT	28.3.18	8.30am	Unit marched to LAWARDE-MAUGER + billeted in a Ca[illegible]	[initials]

D. D. & L., London, E.C.
(A7853) Wt. W807/M1672 350,000 4/17 Sch. 52a Forms/C/2118/14

Instructions regarding War Diaries and Intelligence Summaries are contained in F. S. Regs., Part II, and the Staff Manual respectively. Title pages will be prepared in manuscript.

WAR DIARY
or
INTELLIGENCE SUMMARY.
(*Erase heading not required.*)

Army Form C. 2118.

Place	Date	Hour	Summary of Events and Information	Remarks and references to Appendices
LAWARD	28.3.18		Rejoined from duty with 108th I.A. Surplus Transport under Capt Tewkesbury proceeded to ABBEVILLE	
	29.3.18	6 PM	Unit marched to NAMPS AU VAL. No billets being available in	[illegible]
			any of the villages around about the Unit bivouacked outside the village	
			of NAMPS AU VAL.	
NAMPS AU VAL	30.3.18		Unit marched into village & found shelter from rain which was falling	
			fairly heavily	[illegible]
			During the day ADMS visited Unit & gave us orders to send transport	
			which remained with us viz one GS one limbered, one ambulance wagon & one	
			water cart to GAMACHES. Remainder to march to SALEUX to	
			Entrain. Train to leave at midnight 30-31.	
SALEUX	30.3.18		Unit arrived at SALEUX at 11 PM, and remained at Station	
			until 4 AM 1st April	
	1.4.18		No trains arriving billets in village were found but as trains	
			were hourly expected it was impossible to occupy them. Shelter	[illegible]
			& food were available at Station	

D. D. & L., London, E.C.
(A7883) Wt. W593/M1672 350,000 4/17 Sch. 52a Forms/C/2118/14

Confidential

Apr. 1918. 24

War Diary

of

109th. Field Ambulance.

from 1st. April 1918 to 30th. April 1918.

VOLUME XXXI.

Lt. Colonel
R.A.M.C.

Army Form C. 2118.

WAR DIARY
or
INTELLIGENCE SUMMARY.
(Erase heading not required.)

Instructions regarding War Diaries and Intelligence Summaries are contained in F. S. Regs., Part II. and the Staff Manual respectively. Title pages will be prepared in manuscript.

Place	Date	Hour	Summary of Events and Information	Remarks and references to Appendices
WOINCOURT	1.4.18	10 AM	Unit detrained at GAMACHES and proceeded in lorries to WOINCOURT to billets	
			M.T. & H.T. from NAMPS AU VAL having already arrived.	[illegible]
			Small hospital filled up. 12 patients remaining collected from 8 cc	
	2.4.18	10 AM	Lt Scott proceeded from 108 F.A. to which unit he has been temporarily	
			attached to take over medical charge of 15 R Ir Rifles. Struck off	
			strength.	
			Capt. H.S. Davidson assumed rank of Major under G.R.O. 3448.	
		3 PM	Warning order for move of Division received	
		4 PM	Lt A.F.R. Condor proceeded with Brigade billeting party to new area	[illegible]
			patients remaining 20. Surplus transport from ABBEVILLE returned.	[illegible]
	3.4.18		Baths arranged for personnel.	
	4.4.18	7 AM	Unit less M.T. (proceeding by road) entrained at WOINCOURT Station	
ROUSBRUGGE	5.4.18	6 AM	Unit detrained personnel in lorries to DIRTY BUCKET Camp. Transport	
			to same place. 32 patients brought with unit	[illegible]
DIRTY BUCKET CAMP.		3 PM	Major Davidson & Lt Perrett returned from leave.	[illegible]
			patients remaining 35	[illegible]

A6945 Wt. W11422/M1160 350,000 12/16 D. D. & L. Forms/C./2118/14.

Army Form C. 2118.

WAR DIARY
or
~~INTELLIGENCE SUMMARY.~~
(Erase heading not required.)

Instructions regarding War Diaries and Intelligence Summaries are contained in F. S. Regs., Part II. and the Staff Manual respectively. Title pages will be prepared in manuscript.

Place	Date	Hour	Summary of Events and Information	Remarks and references to Appendices
DIRTY BUCKET CAMP	6.4.18	3 PM	D.R.S at GWALIA FARM taken over from 141 Fd. Ambce. Portion of personnel remaining at DIRTY BUCKET pending departure of 141 Fd. Amb.	[illegible]
GWALIA	7.4.18	3 PM	Major Davidson detailed to 108 Fd. as Surgical Specialist (ADMS)	[illegible]
		6 PM	ADMS visited DRS	
	8.4.18	12.30 PM	ADMS inspected Camp. Patients remaining 86	[illegible]
	9.4.18	3 PM	4 Officers of Med. Res. Corps U.S. Army reported for duty. Lts. Hanlon, Mosty, Johnson & Regan. Patients remaining 119.	[illegible]
	10.4.18	5 PM	Warning order to be prepared to take over CANADA FARM in addition to GWALIA. One OR MISSING since 21 inst. reported. Patients remaining 137.	[illegible]
	11.4.18		Routine. Patients remaining 151	[illegible]
	12.4	8 hours	ADMS visited Camp & rearrangements of wards being carried out. Patients remaining 168	[illegible]

A6945 Wt. W11422/M1160 350,000 12/16 D. D. & L. Forms/C./2118/14.

Instructions regarding War Diaries and Intelligence Summaries are contained in F. S. Regs., Part II. and the Staff Manual respectively. Title pages will be prepared in manuscript.

WAR DIARY
or
INTELLIGENCE SUMMARY.
(Erase heading not required.)

Army Form C. 2118.

Place	Date	Hour	Summary of Events and Information	Remarks and references to Appendices
GWALIA FARM	13.4.18	11 AM	74 OR reinforcements joined.	
		11.30 AM	A.D.M.S. Conference at GWALIA. O.C. & Ons of Fd Amb[ce]	
			109 FA to be ready to convert D.R.S. to M.D.S.	
			patients remaining 190	[illegible]
	14.4.18		Routine. Patients remaining 140. 2 G.S. wagons daily to 108 F.A.	[illegible]
	15.4.18		Major Davidson rejoined from 108 F.A. Patients remaining 131	[illegible]
	16.4.18		Lt Hagan detailed to see sick at SIEGE CAMP daily	
			Patients remaining 132	[illegible]
	17.4.18		1 NCO & 12 men detailed to CANADA FARM to remove surplus Equipment &	
			hold Camp on departure of 30th Divisional F.A.	[illegible]
		3 PM	A.D.M.S. inspected Camp. Patients remaining 148	
	18.4.18		D.D.M.S. II Corps inspected Camp. Patients remaining 162.	[illegible]
	19.4.18		C.O. visited Dressing Station DUHALLOW to make arrangements to	
			remove Huts & re-erect same at GWALIA	
		3 PM	3 NCOs & 15 men detailed for above work. Also party to be accommodated	
			by 108 FA. G.S. wagons of 109 FA to transport huts to GWALIA	[illegible]

A6945 Wt. W11422/M1160 350,000 12/16 D. D. & L. Forms/C./2118/14.

Instructions regarding War Diaries and Intelligence Summaries are contained in F. S. Regs., Part II. and the Staff Manual respectively. Title pages will be prepared in manuscript.

WAR DIARY
or
~~INTELLIGENCE~~ SUMMARY.
(*Erase heading not required.*)

Army Form C. 2118.

Place	Date	Hour	Summary of Events and Information	Remarks and references to Appendices
GWALIA	19.4.18	Cont^d	~~[illegible]~~ S... the Supervision of double Nissen + 1 small Nissen to be removed	
			patients remaining 146.	[illegible]
	20.4.18		Work of removing huts in progress, all wagons employed.	
			Patients remaining 165	[illegible]
	21.4.18		Routine. Lt Ewart arranging for the removal of Stores at	
			Canada Farm.	
		4.30 PM	A.D.M.S. visited Camp. Patients remaining 155	[illegible]
	22.4.18		Erection of Huts from Duhallow Commenced. Patients remaining 189	[illegible]
	23.4.18		Gas Ward completed. Oxygen appliances for 9 patients, alkaline	
			baths + ~~[illegible]~~ drugs provided	
		3 PM	D.D.M.S. II Corps + A.D.M.S. 36 Div inspected the Camp + Hospital	
			Party from Duhallow rejoined. 32 G.S. wagon loads having been	
			carried to GWALIA. 5 Huts + miscellaneous stores + Equipment being	
			brought down.	[illegible]
			Patients remaining 176.	
	24.4.18		Routine. Patients 143	

Instructions regarding War Diaries and Intelligence Summaries are contained in F. S. Regs., Part II. and the Staff Manual respectively. Title pages will be prepared in manuscript.

Army Form C. 2118.

WAR DIARY
or
~~INTELLIGENCE SUMMARY.~~
(Erase heading not required.)

Place	Date	Hour	Summary of Events and Information	Remarks and references to Appendices
GWALIA	25-4-18		Under instructions from A.D.M.S. all unit equipment ~~packs~~ not in use packed on wagons. Patients remaining 170	[illegible]
	26-4-18	6 PM	Conference at A.D.M.S. office:– In consequence of line being withdrawn D.R.S. to be M.D.S. & 109 F.A. to take over evacuation of wounded from 108 F.A. All sick at GWALIA to be sent to new D.R.S. at TUBBY CAMP.	
		8 PM	Capt Russell detailed to post 5 O.R. with wheeled stretchers at each R.A.Ps. viz. ESSEX FARM and DUHALLOW, a motor amb. car posted at DAWSONS CORNER	
			Patients remaining 183	[illegible]
	27-4-18	9 AM	Owing to line still maintained East of CANAL BANK R.A.Ps still at HILLTOP FARM & WEILTJE. Capt Russell & 6 O.R. detailed to form car post at DUHALLOW. Capt Russell to remain and supervise evacuation	
			During the day all sick transferred to 110th F.A. and M.D.S. formed at GWALIA. A large number of casualties	

A6945 Wt. W11422/M1160 350,000 12/16 D. D. & L. Forms/C./2118/14.

Instructions regarding War Diaries and Intelligence Summaries are contained in F. S. Regs., Part II. and the Staff Manual respectively. Title pages will be prepared in manuscript.

WAR DIARY
or
~~INTELLIGENCE~~ SUMMARY.
(Erase heading not required.)

Place	Date	Hour	Summary of Events and Information	Remarks and references to Appendices
GWALIA	27.4.18	Cont	Collected & evacuated. Chiefly from HAGEL DUMP explosion	
			119 wounded & 204 sick being dealt with	
		7PM	2 officers ~~from~~ 108 FA reported for duty with 1st & 9th R Ir Fus.	
			Those officers directed to their units	
			All transport surplus to actual needs sent to 108 FA PROVEN.	[illegible]
	28.4.18		All salvage stores & surplus B.R.C stores to be sent by light	
			railway from STEENSJE siding to PROVEN to Corps dump.	
			Stores required by 110 FA to TUBBY by horse transport	
			Lt A F R Condon evacuated to CCS sick & struck off strength	[illegible]
	29.4.18		Remainder of stores sent to PROVEN. 23 truck loads in all	
			Lt J J Hanlon MO.RCUSA & struck off. [illegible] at BRIELEN	
	30.4.18		Routine	[illegible]

Confidential

War Diary

of

109th. Field Ambulance.

from 1st. May 1918 to 31st. May 1918.

VOLUME XXXII.

[signature] Lt-Colonel RAMC
Comdg. 109th. Fld. Amb.

23 May 1918

Army Form C. 2118.

WAR DIARY
or
INTELLIGENCE SUMMARY.
(Erase heading not required.)

Instructions regarding War Diaries and Intelligence Summaries are contained in F. S. Regs., Part II. and the Staff Manual respectively. Title pages will be prepared in manuscript.

Place	Date	Hour	Summary of Events and Information	Remarks and references to Appendices
GWALIA FARM	1.5.18	3 PM	Remainder of Horse Transport less one limber and one water cart moved to PROVEN	[illegible]
	2.5.18	6 PM	ADMS visited Camp. ADMS arranging for train service on Light Railway from STEENTJE to convey sick to 110th Fd Ambce	[illegible]
	3.5.18		Routine	
	4.5.18	[illegible]	Train Service for sick & wounded started to 110 Fd Amb at TUBBY FARM from STEENTJE Siding to SYDNEY SIDING 110th Fd Amb to meet trains with horse Amb wagons	[illegible]
	5.5.18	11 AM	Conference of O.C. Fd Ambces at office of A.D.M.S. – Personnel Collecting [illegible] to wear brassard. Arrangements in event of Enemy attack discussed. O.C. 109 FA to reinforce DUHALLOW with one bearer subdivision. 108 FA to send 1 bearer Sub-division with their M.A. cars to GWALIA. 109th FA to notify ADMS of attack. Sergt W TOZER A.S.C. M.T. awarded the medal.	[illegible]
		3 PM	Lt Mosby rejoined from DUHALLOW	[illegible]
	6.5.18		Capt J.W. BRIDE RAMC reported his arrival for duty & taken on Strength.	[illegible]
	7.5.18	3 PM	ADMS & O.C. visited ADS & RAPs at DUHALLOW	
			owing to heavy rain the sandbagging on dug outs at DUHALLOW slipped down	

D. D. & L., London, E.C. (A7883) Wt. W803/M1672 350,000 4/17 Sch. 52a Forms/C/2118/14

Army Form C. 2118.

Instructions regarding War Diaries and Intelligence Summaries are contained in F. S. Regs., Part II, and the Staff Manual respectively. Title pages will be prepared in manuscript.

WAR DIARY
or
~~INTELLIGENCE SUMMARY.~~
(Erase heading not required.)

Place	Date	Hour	Summary of Events and Information	Remarks and references to Appendices
GWALIA FARM	7-5-18	7 PM	Working party of 10 O.R. detailed to proceed to DUHALLOW to rebuild dugouts under direction of 2 Sappers of 121 Co R.E.	[initials]
	8-5-18		Concrete [illegible] obtained from C.R.E. & conveyed by No 12 L.R.O. Coy to DUHALLOW for dug outs.	
		1. PM.	D.M.S. 2nd Army & D.D.M.S. II Corps inspected GWALIA FARM and expressed his appreciation of the arrangements & condition of the Camp.	[initials]
	9-5-18		Routine. List of Equipment received from A.D.M.S. for Mobile Dressing Station. This Equipment to be packed on one G.S. wagon so that it can be readily transferred to a [illegible] a Car for use when required.	
	10-5-18		2 G.S. wagons detailed for duty with Agricultural Officer LALOVIE	[initials]
	11-5-18		A.D.M.S. & O.C. visited A.D.S. & forward R.A.P.s O.C. to supply Lime	
		3 PM	to whitewash interior of Dug out at St JEAN which is very dark. Capt J.W. Bride detailed for duty at DUHALLOW.	[initials]
	12-5-18		Lt S.T. Ragan to see sick daily of rear lines of 108th & 109th Bdes in neighbourhood of INTERNATIONAL CORNER	
	13-5-18		Routine. O.C. visited DUHALLOW to inspect progress of dugouts	[initials]

D. D. & L., London, E.C.
(A7883) Wt. W809/M1672 350,000 4/17 Sch. 52a Forms/C/2118/14

Instructions regarding War Diaries and Intelligence Summaries are contained in F. S. Regs., Part II. and the Staff Manual respectively. Title pages will be prepared in manuscript.

WAR DIARY
or
~~INTELLIGENCE~~ SUMMARY.
(Erase heading not required.)

Army Form C. 2118.

Place	Date	Hour	Summary of Events and Information	Remarks and references to Appendices
GWALIA FARM	14.5.18		Arrangements made to retain the slighter gassed cases.	[illegible]
	15.5.18	noon	Major Davidson relieved Capt Russell i/c DUHALLOW.	
			3 Nissen Huts not in use at GWALIA taken down + sent by No 12 L. R. O. Coy to 110 Fd Amb'ce	
		3 PM	ADMS inspected Hospital. Gassed cases remaining 18. Suffering for the most part from BLUE X gas, a few from mustard gas. For the latter Sod bicarb employed either as lotion or paste, 1% sol in eyes. For both varieties – inhalation of Tr. Benz Co alone on boiling water, or simple inhalation of a sol of Tr. Benz Co Eucalyptus, Chloroform Creosote & Tannic. 18 cases remaining	[illegible]
	16.5.18		Routine. Gassed cases remaining 35.	[illegible]
	17.5.18		Lt. Ragan detailed to see sick of 13th R Ir Rifles	
	18.5.18	11 AM	OC visited Transport Lines PROVEN	
		noon	ADMS inspected GWALIA FARM	
		4 PM	Capt Brown C.R. RAMC reported his arrival for duty & taken on strength	[illegible]
			Gassed cases remaining 38.	[illegible]
	19.5.18		Capt Russell authorised to wear major's badges of rank	

D. D. & L., London, E.C. (A7883) Wt. W809/M1672 350,000 4/17 Sch. 52a Forms/C/2118/14

Instructions regarding War Diaries and Intelligence Summaries are contained in F. S. Regs., Part II. and the Staff Manual respectively. Title pages will be prepared in manuscript.

Army Form C. 2118.

WAR DIARY or ~~INTELLIGENCE SUMMARY.~~

(Erase heading not required.)

Place	Date	Hour	Summary of Events and Information	Remarks and references to Appendices
GWALIA FARM	19.5.18		1 NCO + 10 privates detailed for duty at ADS DUHALLOW (by ADMS instructions) gassed cases remaining 42. 2 bicycles sent to the 2 RAPs to assist communication with ADS	[illegible]
	20.5.18	3PM	Routine. O.C. visited Car post at BRIELEN & arranged for personnel to withdraw to another concrete shelter at RED CHATEAU ELVERDINGHE in the event of heavy shelling. Gassed cases remaining 43.	[illegible]
	21.5.18		Routine. Gassed cases remaining 45.	[illegible]
	22.5.18	5PM	ADMS visited GWALIA.	
		6PM	O.C. visited DUHALLOW and arranged for telephonic communication between 109 Bde Signals & ADS. Gas patients remaining 49.	[illegible]
	23.5.18		Routine. Gassed patients remaining 50.	[illegible]
	24.5.18		Routine " " " 53.	[illegible]
	25.5.18	3PM	O.C. visited transport lines.	
		5.30PM	ADMS visited GWALIA. Patients remaining 56.	[illegible]
	26.5.18	2PM	ADMS visited GWALIA and attended Church Parade. Convalescent gas patients sent to 110 Fd Ambce. Remaining 27	
	27.5.18		Lt Ragan MORC USA evacuated to CCS suffering from nephritis	

D. D. & L., London, E.C. (A7883) Wt. W593/M1672 350,000 4/17 Sch. 52a Forms/C/2118/14

Instructions regarding War Diaries and Intelligence Summaries are contained in F. S. Regs., Part II. and the Staff Manual respectively. Title pages will be prepared in manuscript.

Army Form C. 2118.

WAR DIARY
or
~~INTELLIGENCE SUMMARY.~~
(Erase heading not required.)

Place	Date	Hour	Summary of Events and Information	Remarks and references to Appendices
GWALIA FARM	27.5.18		Capt Moran RAMC 100th FA visited GWALIA to see Dental cases. Did a few Extractions & arranged for further treatment for those requiring it. Capt Moran being a L.D.S.	
		5. PM	5 O.R. of unit wounded at DUHALLOW. 3 Evacuated to CCS	
			Patients remaining (Gassed) 33	[illegible]
	28.5.18		Capt Moran saw further Dental cases	
			Capt Brown relieved Capt Bride at Duhallow. gassed patients remaining 35	[illegible]
	29.5.18	4PM	C.O. attended Conference at office of A.D.M.S. to arrange a uniform scheme for G.H.Q & unit signs on Vehicles. This was postponed.	[illegible]
			~~[illegible]~~ 3 Medical officers & 8 O.R. of 77 Division U.S. Army joined for instruction. Major Russell to be acting Major with D.M.S. 2nd Army P13/133 patients gassed remaining 30	[illegible]
	30.5.18		Major Russell detailed to see sick of Battalion Classes at W camp daily patients gassed remaining 29.	[illegible]
			~~[illegible]~~	
	31-5-18	3.45 P.M.	A.D.M.S & C.O. Visited H^d Q^rs 33 Division to reconnoitre Camps in Event of move Gassed Cases remaining 30.	[illegible]

D. D. & L., London, E.C. (A7883) Wt. W503/M1672 350,000 4/17 Sch. 52a Forms/C/2118/14

Confidential

War Diary

of

109th. Field Ambulance.

From 1st. June 1918. to 30th. June 1918.

VOLUME XXXIII.

[illegible signature]

Lt. Colonel
R.A.M.C.

26
June 1918.

33.

Instructions regarding War Diaries and Intelligence Summaries are contained in F. S. Regs., Part II, and the Staff Manual respectively. Title pages will be prepared in manuscript.

WAR DIARY
or
~~INTELLIGENCE~~ SUMMARY.
(Erase heading not required.)

109 Field Ambnce.

Army Form C. 2118.

Place	Date	Hour	Summary of Events and Information	Remarks and references to Appendices
GWALIA FARM	1.6.18	12.30pm	Warning order received Division to be relieved by Belgians. Patients remaining 19.	[initials]
	2.6.18		Belgian Director of medical services inspected the camp & A.D.S. prior to taking over	[initials]
		4PM	A.D.M.S & C.O. visited camp at 27/L 3 a 8.4. occupied by 1/1 W.R. F^d Amb^ce on main Road between POPERINGHE and S^t JAN TER BIEZEN a possible site for Unit on relief by Belgians. Arrangements made to take over and	
		7.PM	Lt Mosby and 4 OR detailed to take over site and hold camp until arrival of unit. Patients remaining 20	[initials]
	3.6.18		109 F.A. to be relieved in Line night of 5th-6th. Routine patients remaining 14.	[initials]
	4.6.18	9.30am	9 Belgian Officers arrived to take over GWALIA FARM. Enemy shelled Camp one direct hit on Farm House killing one Belgian employed by farmer. Several shells burst between Huts & billet. all patients & personnel having been removed from Camp at commencement of shelling only one casualty was caused and that slight.	[initials]

D. D. & L., London, E.C. (A7883) Wt. W593/M1672 350,000 4/17 Sch. 52a Forms/C/2118/14

Army Form C. 2118.

Instructions regarding War Diaries and Intelligence Summaries are contained in F. S. Regs., Part II. and the Staff Manual respectively. Title pages will be prepared in manuscript.

WAR DIARY
or
~~INTELLIGENCE SUMMARY.~~

(Erase heading not required.)

Place	Date	Hour	Summary of Events and Information	Remarks and references to Appendices
GWALIA FARM	4.6.18		All patients transferred to D.R.S. or evacuated to C.C.S.	[illegible]
		7 P.M.	Lt. Johnston + 27 O.R. proceeded in advance to new Camp.	
	5.6.18	10 AM	Major Russell proceeded on 14 days leave	
		3 PM	Capt C R Brown + 12 O R rejoined from Line. Major Davidson + remainder of party remained to hand over ADS + R.A.Ps to 12th Belgian Inf Division on relief	
	6.6.18	9 AM	Major Davidson + party rejoined, the relief of Division having been completed without a casualty.	
			One M A Car left at GHENT COTTAGES for Divisional Artillery till their relief	
		10 AM	Camp handed over to Belgians	[illegible]
		10.30 pm	Unit moved	[illegible]
SCHOOL CAMP 27/G 3 a 8.4.		noon	Unit arrived.	[illegible]
	7.6.18		Sick of 107 + 109th Inf Bdes. R.Es + the R Ir R (P) also 173 Bde R F A on arrival collected by horse wagons + conveyed to 110th Fd Amb	
			One NCO detailed for duty at ROADCAMP Baths to inspect men bathed for skin disease	[illegible]

D. D. & L., London, E.C.
(A7883) Wt. W593/M1672 350,000 4/17 Sch. 52a Forms/C/2118/14

Instructions regarding War Diaries and Intelligence Summaries are contained in F. S. Regs., Part II. and the Staff Manual respectively. Title pages will be prepared in manuscript.

WAR DIARY
or
INTELLIGENCE SUMMARY.
(Erase heading not required.)

Army Form C. 2118.

Place	Date	Hour	Summary of Events and Information	Remarks and references to Appendices
SCHOOL CAMP	8.6.18	8 AM	Amb. Car rejoined from GHENT COTTAGES	[illegible]
		10 AM	Lt. Johnson 1 NCO + 2 OR detailed for duty with troops at musketry at RUBROUCK near BOLLEZEELE and to remain as long as any troops are in that area.	[illegible]
			Sick of Battalion at BOIS St. ACAIRE to be collected by 109 F.A. on request.	[illegible]
		10.30 AM	Lt. Mosby detailed for temporary duty with 15 R Ir. Rif vice Lt Scott sick.	[illegible]
		4 PM	A.D.M.S. visited camp.	
		5 PM	22 OR rejoined from Transport Lines PROVEN	
	9.6.18		Routine	[illegible]
	10.6.18	11 AM	G.O.C. 36 Division inspected Camp.	[illegible]
			One N.C.O detailed to attend course of instruction at 2nd Army San School.	
	11.6.18		Routine	
	12.6.18		Under instruction of ADMS Capt Brown proceeded to see sick of 153 Bde R.F.A.	[illegible]
		noon	Capt Brown reported that sick of 153 Bde are being seen by M.O.	
		6 PM	CO. visited transport lines	

D. D. & L., London, E.C. (A7883) Wt. W803/M1672 350,000 4/17 Sch. 52a Forms/C/2118/14

Instructions regarding War Diaries and Intelligence Summaries are contained in F. S. Regs., Part II. and the Staff Manual respectively. Title pages will be prepared in manuscript.

Army Form C. 2118.

WAR DIARY
or
~~INTELLIGENCE~~ ~~SUMMARY.~~

(Erase heading not required.)

Place	Date	Hour	Summary of Events and Information	Remarks and references to Appendices
SCHOOL CAMP	13.6.18	8.30 AM	Capt. Brown proceeded to see sick of 173 Bde R.F.A.	
		11 AM	Lt Perritt detailed to represent C.O at conference held by A.D.M.S to arrange a uniform scheme for painting wagons	[signature]
	14.6.18		Routine	
	15.6.18	3 PM	A.D.M.S No 9414. Lt J Scott from 15 R Ir Rif to be taken on Strength from 17th inst vice Lt Mosby who is posted to medical charge of that Battalion	[signature]
	16.6.18	11 AM	Major Davidson attended Court of Inquiry at 108 Fd Amb re cause of fire at that Unit's Camp	[signature]
	17.6.18		2 N.C.O. detailed for Course of instruction at Corps Skin Depot.	
		3 PM	A.D.M.S & C.O proceeded to VLAMERTINGHE to make arrangements to salve Nissen Huts for Div Rest Station. Huts selected at ORILLA and No 12 L.R.O. Coy agreed to convey them to PUGWASH	[signature]
		5 PM	Lt Scott reported his arrival for duty from 15 R Ir Rif and taken on strength.	
		8 PM	One N.C.O + 11 O.R. proceeded to ORILLA to salve Huts.	
	18.6.18	4 PM	Lt Scott detailed for temporary duty as M.O i/c 171 Tunnelling Co R.E.	[signature]

D. D. & L., London, E.C. (A7883) Wt. W593/M1672 350,000 4/17 Sch. 52a Forms/C/2118/14

Instructions regarding War Diaries and Intelligence Summaries are contained in F. S. Regs., Part II. and the Staff Manual respectively. Title pages will be prepared in manuscript.

WAR DIARY or INTELLIGENCE SUMMARY.

(Erase heading not required.)

Army Form C. 2118.

Place	Date	Hour	Summary of Events and Information	Remarks and references to Appendices
SCHOOL CAMP	19.6.18	3PM	Capt. Bride detailed to take over medical charge of 1 R Innis Fus., struck off strength.	
			2 Huts delivered to PUGWASH for 110 FA (DRS)	[illegible]
			C.O. visited transport lines.	
	20.6.18		Routine. C.O. visited working Party at ORILLA	[illegible]
	21.6.18		Major Russell returned from leave	[illegible]
	22.6.18	11AM	ADMS visited camp. One nissen hut erected at SCHOOL CAMP.	[illegible]
	23.6.18	2.30PM	One water cart with personnel + mules detailed to report for duty with II Corps Works Battalion	[illegible]
		3PM	C.O. visited transport lines. 2 Huts sent to DRS.	
	24.6.18	11AM	Conference held by ADMS to consider reduction of Equipment, C.O. + D + QM attended.	[illegible]
	25.6.18	12.30PM	ADMS wire 2 Tent Sub Division with 2 Officers to take over II Corps Rest Station at BOLLEZEELE	
		2PM	C.O. visited Office of ADMS to arrange above. One Officer + 6 OR to proceed to II Corps Rest Station at 6 PM as advance party, with one Car	[illegible]

D. D. & L., London, E.C. (A7883) Wt. W801/M1672 350,000 4/17 Sch. 52a Forms/C/2118/14

Instructions regarding War Diaries and Intelligence Summaries are contained in F. S. Regs., Part II. and the Staff Manual respectively. Title pages will be prepared in manuscript.

WAR DIARY
or
~~INTELLIGENCE~~ SUMMARY.

(*Erase heading not required.*)

Army Form C. 2118.

Place	Date	Hour	Summary of Events and Information	Remarks and references to Appendices
SCHOOL CAMP.	26.6.18	7.30	Major Davidson + 5 OR proceeded to take over II Corps Rest Station. Capt Brown to return in Car + Take remainder of tent sub-division by rail from TROIS ROIS Station at 4 PM	[illegible]
	27.6.18	noon	CO. + QM visited II Corps Rest Station.	[illegible]
	28.6.18		Routine.	[illegible]
	29.6.18		CO visited transport lines	[illegible]
	30.6.18		Tents pitched on aerodrome for use of Divisional Horse Show on 1.7.18.	[illegible]

2353 Wt. W2541/1454 700,000 5/15 D. D. & L. A.D.S.S./Forms/C. 2118.

WO 95/3131.
34

Confidential

War Diary

of

109th Field Ambulance

from 1st. July 1918. to 31st. July 1918.

VOLUME XXIII.

[signature]
Lt. Colonel
R.A.M.C.

19

8.11.18

Instructions regarding War Diaries and Intelligence Summaries are contained in F. S. Regs., Part II. and the Staff Manual respectively. Title Pages will be prepared in manuscript.

WAR DIARY
or
~~INTELLIGENCE SUMMARY~~
(Erase heading not required.)

Army Form C. 2118.

Place	Date	Hour	Summary of Events and Information	Remarks and references to Appendices
SCHOOL CAMP	1.7.18		Divisional Horse Show. Major Russell in charge of medical arrangements.	[illegible]
		5.30 PM	Conference at Office of A.D.M.S. re arrangements of move of Field ambulances with Division. F.As to affiliated Brigade Groups.	[illegible]
		8 PM	Orders issued to Major Davidson O/C II Corps Rest Station to return all Horse transport to SCHOOL CAMP. H.T. & Details at PROVEN to rejoin tomorrow	[illegible]
	2.7.18	8 AM	Sergt. Gordon proceeded with M.A. Car & 109 Bde Billeting party to new area	[illegible]
			H.T. from II Corps Rest Station rejoined.	
		11.30 AM	H.T. & details rejoined from PROVEN.	
		2 PM	Bde order No 40. F.A. to meet 109 Bde at WATOU 6.35 AM. 3rd inst	
		4 PM	II Corps Rest Station handed over by Major Davidson to 104th F.A. Major Davidson & party to rejoin in new area	[illegible]
		9 PM	Water Cart & personnel rejoined from II Corps Works Batn	
	3.7.18	5.30 AM	Unit moved off	[illegible]
TROIS ROIS SHEET 27.O.6409		12.30 PM	Unit arrived. Carrying 15 Patients	

2449 Wt. W14957/M90 750,000 1/16 J.B.C. & A. Forms/C.2118/12.

Instructions regarding War Diaries and Intelligence Summaries are contained in F. S. Regs., Part II. and the Staff Manual respectively. Title Pages will be prepared in manuscript.

WAR DIARY
or
INTELLIGENCE SUMMARY
(Erase heading not required.)

Army Form C. 2118.

Place	Date	Hour	Summary of Events and Information	Remarks and references to Appendices
TROIS ROIS	4.7.18	10 AM	Major Davidson Capt. Brown + Personnel returned from II Corps R.S. also Lt. H. F. Johnson + 20 OR from Inf. Detachments at RUBROUCK. Sick of Brigade to be collected daily.	
		6.30 PM	Concert by Unit troupe. Patients remaining 23.	
	5.7.18		Routine	
		6.30 PM	Orders from A.D.M.S. for Unit to be in reserve + ready to move. Patients remaining 30.	
	6.7.18		Sick of 153 Bde RFA and 36 D.A.C. to be collected daily.	
			Drill, Stretcher drill + training from 8 AM to noon. Patients remaining 30	
	7.7.18		Training as before.	
		4 AM	Majors Davidson + Russell proceeded to OXELAERE to examine 8 offrs and 50 OR for category. (13th Gloster Regt.) Unit being outside divisional area O.C. proceeded to reconnoitre for a new camp. Suitable fields in neighbourhood of KORTEN LOOP. Patients remaining 39.	

Instructions regarding War Diaries and Intelligence Summaries are contained in F. S. Regs., Part II. and the Staff Manual respectively. Title Pages will be prepared in manuscript.

WAR DIARY
or
~~INTELLIGENCE SUMMARY~~
(Erase heading not required.)

Army Form C. 2118.

Place	Date	Hour	Summary of Events and Information	Remarks and references to Appendices
TROIS ROIS	8.7.18	8.30	Training as before	
		11.30	Harness inspection	
		Noon	orders from Division to vacate Camp by 9 AM 9th inst.	
		1 PM	Major Russell + Lt Perritt proceeded to KORTEN LOOP and selected a site at 27/P. 26 d.7.8.	
			Patients remaining 61.	[illegible]
	9.7.18	8.30 AM	Unit moved to	[illegible]
27/P.26.d.7.8		11.30 AM	Unit arrived. Personnel in tents. Patients in a barn. Remaining 60	
	10.7.18		Sick of ~~[illegible]~~ details of Brigades to be seen daily in BAVINCHOVE AREA	[illegible]
			Patients remaining 39.	
	11.7.18		All patients transferred to 108 FA DRS.	[illegible]
	12.7.18		Sports arranged postponed owing to rain.	[illegible]
			One water cart & personnel & mules proceeded for duty to 36 Divisional Reception Camp MILLAIN	

Army Form C. 2118.

Instructions regarding War Diaries and Intelligence Summaries are contained in F. S. Regs., Part II. and the Staff Manual respectively. Title Pages will be prepared in manuscript.

WAR DIARY
or
INTELLIGENCE SUMMARY

(Erase heading not required.)

Place	Date	Hour	Summary of Events and Information	Remarks and references to Appendices
27/P.26.d.7.8	13-7-18		Routine. Training 2 wagons G.S. to report daily to 36 Div. R.D.O. to convey men returning from leave to their transport lines.	Sh
	14-7-18	1 PM	Orders from A.D.M.S. to hold in readiness 1 Bearer Subdivision	
		4 PM	Capt. Brown Lt. H.7 Johnston, 6 O.R. Ramc. with 2 O.R. M.T. A.S.C. proceeded to A.D.S. 110th F.A. for instruction in the line.	Sh
	15-7-18		1 O.R. proceeded to II Army Rest Camp. 3 O.R. returned.	
		6 PM	Orders from A.D.M.S. for Capt Brown to take over temporary medical charge of 9th R. Ir. Fus. Majors Dawson & Russell to be attached to 110th Fd. Amb. for instruction in the line. Lt. Johnston to rejoin	Sh
	16-7-18	9 AM	Ford car driver detailed for duty to A.D.M.S. Capt E.H. King MORC USA reported for duty from medical charge of R.Es & taken on strength Medical orderly driver Maltese cart. Horse & Equipment attached from R.Es.	Sh

2449 Wt. W14957/M90 750,000 1/16 J.B.C. & A. Forms/C.2118/12.

Instructions regarding War Diaries and Intelligence Summaries are contained in F. S. Regs., Part II. and the Staff Manual respectively. Title Pages will be prepared in manuscript.

WAR DIARY

or

~~INTELLIGENCE SUMMARY~~

(Erase heading not required.)

Army Form C. 2118.

Place	Date	Hour	Summary of Events and Information	Remarks and references to Appendices
27/P.26.d.7.8.	16.7.18	Cont 10PM	Warning re concentration of A.A. Gun fire in event of E.A. attack.	[illegible]
	17.7.18		Lt Johnson detailed to carry out inoculation of Brigade details at BAVINCHOVE	[illegible]
		3PM	A.D.M.S visited Camp.	
			Majors Russell and Dawson rejoined from Line	
			Sergt Woolman detailed to relieve Sergt. Robinson N.C.O. i/c Divisional Surplus Baggage store at AUDRUICQ	[illegible]
			Revetted splinter proof bank round Horse lines in progress.	
		4PM	A.D.M.S. - A Dentist will attend on Fridays & Saturdays.	
			- 109th F.A. to send for horsed ambce wagons sick from 110th F.A. to 108 Div R.S. 108th to send for them on other days	
			Cricket match against Div H.Q.	[illegible]
	18.7.18		8 O.R. rejoined from Line (110th F.A.)	[illegible]
	19.7.18		Routine. Cook House erected & finished.	[illegible]
	20.7.18		Despatch Rider rejoined from duty from A.D.M.S. One D Rider detailed for duty with 110 F.A	[illegible]

2449 Wt. W14957/M90 750,000 1/16 J.B.C. & A. Forms/C.2118/12.

Instructions regarding War Diaries and Intelligence Summaries are contained in F. S. Regs., Part II. and the Staff Manual respectively. Title Pages will be prepared in manuscript.

WAR DIARY
or
~~INTELLIGENCE~~ SUMMARY
(Erase heading not required.)

Army Form C. 2118.

Place	Date	Hour	Summary of Events and Information	Remarks and references to Appendices
27/P.26d.7.8	20.7.18	Cont	41193 Pte Rainey J. mentioned in despatches (R.A.M.C. orders)	
	21.7.18	10.30 AM	A.D.M.S visited unit to inspect dental cases recommended for dentures	
			Sports	
		2 PM	Lt Scott reported from duty with 171 Tunnelling Co R.E.	
	22.7.18		Routine	
	23.7.18		Routine Bde orders (109) Relief of 108 Inf Bde night of 23/24th	
	24.7.18		Lt Johnson detailed to follow with M.A.C. Div details on march to BONNINGUES Training Camp.	
	25.7.18	7 AM	Lt Johnson visits Details at BONNINGUES. Routine Shelter for horses being constructed.	
	26.7.18		orders from A.D.M.S for a M.O. to relieve ~~Capt~~ Lt Mosby M.O.R.C. U.S.A. M.O. i/c 15 R.Ir.Rif. Lt Johnson detailed.	
	27.7.18		Routine. One G.S. wagon detailed to report nightly at 8 PM to X Corps R.E. Dump GODWAERSVELDE	

2449 Wt. W14957/M90 750,000 1/16 J.B.C. & A. Forms/C.2118/12.

Instructions regarding War Diaries and Intelligence Summaries are contained in F. S. Regs., Part II. and the Staff Manual respectively. Title pages will be prepared in manuscript.

WAR DIARY

or

~~INTELLIGENCE~~ SUMMARY.

(Erase heading not required.)

Army Form C. 2118.

Place	Date	Hour	Summary of Events and Information	Remarks and references to Appendices
27/P.26 d 7.8	28.7.18	10 a.m.	A.D.M.S. visited Camp	
			Lt. Mosty reported on relief by Lt. Johnson	
	29.7.18	noon	C.O. attended Conference at office of A.D.M.S. arrangements made for disposal of surplus transport if necessary.	
			40 Stretchers 40 blankets + 3 wheeled stretchers sent to 110 F.A.	
	30.7.18	2.30 PM	A.D.M.S. inspected unit on parade	
	31.7.18		Routine	

A7092 Wt. W128 9/M1293 750,000. 1/17. D. D & L. Ltd. Forms/C2118/14.

Confidential

War Diary

of

109 th. Field Ambulance.

from 1 st. August 1918. to 31 st. August 1918.

VOLUME - XXXV.

[illegible] Lt. Colonel. RAMC
Commanding.

Instructions regarding War Diaries and Intelligence Summaries are contained in F. S. Regs., Part II. and the Staff Manual respectively. Title pages will be prepared in manuscript.

WAR DIARY

or

~~INTELLIGENCE SUMMARY.~~

(Erase heading not required.)

Army Form C. 2118.

Place	Date	Hour	Summary of Events and Information	Remarks and references to Appendices
PARKSIDE (P 26.d.8.6.	1.8.18		Routine	[illegible]
	2.8.18		Routine. F.A. Troupe gave performance at D.R.S. 108 F.A.	[illegible]
	3.8.18	11 AM	2 O.R. reinforcement reported for duty.	
			3 O.R. detailed to attend Special Church Parade on Sunday 4th inst and to be attached to 110th F.A. until after Parade.	[illegible]
			Training of personnel carried on during week.	[illegible]
	4.8.18	11 AM	A.D.M.S. inspected Camps and afterwards attended Church Parade	
		3 PM	Capt King M.O.R.C. U.S.A. detailed as temporary M.O. i/c 12 R. Ir. Rifles.	[illegible]
	5.8.18	2 PM	Major Russell M.C. with A.D.M.S. categorised personnel of 121 Lab Co.	[illegible]
			Routine training	
	6.8.18		Secret code No 6 to come into use night of 7/8th	[illegible]
		8 PM	Troupe performed at R.A.F. Camp.	[illegible]
	7.8.18	6 PM	Troupe performed at Camp of 161 Labour Co.	
	8.8.18	3 PM	Capt A.Y.R. Conder reported his arrival for duty	[illegible]
	9.8.18		Routine training.	
		3 PM	A.D.M.S. No 475 "Hold M.O. in readiness for temporary duty with 1st R. Ir. Reg"	[illegible]

D. D. & L., London, E.C.
(10340) Wt W5300/P713 750,000 3/18 E 2688 Forms/C2118/16.

Instructions regarding War Diaries and Intelligence Summaries are contained in F. S. Regs., Part II. and the Staff Manual respectively. Title pages will be prepared in manuscript.

WAR DIARY
or
~~INTELLIGENCE~~ SUMMARY.
(Erase heading not required.)

Army Form C. 2118.

Place	Date	Hour	Summary of Events and Information	Remarks and references to Appendices
PARKSIDE 27/P.26.d.8.6	10.8.18	7AM	Capt CR Brown returned from duty with 9th R.Ir.Fus. and	
		9AM	proceeded on leave to U.K. for 14 days	
		2PM	2 O.R detailed to represent Unit at Special Church Parade to be held on 11th at TERDEGHEM.	
			During the week unit underwent training in stretcher bearing, drill and gas treatment.	
	11.8.18	11AM	Special Church Parade at TERDEGHEM of representatives from 2nd Army Units. H.M. the King present. After Parade the troops marched past His Majesty. This Unit represented by 2 O.R.	
		1PM	A.D.M.S. inspected Camp + Dental Cases.	
			1 N.C.O + 17 O.R detailed to report to C.R.E for work at A.D.S at LE ROSSIGNOL S.E of MONT DES CATS.	
			Lt + Qr Perrott proceeded under instructions of A.D.M.S. for temporary duty with 108 F.A. to assist in D.R.S.	
	12.8.18	5PM	Major Russell M.C ~~[illegible]~~ proceeded to take charge of A.D.S. + Evacuation of wounded from Line.	
		"	1 N.C.O. detailed to attend course of instruction at X Corps Gas School	

D. D. & L., London, E.C.
(10340) Wt W5300/P715 750,000 3/18 E 2688 Forms/C2118/16.

Instructions regarding War Diaries and Intelligence Summaries are contained in F. S. Regs., Part II. and the Staff Manual respectively. Title pages will be prepared in manuscript.

WAR DIARY
or
INTELLIGENCE SUMMARY.
(*Erase heading not required.*)

Army Form C. 2118.

Place	Date	Hour	Summary of Events and Information	Remarks and references to Appendices
PARKSIDE (27/P.26.d.8.6	13.8.18	Noon	Capt A F A Conder proceeded to assist Major Russell at A.D.S. and supervise salvage of building material from forward area.	[initials]
			Unit with 1107A ~~[illegible]~~ selected to represent Rawl of Division at X	
	14.8.18		Corps Horse Show on 31st inst. 1 Horsed Amb. and Water Cart.	[initials]
	15.8.18		Routine, work of improving Camp in progress.	
	16.8.18	7 PM	Water Cart + personnel on detachment at 36 Divisional Reception Camp rejoined.	[initials]
		8 PM	1 NCO + 30 OR detailed for Salvage work in forward area under Capt Conder.	[initials]
	17.8.18		Routine. Training continued during week.	
	18.8.18	11 AM	ADMS visited Camp + inspected dental Cases.	
			2 G.S. Wagons + teams detailed for Salvage work in front area to proceed at 11 P.M. nightly	[initials]
	19.8.18	8 AM	2 Wagons limbered proceeded for Div. Fatigues at Les Trois Rois	
		3 PM	ADMS No 625. Two dentists will attend [illegible] on Fridays.	[initials]
	20.8.18	3 PM	Capt T Scott proceeded for Tempy duty with 1st R Ir Rifles	[initials]

D. D. & L., London, E.C.
(10340) Wt W5300/P713 750,000 3/18 E 2688 Forms/C2118/16.

Instructions regarding War Diaries and Intelligence Summaries are contained in F. S. Regs., Part II. and the Staff Manual respectively. Title pages will be prepared in manuscript.

WAR DIARY
or
~~INTELLIGENCE SUMMARY.~~
(Erase heading not required.)

Army Form C. 2118.

Place	Date	Hour	Summary of Events and Information	Remarks and references to Appendices
PARKSIDE 27/P.26.d.86	21.8.18	11 AM	Consulting Surgeon 2nd Army Col Fullerton CMG examined Lt H.P. Mosby MORC U.S.A. M.O. 15 R Ir Rif and advised operation for Gall Stones	
		5 PM	3 M.A. Cars proceeded for duty with 110 FA.	
	22.8.18	9 AM	[illegible]. 3 M.A. Cars rejoined from 110 FA. Routine.	
		11 AM	S.S. Major working nightly under Corps R.Es. Cancelled.	
	23.8.18		Lt H.P. Mosby Evacuated sick for operation	
		6 PM	3 M.A. Cars proceeded to 110 FA for duty.	
	24.8.18	7 AM	C.O. proceeded to VIII Corps Horse Show to judge in Heavy Draught and R.A.M.C. Classes.	
		3 PM	3 Cars from 110 FA rejoined.	
	25.8.18	9 AM	Major Davidson proceeded on leave 14 days to U.K.	
		11 AM	Capt E.H. King rejoined from duty with 12 R Ir Rifles	
		11.30 AM	A.D.M.S. visited Camp. and inspected Dental Cases	
	26.8.18	noon	Capt C.R. Brown rejoined from leave.	
	27.8.18	2 PM	Lt H.F. Johnson M.O.R.C.U.S.A. arrived from 15 R Ir Rifles slightly gassed to Convalesce.	

D. D. & L., London, E.C.
(10340) Wt W5300/P713 750,000 3/18 E 2688 Forms/C2118/16.

Instructions regarding War Diaries and Intelligence Summaries are contained in F. S. Regs., Part II. and the Staff Manual respectively. Title pages will be prepared in manuscript.

WAR DIARY
or
INTELLIGENCE SUMMARY.
(Erase heading not required.)

Army Form C. 2118.

Place	Date	Hour	Summary of Events and Information	Remarks and references to Appendices
PARKSIDE 27/P 26. d. 8.6	28.8.18	3.30 am	1 N.C.O. + 17 O.R. rejoined from work on A.D.S.	JCu
		9. PM	A.D.M.S. no 708, Collect sick of 107 Inf Bde from 29th Inst.	
		7.30 AM	2 N.C.Os proceeded for duty to Divisional Baths to detect Skin diseases	
	29.8.18		sick of 107 Bde Collected. Bde in St MARIE CAPPEL area.	JCu
	30.8.18	1. AM	On Relief of Division Major Russell + Capt Cowder rejoined from A.D.S.	
		10 AM	Capt King + 10 O.R. proceeded to take over Reserve Dressing Station at 27/Q 11. d. 2.7 from 105 F.A.	
		"	2 Horse Ambulances from 110th F.A. reported for duty to assist in Collecting sick of Division	JCu
		9 P.M.	C.O attended Conference at Office of A.D.M.S., The Enemy having retired from his line from which the Division was relieved yesterday the Division is recalled to relieve the 35 Div. and 109 F.A. is detailed to take over the Evacuation of line from 105 F.A. from 31st	JCu
	31.8.18	8. AM	Major Russell + Capt Cowder + 30 O.R. proceeded to take over a Dressing Station at LE ROSSIGNOL + to undertake Evacuation of line	JCu

D. D. & L., London, E.C.
(10340) Wt W5300/P713 750,000 3/18 E 2888 Forms/C2118/16.

Instructions regarding War Diaries and Intelligence Summaries are contained in F. S. Regs., Part II. and the Staff Manual respectively. Title pages will be prepared in manuscript.

WAR DIARY
or
INTELLIGENCE SUMMARY.
(Erase heading not required.)

Army Form C. 2118.

Place	Date	Hour	Summary of Events and Information	Remarks and references to Appendices
PARKSIDE 27/~~[illegible]~~ P.26.d.8.6.	31.8.18	9 AM	Cont. Capt Brown + 30 O.R. proceeded to take over M.D.S at 27/Q22 c.4.3 from 105 F.A.	[illegible]
		3 PM	Remainder of Unit moved to	[illegible]
Q.22 c.3.3 East of EECKE	"	5 PM		
		5.30 PM	5 M.A. cars from 108 + 110 F.As also 2 cars from X Corps M.A.C reported for Duty.	[illegible]
		10 PM	The Enemy having retired beyond REVELSBURG Capt Brown + 29 O.R. proceeded with Cars to Establish a forward Dressing Station at R.28.b.5.6, Major Russell + Capt Corder with own cars evacuating wounded from line as it advances, R.A.Ps on REVELSBURG HILL. Evacuation through BAILLEUL	
		10.30 PM	Duties of A.D.M.S. taken over by C.O. A.D.M.S proceeding on leave.	[illegible]

D. D. & L., London, E.C. (10340) Wt W5300/P715 750,000 3/18 E 2688 Forms/C2118/16.

Confidential

War Diary

of

109th Field Ambulance

for

month of September, 1918.

VOL. No. XXXVI

4th Octr., 1918.

H. S. Davidson
Major, R.A.M.C.
A/Commanding 109 F.A.

Army Form C. 2118.

WAR DIARY
or
INTELLIGENCE SUMMARY.
(Erase heading not required.)

Instructions regarding War Diaries and Intelligence Summaries are contained in F. S. Regs., Part II. and the Staff Manual respectively. Title pages will be prepared in manuscript.

Place	Date	Hour	Summary of Events and Information	Remarks and references to Appendices
27/Q22.C4.3. (EECKE)	1.9.18	9.30 Am	C.O. visited 108 F.A. & arranged with C.O. latter unit to relieve 109 FA at EECKE when required.	[illegible]
		12.30 PM	C.O. proceeded to forward area and visited RAPs of Battalions of Brigade in Line. East of Ravelsberg Hill. Car 1200 yards behind Forward RAP (2 R Innis was at S.17.d.4.8.). 10 RAMC bearers attached to each of the 3 RAPS.	[illegible]
			Road unsuitable for wheeled stretchers.	
		6.PM	CO visited 108 Bde (who are taking over line) at WHITE CHATEAU and arranged with Brigadier for Evacuation.	[illegible]
		7PM	CO visited A.D.S. at R.28.b.5.6.	[illegible]
			Casualty [illegible] for previous 24 hours. 1 officer. 22 O.R.	
		9.PM	Capt E.H. King MRCUSA proceeded for temporary duty with 2 R Ir. Rifles	[illegible]
	2.9.18	10 Am	CO proceeded to A.D.S. R.28.b.5.6. Working Party obtained from Hallowes Company to roof A.D.S. also party of Sappers from CRE to prepare a damaged house at Asylum Gates (S.14.b.2.4) as an A.D.S.	[illegible]
		11 Am	Major Sowerby attached for duty from 108 Fd Ambce.	
			RAPs moving forward. Major Russell & Capt Conder keeping in touch with Battalions of 108 Bde now in line.	[illegible]
			Casualties previous 24 hours 7 off. + 44 OR.	

Instructions regarding War Diaries and Intelligence Summaries are contained in F. S. Regs., Part II. and the Staff Manual respectively. Title pages will be prepared in manuscript.

WAR DIARY
or
~~INTELLIGENCE~~ SUMMARY.
(Erase heading not required.)

Army Form C. 2118.

Place	Date	Hour	Summary of Events and Information	Remarks and references to Appendices
27/Q22 c.4.3. (EECKE)	3.9.18	8AM	Unit moving to ROCH FARM 27/R28.b.5.6	[initials]
ROCH FARM	3.9.18	10AM	During ~~previous~~ evening car post + bearers moved forward to 28/T.19.b.5.5 a car + 2 orderlies with dressings etc being left at old post on reverse slope of REVELSBURG HILL at 28/S.16.c.5.4. to collect casualties from Infantry + Artillery in neighbourhood.	[initials]
		Noon	an A.D.S. established at NEUVE EGLISE at T.8.d.3.1. Wounded evacuated thence by road through DRANOUTRE. a car + 3 orderlies being left at previous post T.19.b.5.5 for support Brigade and Artillery. a telephone connection established between A.D.S + M.D.S.	
		"	Camp at 27/Q22 c.4.3. taken over by 108 F.A. Casualties previous 24 hours 4 off 102 O.R.	[initials]
	4.9.18		Lt H.G. Johnston evacuated + gassed + struck off strength.	[initials]
		Noon	Dressing station established at House opposite Asylum Gate BAILLEUL. Capt Morham (110 F.A.) in charge. all wounded ex slight gassed will be treated here and evacuated by M.A.C. Cars.	
		5PM	A.D.S. moved forward to T.9.d.6.3 EMU FARM. Capt Brown proceeded for duty at A.D.S. Cars now using BAILLEUL — ARMENTIERES Road. Road forward of A.D.S. practicable for Cars almost	

(10340) Wt W5300/P713 750,000 3/18 E 2688 Forms/C2118/16. D. D. & L., London, E.C.

Instructions regarding War Diaries and Intelligence Summaries are contained in F. S. Regs., Part II. and the Staff Manual respectively. Title pages will be prepared in manuscript.

WAR DIARY
or
INTELLIGENCE SUMMARY.
(Erase heading not required.)

Army Form C. 2118.

Place	Date	Hour	Summary of Events and Information	Remarks and references to Appendices
ROCH FARM	4.9.18	Cont.	to R.A.P.s. Telephone installed	
			Casualties previous 24 hours 2 offs. 65 O.R.	
			Baths + changes of clothing at all 3 dressing stations, also gas centre at 108 FA	[illegible]
	5.9.18	9 am	Capt J. Scott proceeded to report for duty to D.D.M.S. III Corps. Struck off strength.	[illegible]
			Evacuation proceeding satisfactorily	
			C.O visited A.D.S. + inspected divisional baths.	
			Casualties previous 24 hours. Offs 3 OR 170.	
	6.9.18		C.O visited forward area with A. A.Q.M.G. also Brigadier. Reconnoitred cellars in Asylum with a view to forming a M.D.S.	[illegible]
			Lt. Chapman reported to relieve Capt King M.O. i/c 2 R. Ir. Rifs. not required.	
			Lorries obtained from S.M.T.O. to convey sick + lightly wounded to 108 F.A. Lorries to report daily.	[illegible]
			Casualties previous 24 hours. Offs 1- OR 43	
			2 O.R. 109 F.A. wounded	
	7.9.18	10 am	Capt C R Brown proceeded to take medical charge of 2 R. Ir. Rifs vice Capt King gassed + evacuated.	
			2 O.R. 109 F.A. wounded.	
			Casualties previous 24 hours Offs 13. OR 330. practically all gas. (Shell)	

(10340) Wt W5300/P713 750,000 3/18 ... London, E.C. E 2688 Forms/C2118/16.

Instructions regarding War Diaries and Intelligence Summaries are contained in F. S. Regs., Part II. and the Staff Manual respectively. Title pages will be prepared in manuscript.

WAR DIARY
or
~~INTELLIGENCE SUMMARY.~~
(Erase heading not required.)

Army Form C. 2118.

Place	Date	Hour	Summary of Events and Information	Remarks and references to Appendices
ROCK FARM	8.9.18	1 AM	EMU FARM evacuated by order of DIV. on account of suspected mines. A.D.S. Established in house at T 9. d. 30.05. R.E's arranging to make some cover	[signature]
			1 O.R 109 F.A. wounded.	[signature]
			1 N.C.O to inspect skins at Recept Camp Baths.	
			1 N.C.O + 10 O.R relieve a similar number at A.D.S.	
	9.9.18	11 AM	1 off + 20 O.R. 108 F.A. ~~[illegible]~~ proceed to A.D.S. preparatory to 108 F.A. taking over Evacuation of line.	[signature]
		6 PM	7 O.R Reinforcements reported for duty	
			Casualties 1 off 46 O.R	
	10.9.18	6 PM	Capt Conder proceeded for temporary duty to X Corps as D.D.M.S. during Major Berry's absence on leave, CO visited A.D.S.	[signature]
			Casualties 3 O.R	
	11.9.18	9 AM	Unit moved to 27 Q 22 C 43. replacing 108 F.A.	[signature]
		Noon	108 F.A took over Evacuation of line. Major Russell remaining to assist at A.D.S.	[signature]
Q.22 C.3.4.	~~12 noon~~	12 noon	Unit arrives. taking over D.R.S. + 347 patients.	

D. D. & L., London, E.C. (10340) Wt W5300/P713 750,000 3/18 E 2688 Forms/C2118/16.

Instructions regarding War Diaries and Intelligence Summaries are contained in F. S. Regs., Part II. and the Staff Manual respectively. Title pages will be prepared in manuscript.

WAR DIARY
or
INTELLIGENCE SUMMARY.
(Erase heading not required.)

Army Form C. 2118.

Place	Date	Hour	Summary of Events and Information	Remarks and references to Appendices
Q22 C. 4.3.	12/9/18	–	Sick of Troops in neighbourhood collected.	
			Routine. patients remaining 354	[initials]
	13.9/18		Routine. patients remaining 368	[initials]
	14.9/18		Routine improvements to Cook House. Also Bathing accommodation increased. patients remaining 336	[initials]
	15/9/18		Major Russell a casualty. gassed shell admitted to 109 F.A.	[initials]
		11 AM	D.D.M.S. inspected D.R.S. C.O. absent (at H.Qrs)	
			Sutton Farm at BERTHEN allotted to D.D.M.S. for proposed D.R.S. 1 N.C.O + 6 O.R. sent as holding party.	
			patients remaining 332	[initials]
	16/9/18	2 PM	C.O with officer of 122 Fd Co R.E. inspected Sutton Farm and arranged for R.E. Party ~~with~~ and party of 109 F.A. to begin work on farm tomorrow.	

D. D. & L., London, E.C.
(10340) Wt W5300/P715 750,000 3/18 E 2688 Forms/C2118/16.

Instructions regarding War Diaries and Intelligence Summaries are contained in F. S. Regs., Part II. and the Staff Manual respectively. Title pages will be prepared in manuscript.

WAR DIARY
or
~~INTELLIGENCE SUMMARY.~~
(Erase heading not required.)

Army Form C. 2118.

Place	Date	Hour	Summary of Events and Information	Remarks and references to Appendices
~~27~~ O.22.C.4.3	17th Sept.	8 AM	One NCO and nine OR proceeded to [illegible] Farm as a working ~~party~~ and construction party with 3 G S wagons and Teams.	[illegible]
		4 PM	Corps Commander inspected camp and expressed himself as pleased with arrangements.	
			Patients remaining 420.	
	18th Sept	8 AM	15 O.R. proceeded for duty at A D S of 108th F.A. 1 O.R. [illegible] to BERTHEN.	[illegible]
			Patients remaining 375.	
	19th Sept.	10 AM	Major [illegible] Davidson attended conference with A D M S, with O.C. 108th F.A. and A D M S 36th Div [illegible].	[illegible]
		2 PM	Lt Col R. [illegible] proceeded on 14 days leave.	
		2 PM	15 O R rejoined from 108th F A	[illegible]
			1 NCO and 2 OR reported for duty with Divisional Baths.	
			Patients remaining 374.	
	20th Sept.	7 PM	Capt J. H. Swan reported for duty and taken on strength	[illegible]
		3 PM?	Capt [illegible] reported for duty from 108th F A	
			Patients remaining 350	

D. D. & L., London, E.C.
(10340) Wt W5300/P715 750,000 3/18 E 2688 Forms/C2118/16.

Instructions regarding War Diaries and Intelligence Summaries are contained in F. S. Regs., Part II. and the Staff Manual respectively. Title pages will be prepared in manuscript.

WAR DIARY
or
~~INTELLIGENCE SUMMARY.~~

(*Erase heading not required.*)

Army Form C. 2118.

Place	Date	Hour	Summary of Events and Information	Remarks and references to Appendices
27/O.22.c.4.8	21st Sept	2 PM	Capt R. A. Appleton 110th F.A. reported for duty	
		3 PM	Capt R. A. Appleton detailed for duty with 36th Divl Reception Camp	
		[illegible]	Capt Lindsay rejoined 110th F.A.	[illegible]
		6 PM	Capt Chapman detailed for temporary duty as M.O. i/c 9th Royal Inniskilling Fusiliers	
			Patients remaining 3[illegible]	
	22nd Sept	[illegible]	[illegible] 108th and 109th Brigades	
		[illegible]	[illegible] with [illegible] Wagons and Team.	[illegible]
			Patients remaining 3[illegible]	
	[illegible]	[illegible]	[illegible] OCHTEZEELE. Capt J [illegible] and 2/[illegible] for duty [illegible]	
		[illegible]	[illegible]	[illegible]
			Patients remaining 324	
	24th Sept	[illegible]	[illegible]	
			[illegible] Ambulance [illegible] Loading party	
			[illegible]	[illegible]
		4 PM	[illegible] camp	
			Patients remaining 362	

D. D. & L., London, E.C.
(10340) Wt W5300/P713 750,000 3/18 E 2688 Forms/C2118/16.

Army Form C. 2118.

WAR DIARY
or
INTELLIGENCE SUMMARY.
(Erase heading not required.)

Instructions regarding War Diaries and Intelligence Summaries are contained in F. S. Regs., Part II. and the Staff Manual respectively. Title pages will be prepared in manuscript.

Place	Date	Hour	Summary of Events and Information	Remarks and references to Appendices
27/C.22.c.4.3	25th Sept.	9 P.M.	Bearer Sub-division (Sgt Butler in charge) proceeded for duty with 108th F.A. Patients remaining 371.	H.F.
	26th Sept.	Noon.	Patients remaining 371.	H.F.
	27th Sept.	7 P.M.	A.D.M.S. secret O/425 received	
		7 P.M.	Capt A.F.R. CONDER rejoined from temporary duty with D.D.M.S. Xth Corps.	
		11 P.M.	Capt C.R. BROWN. rejoined from temporary duty with 2nd R. Irish Rifles. Patients remaining 366	H.F.
	28th Sept	1 P.M.	Capt C.R. Brown and Capt A.F.R. Conder detailed for temporary duty with 110th Field Ambulance. A.D.M.S. Secret O/936 received Patients remaining 342	H.F.
	29th Sept.	2.45 P.M.	A.D.M.S. C3 received. 1 N.C.O. and 3 O.R. sent to GWALIA FARM. Ohold. Capt SWAN with personnel and patients from OCHTEZEELE transferred to GWALIA FARM. Patients remaining 334.	H.F.

D. D. & L., London, E.C.
(10340) Wt W5300/1713 750,000 3/15 E 2688 Forms/C2118/16.

Army Form C. 2118.

Instructions regarding War Diaries and Intelligence Summaries are contained in F. S. Regs., Part II. and the Staff Manual respectively. Title pages will be prepared in manuscript.

WAR DIARY
or
~~INTELLIGENCE SUMMARY.~~

(Erase heading not required.)

Place	Date	Hour	Summary of Events and Information	Remarks and references to Appendices
27/O22.c 4.3	30th Sept. '18	Noon	Patients remaining 317.	~~R.S.~~

D. D. & L., London, E.C. (10340) Wt W5300/1713 750,000 3/15 E 2688 Forms/C2118/16.

"Regt. No.182."

penetrated to the western edge, capturing, after a stubborn fight, the party of the 17/Manchester still in the wood. At the

Confidential

War Diary

of

109th Field Ambulance.

from 1st. October 1918. To. 31st. October 1918.

VOLUME XXXVI.

H. S. Davidson Major RAMC
Commanding.

8/1918

3

Vol 36

109/A/7

Instructions regarding War Diaries and Intelligence Summaries are contained in F. S. Regs., Part II. and the Staff Manual respectively. Title pages will be prepared in manuscript.

WAR DIARY
or
~~INTELLIGENCE SUMMARY.~~
(Erase heading not required.)

Army Form C. 2118.

Place	Date	Hour	Summary of Events and Information	Remarks and references to Appendices
~~[illegible]~~ 27/Q22.c.1.3	1st Oct.	1 P.M.	Sgt Gordon and 19 O.R. proceeded to GWALIA FARM. Patients remaining 297	[illegible]
28/A23 a 1.0.	2nd Oct.	5 P.M. 5.30 P.M.	Unit moved to GWALIA FARM. Holding party of 4 O.R. and Q.M.S. left behind. A.D.M.S. Secret No O/939 received. Patients remaining 258.	[illegible]
28/A23.a.1.0.	3rd Oct.	1 P.M. 2 P.M.	A.D.M.S. ~~visited~~ camp and inspected A.D.M.S. Secret No O/942 received Patients remaining 250.	[illegible]
—	4th Oct.	8 A.M.	Capt. Swan and 20 O.R. proceeded for duty with 108th F.A. Prison YPRES. Patients remaining 243.	[illegible]
	5th Oct.	7.30.	Rev. Clark C.F. attached to unit. Capt A.F.R. Conder returned from duty with 110th F.A. Patients remaining 258	[illegible]

D. D. & L., London, E.C.
(10340) Wt W5300/P713 750,000 3/15 E 2688 Forms/C2118/16.

Instructions regarding War Diaries and Intelligence Summaries are contained in F. S. Regs., Part II. and the Staff Manual respectively. Title pages will be prepared in manuscript.

WAR DIARY
or
~~INTELLIGENCE SUMMARY.~~
(Erase heading not required.)

Army Form C. 2118.

Place	Date	Hour	Summary of Events and Information	Remarks and references to Appendices
28/A 23 a 1.0	6th Oct.	01.00	Clocks put back one hour Summer Time to Winter time	[illegible]
		11.00	Major A.S. Davidson attended conference at A.D.M.S. Office	
			Capt C.R. Brown returned from duty with 110 F.A. (P.O.W. Cage)	
			Patients remaining 252.	
28/A 23 c 1.0	7 Oct.	13.00	A.D.M.S. inspected camp	[illegible]
			Major W. Russell M.C. awarded bar to M.C.	
			20 O.R. returned from duty with 108th F.A.	
			Patients remaining 245	
28/A 23 c 1.0	8th Oct.	14.00	Capt A.F.R. Conder and 1 O.R. proceeded for duty with 110th F.A.	[illegible]
			Secret A.D.M.S. No 0/965 received	
			Patients remaining 234.	
[illegible]	9th Oct.	16.00	Secret ADMS. No 0/940 received.	[illegible]
			Patients remaining 222.	
28/A 23 c 1.0	10th Oct.	15.00	Capt A. Swan rejoined from duty with 108th Fd Amb.	[illegible]
			Patients remaining 234.	
28/A 23 c 1.0	11th Oct.		Routine. Patients remaining 270.	[illegible]

D. D. & L., London, E.C.
(10340) Wt W5300/1713 750,000 3/18 E 2688 Forms/C2118/16.

Instructions regarding War Diaries and Intelligence Summaries are contained in F. S. Regs., Part II. and the Staff Manual respectively. Title pages will be prepared in manuscript.

WAR DIARY
or
INTELLIGENCE SUMMARY.
(Erase heading not required.)

Army Form C. 2118.

1

Place	Date	Hour	Summary of Events and Information	Remarks and references to Appendices
28/A 23 a 1.0.	12th Oct.	9.00	One bearer subdivision with Sgt Hall R. proceeded for temporary duty with 100th F.A. Patients remaining 285.	[illegible]
28/A 23 a 1.0.	13 Oct.	12.00	D.D.M.S. II Corps visited and inspected camp. Patients remaining 280.	[illegible]
28/A 23 a 1.0.	14th Oct	9.00	Capt. J. Morham rejoined 110 F.A. Casualty R.A.M.C. personel (A/Cpl J. Rowley wounded by shell) Patients remaining 296	[illegible]
28/A 23 a 1.0.	15th Oct		Major W. Russell proceeded on leave from [illegible] to [illegible]. Patients remaining 305	[illegible]
28/A 23 a 1.0.	16th Oct		Routine Patients remaining 295.	[illegible]
28/A 23 a 1.0.	17 Oct		Patients remaining 291.	[illegible]
28/A 23 a 1.0.	18th Oct	17.00	A.D.M.S. visited camp. Patients remaining 280	[illegible]
28/A 23 a 1.0.	19th Oct	12.00	Lt W. E. Pirritt proceeded on leave from 20/10/18 to 3/11/18. Patients remaining 240	[illegible]

D. D. & L., London, E.C.
(10340) Wt W5300/P713 750,000 3/18 E 2688 Forms/C2118/16.

Instructions regarding War Diaries and Intelligence Summaries are contained in F. S. Regs., Part II. and the Staff Manual respectively. Title pages will be prepared in manuscript.

WAR DIARY
or
INTELLIGENCE SUMMARY.
(Erase heading not required.)

Army Form C. 2118.

Place	Date	Hour	Summary of Events and Information	Remarks and references to Appendices
20/ [illegible]	20 Oct.	17.00	Secret A.D.M.S. [illegible]/1109 received. Patients remaining 216.	[illegible]
21/ [illegible]	21 Oct.	8.00	One Tent Subdivision proceeded for temporary duty with Advanced Operating Centre. Patients remaining 197.	[illegible]
[illegible]	22nd Oct.	00.05	Equipment & transport of Tent Subdivision proceeded to Advanced Operating Centre MOORSEELE.	[illegible]
		2.00	Order cancelled and transport etc returned. Patients remaining 175.	[illegible]
23/ [illegible]	23 Oct.	9.00	M.O. detailed to see the sick at the Field Punishment Compound CATERPILLAR CORNER daily.	[illegible]
		11.30	A.D.M.S. [illegible] Warning order received to move to LEDEGHEM. Patients remaining 159.	
24/ [illegible]	24 Oct.	[illegible]	Tent Subdivision to proceed from Corps Operating Centre to LEDEGHEM. [illegible] A.H.A. wagon, 2 G.S. wagons [illegible] proceeded to LEDEGHEM. Patients remaining 162.	[illegible]

D. D. & L., London, E.C.
(10340) Wt W5300/1713 750,000 3/18 E 2688 Forms/C2118/16.

Instructions regarding War Diaries and Intelligence Summaries are contained in F. S. Regs., Part II. and the Staff Manual respectively. Title pages will be prepared in manuscript.

WAR DIARY
or
INTELLIGENCE SUMMARY.
(Erase heading not required.)

Army Form C. 2118.

Place	Date	Hour	Summary of Events and Information	Remarks and references to Appendices
21/A 13 a 1.0.	25th Oct		Patients remaining 136.	
	26 Oct.	11.00	Secret A.D.M.S. Memo No 0/1202 received (Instructions re move to LEDEGHEM) (via NOORDHOFWIJK) Patients remaining 133	
LEDEGHEM.	27 Oct.	09.00	Unit with patients moved from GWALIA FARM via NOORDHOFWIJK siding Camp Back YPRES and light railway to LEDEGHEM arriving 14.00. Transport proceeded by road. Patients remaining 123.	
BELLEGHEM	28 Oct.	08.00	Capt A.F.R. Conder and 8 O.R. arrived & took over from 102 F.A. at BELLEGHEM	
		13.00	Unit moved to BELLEGHEM arriving 18.30. Patients transferred by road and motor lorry to 108 F.A. Patients remaining 29.	
	29. Oct.		[illegible] prepared [illegible] Patients remaining 36.	

(10340) Wt W5300/P715 750,000 3/18 E 2688 Forms/C2118/16. D. D. & L., London, E.C.

Army Form C. 2118.

WAR DIARY
or
INTELLIGENCE SUMMARY.

(Erase heading not required.)

Instructions regarding War Diaries and Intelligence Summaries are contained in F. S. Regs., Part II. and the Staff Manual respectively. Title pages will be prepared in manuscript.

Place	Date	Hour	Summary of Events and Information	Remarks and references to Appendices
Beaulencourt [illegible]	30th Oct.	1500	Capt C. R. Brown proceeded for temporary duty to M. O. [illegible] 76th Army Brigade R.F.A. Position [illegible] nil.	[illegible]
	31st Oct.		Routine.	[illegible]

D. D. & L., London, E.C.
(10340) Wt W5300/P715 750,000 3/18 E 2688 Forms/C2118/16.

Secret

War Diary

of

109th Field Ambulance

for month of November, 1918.

VOL. XXXVIII

1st Decr., 1918

J.H.S. Davidson, Lt-Col., R.A.M.C.,
Commanding 109th Field Amb.

Army Form [redacted]2118.

WAR DIARY
or
INTELLIGENCE SUMMARY.
(Erase heading not required.)

Instructions regarding War Diaries and Intelligence Summaries are contained in F. S. Regs., Part II. and the Staff Manual respectively. Title pages will be prepared in manuscript.

Place	Date	Hour	Summary of Events and Information	Remarks and references to Appendices
BELLEGHEM 29/N27.C.	1/11 18	16.00	Secret A.D.M.S. No1234 received.	HG
	2/11 18	12.00	Sick of 109th Brigade and 107th in their new area to be collected.	
		22.30	Instructions received from A.D.M.S.: that unit moves to STERHOEK on 4/11 18.	HG
	3/11 18	12.00	Sick of 109th Brigade only to be collected by this unit.	
		14.00	O.C. and A.D.M.S. went to STERHOEK to see billets. Found them scattered but a chateau suitable for a small hospital for sick officers or O.R.	HG
		18.00	Capt. C. R. Brown rejoined from duty with 96th Army Brigade R.F.A.	
STERHOEK 29/M35.c.3.3	4/11 18	12.30	Unit moved from BELLEGHEM. Arrived STERHOEK 14.30.	HG
	5/11 18	21.00	Sick of Divisional Artillery (153 Bde R.F.A., 173 Bde. R.F.A., 36th Divn T.M.B.) to be collected from HQ 6th.	HG
	6/11 18	10.00	Ford Car and Pte Matthews detailed for duty with A.D.M.S.	
			Cpl. McCrum and Pte Tedder detailed for duty with O.C. Baths	
		13.00	A/Q.M. W.E. Perrott returned from leave.	HG
		15.00	Capt. H. Swan detailed for temporary duty as M.O. i/c 36th Division Reception Camp.	

D. D. & L., London, E.C.
(10340) Wt W5300/P713 750,000 3/18 E 2688 Forms/C2118/16.

Instructions regarding War Diaries and Intelligence Summaries are contained in F. S. Regs., Part II. and the Staff Manual respectively. Title pages will be prepared in manuscript.

WAR DIARY
or
~~INTELLIGENCE SUMMARY.~~
(Erase heading not required.)

Army Form C. 2118.

Place	Date	Hour	Summary of Events and Information	Remarks and references to Appendices
STERHOEK 2⁰/M 35. c. 3. 3.	7/11 18.	14:00	Capt. C. R. Brown detailed to see the sick of the D.A.C. daily.	~~A.S.D.~~
	8/11 18		Routine.	~~A.S.D.~~
	9/11 18	11.00	O.C. attended conference at A.D.M.S. office on various matters.	A.S.D.
		14:00	Lt A. Millenberger M.O.R.C.; U.S.A reported for duty and taken on the strength.	
		15:00	Notification of the award of the M.M. to ~~Pte~~ Pte E. Turney and Pte J. Hunt.	
	10/11 18	9.00	Authority received for Major Davidson to wear the badges of rank of Lt. Col. whilst a/Commanding the 109th Field Ambulance.	
		14.30.	Special combined Church Parade service of the three Field Ambulances. An especially vivid service contrasted with the congratulations which the A.D.M.S. conveyed to the Officers and men for their work in the recent fighting.	
		16.00	2 Wolsley Motor Cars detailed for duty with 108th F.A. at the call of the M.A.C.	
		21.00	A firm rumour from the Corps that the German plenipotentiaries had signed the armistice terms and that for practical purposes the war appeared to be finished. A certain mild excitement was exhibited by both officers and O.R. of the unit, whilst some were even heard to express regret.	

D. D. & L., London, E.C. (10340) Wt W5300/P713 750,000 3/18 E 2688 Forms/C2118/16.

Army Form C. 2118.

WAR DIARY
or
INTELLIGENCE SUMMARY.
(Erase heading not required.)

Instructions regarding War Diaries and Intelligence Summaries are contained in F. S. Regs., Part II. and the Staff Manual respectively. Title pages will be prepared in manuscript.

Place	Date	Hour	Summary of Events and Information	Remarks and references to Appendices
STERHOEK 29/ M35.c.3.3.	10/11 18	21.00	The band of the unit rose to the occasion and played the Marseillaise with great martial ardour to the delight of the civil population and the discomfort of all who wished to sleep. It rendered "God save the King" and as a tribute to the old army "Tipperary" was given with great feeling.	[illegible]
	11/11 18	07.00	23 O.R. detailed for duty at the Baths MOUSCRON to return same day.	[illegible]
		14.00	Find that the rejoicings of yesterday evening were premature but that Armistice was signed this day & cessation of hostilities took place at 11.00.	
	12/11 18	14.00	Sgt W. Butler awarded the M.M.	[illegible]
		16.00	Pte R. [illegible] attached as temporary Medical Orderly 5 [illegible] Bde R.F.A.	
	13/11 18	9.00	[illegible] attached for temporary duty as M.O. to 1st R. [illegible] Fusiliers.	[illegible]
		9.00	4 O.R. detailed for duty at the Baths MOUSCRON.	
	14/11 18	12.00	Capt S.E. Pickson M.C. R.A.M.C. reported for duty and taken on the strength.	[illegible]
	15/11 18	15.00	A.D.M.S. visited the Camp.	[illegible]

D. D. & L., London, E.C.
(10340) Wt W5300/P713 750,000 3/16 E 2688 Forms/C2118/16.

Army Form C 2118.

Instructions regarding War Diaries and Intelligence Summaries are contained in F. S. Regs., Part II. and the Staff Manual respectively. Title pages will be prepared in manuscript.

WAR DIARY
or
INTELLIGENCE SUMMARY.
(Erase heading not required.)

Place	Date	Hour	Summary of Events and Information	Remarks and references to Appendices
STERHOEK. 29/M35.c.3.3.	16/11 18.	9.00	1 N.C.O. & 22 O.R. detailed for temporary duty at Divisional Baths.	[illegible]
	17/11 18.	10.00	D.D.M.S. Xth Corps visited camp.	
			2 M A Cars detailed for duty with No 20 M.A.C.	[illegible]
			2 Horse Ambulance Wagons detailed for duty with 110. F A.	
		12.00	Major W Russell M.C. rejoined from leave.	
	18/11 18.	9.00	1 N.C.O. & 22 O.R. detailed for temporary duty at Divisional Baths.	[illegible]
		15.00	O.C. attended meeting on Education at MOUVERON.	
	19/11 18.	11.00	O.C. and Major Russell M.C. attended conference on Sports and Education at A.D.M.S. office.	
		12.00	Capt C R Brown detailed to duty as M.O. i/c 2nd R. I. Rifles. Struck off strength.	[illegible]
	20/11 18	11.00	D.M.S. Second Army inspect the unit and addressed the personnel.	[illegible]
		15.00	1 M A Car rejoined from duty with No 20 M.A.C.	
	21/11 18.	12.00	1 O.R. as reinforcement ~~taken~~ on strength.	[illegible]
			2 O.R. of 122 Field Coy R.E. attached for instruction in Water cart duties.	
			3 G.S. Wagons detailed for duty at Field Dump WERVICQ	

D. D. & L., London, E.C.
(10340) Wt W5300/P713 750,000 3/18 E 2688 Forms/C2118/16.

Instructions regarding War Diaries and Intelligence Summaries are contained in F. S. Regs., Part II. and the Staff Manual respectively. Title pages will be prepared in manuscript.

WAR DIARY
or
~~INTELLIGENCE SUMMARY.~~
(Erase heading not required.)

Army Form C. 2118.

Place	Date	Hour	Summary of Events and Information	Remarks and references to Appendices
STEERHOEK 29/M35.c 3.3	22/11/18	8.00	1 N.C.O. 24 O.R. detailed for temporary duty at Divisional Baths.	
			3 G.S. Wagons for duty at Fuel dump WERVICQ	
			Sick of 25th Brigade R.G.A. were collected.	[initials]
		14.00	Inter Section Foot ball Competition open to Field Ambulances	
			109th A.S.C. section 5 C Section 109 F.A. 3.	
	23/11/18	8.00	3 G.S. Wagons detailed for duty at Fuel Dump WERVICQ.	[initials]
			Capt J. H. [illegible] rejoined from duty at Divisional Reception Camp.	
	24/11/18	14.30.	Combined Church Parade and Service MOUSCRON.	[initials]
	25/11/18	12.00	Capt J. H. [illegible] RAMC detailed [illegible] with O.C. Divisional Train for a series of lectures to the personnel thereof on the dangers of Venereal Disease.	[initials]
	26/11/18	11.00	Capt A.F.R. Conder attended a meeting of R.A.M.C. [illegible] officers at A.D.M.S. office.	
			Cases of 30 [illegible] [illegible] to be admitted by this division.	
			Extract [illegible] G.H.Q. appointments 17.11.18.	[initials]
			Temp. Capt. (A/major) [illegible] Davidson to be Lt Col whilst commanding Field Ambulance 109. from 19th October '18.	

D. D. & L., London, E.C.
(10340) Wt W5300/P713 750,000 3/18 E 2688 Forms/C2118/16.

Instructions regarding War Diaries and Intelligence Summaries are contained in F. S. Regs., Part II. and the Staff Manual respectively. Title pages will be prepared in manuscript.

WAR DIARY
or
~~INTELLIGENCE~~ SUMMARY.
(Erase heading not required.)

Army Form C. 2118.

Place	Date	Hour	Summary of Events and Information	Remarks and references to Appendices
STEERHOEK 29/M.35.c.3.3.		8.00	3 G.S. Wagons detailed for duty at fuel dump WERVICQ.	[illegible]
	27/11/18.	14.00.	Dental Surgeon to be attached for duty with 108th F.A.	
	28/11/18.	15.00	200 Wooden Beds drawn for use of personnel from C.R.E. 36th DW.	[illegible]
	29/11/18	9.00	1 N.C.O. 22 O.R. detailed for temporary duty at Baths MOUSCRON.	
			Inter Section R.A.M.C. Football Competition	[illegible]
			"B" Section 110 F.A. 4. "B" Section 109th F.A. 2.	
	30/11/18.		Inter section R.A.M.C. Football Competition	[illegible]
			"A" Section 109th F.A. 4. "C" Section 108 F.A. 1.	

D. D. & L., London, E.C.
(10340) Wt W5300/P713 750,000 3/18 E 2688 Forms/C2118/16.

War Diary

by

Lieut-Colonel H. S. Davidson. R.A.M.C.

Commanding 109th Field Ambulance.

December 1918.

Instructions regarding War Diaries and Intelligence Summaries are contained in F. S. Regs., Part II. and the Staff Manual respectively. Title pages will be prepared in manuscript.

WAR DIARY
or
INTELLIGENCE SUMMARY.
(Erase heading not required.)

Army Form C. 2118.

Place	Date	Hour	Summary of Events and Information	Remarks and references to Appendices
STEERHOCK (?)	1st Dec 18		Routine.	[illegible]
	2/12 18	11.00	CO and Lt PERRITT attended conference at A.D.M.S. office re Ceremonial Parade to be held on the third	[illegible]
	3/12 18	7.00	Parade cancelled.	
		14.00	Capt J H Swan detailed for temporary duty with French Mission ROUBAIX.	[illegible]
	4/12		Routine.	[illegible]
	5/12 18	6.00	1 NCO 22 OR attached for temporary duty at the Lazaret Mouscron.	
		10.30	Lt Perritt attended conference of Quarter master in Town hall Mouscron	[illegible]
		4.00	Lt McIlraith (?) rejoined from duty with 1st R Inniskilling Fusiliers	
	6/12 18	11.00	Unit attended Ceremonial parade (Rehearsal) at Aerodrome HALLUIN	
			Lt Perritt acted as Adjutant to A.D.M.S.	
		11.00	Lt McIlraith (?) proceeded on leave.	[illegible]
		11.00	Capt S E Pickin proceeded to temporary duty as M.O. i/c 153 Brigade R.F.A	

A6945 Wt. W11422/M1160 350,000 12/16 D. D. & L. Forms/C./2118/14.

Instructions regarding War Diaries and Intelligence Summaries are contained in F. S. Regs., Part II. and the Staff Manual respectively. Title pages will be prepared in manuscript.

WAR DIARY
or
~~INTELLIGENCE~~ SUMMARY.
(Erase heading not required.)

Army Form C. 2118.

Place	Date	Hour	Summary of Events and Information	Remarks and references to Appendices
STEENWERCK	7/12/18		Capt. A.F.R. Conder with 30 RAMC OR (10 from each Ambulance) were allowed to proceed to ROUBAIX to greet His Majesty who passed through that town en route to LILLE.	[illegible]
	8/12/18	10.00	2 M.A. Cars reported for duty to Railhead P.O.	
		12.00	Sgt. W.H. [illegible] A.S.C. i/c 3 G.S. Wagons drivers and orderlies detailed for duty with [illegible] C. 36th [illegible] Battalion.	[illegible]
	[illegible].12.18	9.00	1 NCO 22 OR detailed for temporary duty at Baths MOUSCRON.	
		9.00	2 NCO (Sgt. W. Butler, Cpl. F. McCann) detailed for duty at Baths RONCQ.	[illegible]
		16.00	Cpl. [illegible] reported from duty with 153 Bde RFA.	
	[illegible].12.18	17.00	Capt. J.H. Swan reported from duty with French Mission ROUBAIX.	[illegible]
	[illegible].12.18		Routine.	[illegible]
	[illegible].12.18		Routine.	
	[illegible].12.18	11.00	Unit attended Ceremonial Parade at MOUSCRON for presentation of [illegible] awarded for gallantry & [illegible] by the Divisional Commander.	[illegible]

A6945 Wt. W11422/M1160 350,000 12/16 D. D. & L. Forms/C./2118/14.

Instructions regarding War Diaries and Intelligence Summaries are contained in F. S. Regs., Part II. and the Staff Manual respectively. Title pages will be prepared in manuscript.

WAR DIARY
or
~~INTELLIGENCE SUMMARY.~~
(Erase heading not required.)

Army Form C. 2118.

Place	Date	Hour	Summary of Events and Information	Remarks and references to Appendices
STEENBECK	11/12 18.	9.00	Capt. J. H. Swan proceeded for duty with 32nd Labour Group	
		14.00	Capt. S. E. Pitkin proceeded for temporary duty with 153 Bde R.F.A.	
	15/12 18.		Routine.	
	16/12 18.	11.00	Unit took part in the Review and March past of the Division at HALLUIN before the Corps Commander.	
	17/12 18.	16.00	Capt. J. H. Swan reported arrival for duty with 32nd Labour Group.	
		16.00.	Sgt. Whittingham with 3 wagons and personnel returned from duty at New Riding School.	
	18/12 18.		Routine	
	19/12 18.	11.00	Photograph taken of the N.C.O.'s of the division.	
	20/12 18		Routine	
	21/12 18.	18.00	"A" Section held a successful convivial gathering.	
			Capt. A. F. R. Conder proceeded to [illegible]	

A5834 Wt. W4973/M687 750,000 8/16 D. D. & L. Ltd. Forms/C.2118/13.

Army Form C. 2118.

Instructions regarding War Diaries and Intelligence Summaries are contained in F. S. Regs., Part II. and the Staff Manual respectively. Title pages will be prepared in manuscript.

WAR DIARY
or
~~INTELLIGENCE~~ SUMMARY.
(Erase heading not required.)

Place	Date	Hour	Summary of Events and Information	Remarks and references to Appendices
STEERHOEK.	22/12 18		Routine.	[illegible]
	23/12 18		Routine	[illegible]
	24/12 18		Routine.	[illegible]
	25/12 18	11	Church Parade (Combined Service).	
		14-15	"Silent" Football Match.	
		17	Christmas Dinner followed by a Concert in File Factory.	W.R.
			Lieut-Col Davidson proceeded on leave to U.K.	
	26/12 18	9	Lieut. A. Mildenberger detailed as M.O. i/c 5th Army R.A. Reinforcement Camp.	W.R.
		12	Capt. S.E. Picken reported arrival from temporary duty with 153 Bde. R.F.A.	
	27/12 18	10	Capt. J.H. Swan detailed for temporary duty with 110th Field Ambulance.	W.R.
	28/12 18	14-45	A/C.O. + Capt. S.E. Picken attended meeting of XI Corps Medical Society.	W.R.
	29/12 18		Routine.	W.R.
	30/12 18		Routine	W.R.
	31/12 18		Routine.	W.R.

A5834 Wt. W4973/M687 750,000 8/16 D. D. & L. Ltd. Forms/C.2118/13.

Confidential.

War Diary

of

109th Field Ambulance

by

Lieut-Colonel H. S. Davidson, R.A.M.C.,

Period:-

From 1st January 1919.

To 31st January 1919.

Army Form C. 2118.

WAR DIARY
or
~~INTELLIGENCE~~ SUMMARY.
(Erase heading not required.)

Instructions regarding War Diaries and Intelligence Summaries are contained in F. S. Regs., Part II. and the Staff Manual respectively. Title pages will be prepared in manuscript.

Place	Date	Hour	Summary of Events and Information	Remarks and references to Appendices
STEERHOEK	1-1-19		Lieut. Miltenberger A. M.O.R.C. U.S.A. taken on strength from 30-12-18.	
		14 hrs	Association Football Final for Medals presented by A.D.M.S. A Sect. 109 F.A. beat A.S.C. 108 F.A.	W.R.
	2-1-19		Routine	W.R.
	3-1-19		Routine	W.R.
	4-1-19		Routine	W.R.
	4-1-19		Routine	W.R.
	5-1-19		Church Parades C. of E. 9-30 Pres. 11-30.	
			Routine.	W.R.
	6-1-19		Routine.	W.R.
	7-1-19		Capt. A. J. R. Conder awarded "The Military Cross."	
			Routine	W.R.
	8-1-19		Routine	W.R.
	9-1-19	14 hrs	Route March.	W.R.
		18 hrs	Capt. A. J. R. Conder rejoined from leave to U.K.	
			Routine	W.R.
	10-1-19	7-30	Bathing Parade.	W.R.

A6945 Wt. W11422/M1160 350,000 12/16 D. D. & L. Forms/C./2118/14.

Instructions regarding War Diaries and Intelligence Summaries are contained in F. S. Regs., Part II. and the Staff Manual respectively. Title pages will be prepared in manuscript.

Army Form C. 2118.

WAR DIARY
or
~~INTELLIGENCE~~ SUMMARY.
(*Erase heading not required.*)

Place	Date	Hour	Summary of Events and Information	Remarks and references to Appendices
STEERHOEK	11-1-19		Lieut + Qmr. W.E. Perritt, S.Sgt Wilson T. + Pte Sterling J. awarded Croix de Guerre by the Belgian Authorities	WR.
	~~12-1-19~~		Routine.	WR.
	12-1-19	11 hrs	8 O.R. attended Church Parade at Roubaix	WR.
		"	Church Parade (Combined Service).	WR.
	13-1-19		Routine	WR.
	14-1-19		One G.S. Wagon + personnel detailed to report to Comdt. Courtrai Animal Demob. Camp for temp. duty.	WR.
			Capt J.H. Swan rejoined from temp. duty with 110 Field Ambce	
	15-1-19		Routine.	WR.
	16-1-19		Routine.	WR.
	16-1-19		Routine	WR.
		11-30 hrs	Capt. A.F.R. Conder detailed to represent Div. RAMC. at Sports Meeting Goffre	WR.
	17-1-19	11-30 hrs	a/C.O. + Lieut. + Qmr. W.E. Perritt attended conference at A.D.M.S. office on Equipment + of a Field Ambulance.	
			Routine.	WR.

Instructions regarding War Diaries and Intelligence Summaries are contained in F. S. Regs., Part II. and the Staff Manual respectively. Title pages will be prepared in manuscript.

WAR DIARY
or
~~INTELLIGENCE SUMMARY~~.
(Erase heading not required.)

Army Form C. 2118.

Place	Date	Hour	Summary of Events and Information	Remarks and references to Appendices
STEERHOEK	18-1-19	11 hrs	Classification of animals by D.A.D.V.S. 36 Division	
			Routine	W.R.
	19-1-19	11.00	Combined Church Parade.	
			One G.S. wagon with personnel rejoined from temp. duty with Courtrai Animal Demob. Camp.	W.R.
	20-1-19		Routine	W.R.
	21-1-19		Routine	W.R.
	22-1-19	10.00	Majors Russell & Picken attended interview at Office of D.M.S. V Army with view to obtaining permanent Commissions.	W.R.
		11.00	Inspection of animals by Demobilization Officer	W.R.
	23-1-19		Routine	W.R.
			No 51297 Sgt McCurdy. R. awarded M.S.M. (D.R.O. 23/1/19. No 25-86)	~~H.G.~~
	24-1-19		Routine	
	25-1-19	10.00	Capt J. H. Swan detailed to report for temporary duty with 1st R. Irish Fusiliers as M.O.	~~H.G.~~

A6945 Wt. W11422/M1160 350,000 12/16 D. D. & L. Forms/C./2118/14.

Instructions regarding War Diaries and Intelligence Summaries are contained in F. S. Regs., Part II. and the Staff Manual respectively. Title pages will be prepared in manuscript.

WAR DIARY
or
~~INTELLIGENCE~~ SUMMARY.
(Erase heading not required.)

Army Form C. 2118.

Place	Date	Hour	Summary of Events and Information	Remarks and references to Appendices
STEERHOEK	26/1/19	11.00	Medical Board inspected P.O.W. Camps at MENIN and GELUWE.	[illegible]
	27/1/19	16.00	Lt Col. H.S. Davidson rejoined from leave	[illegible]
	28/1/19	11.00	Medical Board inspected P.O.W. camp at MOORSEELE	[illegible]
		12.00	Sgt Sweeney and 2 O.R. detailed to report to 3rd Ad. Depot Med Stores LILLE for temporary duty	[illegible]
	29/1/19	16.00	10 O.R. rejoined from temporary duty at 62 C.C.S.	[illegible]
	30/1/19		Routine	[illegible]
	31/1/19	6.00	Major W. Russell. M.C. proceeded to U.K. for duty. Struck off Strength	
		14.00	Capt A.F. R. Condon M.C. detailed for temporary duty with O.C. 33rd Labour Coy.	[illegible]

Feb. 1919

Confidential

War Diary

by

Lieut-Colonel H. S. Davidson. R.A.M.C.

Commanding 109th Field Ambulance.

31

Vol 41

10/1924

Instructions regarding War Diaries and Intelligence Summaries are contained in F. S. Regs., Part II. and the Staff Manual respectively. Title pages will be prepared in manuscript.

WAR DIARY
or
~~INTELLIGENCE SUMMARY.~~
(Erase heading not required.)

Army Form C. 2118.

Place	Date	Hour	Summary of Events and Information	Remarks and references to Appendices
STEERHOEK	1/2/19		Routine.	[illegible]
	2/2/19	11.00	Combined Church Service	[illegible]
	3/2/19		Sgt W. Tozer R.A.M.C. granted Special Leave from 3rd – 17th Feb. (XV Corps No A.L. L/1050/d/31/1/19.)	[illegible]
	4/2/19.		Capt S. E. Picken M.C. appointed Acting Major whilst commanding a Section of a Field Ambulance (Auth. XV Corps No A.C. 5/1/31 36th Div. No 7/3/36A. d. 3-2-19.	[illegible]
	5/2/19.		Routine.	[illegible]
	6/2/19		Routine.	[illegible]
	7/2/19	11.00	[illegible] & Lt [illegible] attended conference at A.D.M.S. Office	[illegible]
	[illegible]		Routine.	[illegible]
	[illegible]		Routine	[illegible]
	[illegible]/2/19		Routine	[illegible]
	[illegible]/2/19		Routine	[illegible]
	[illegible]		Routine.	[illegible]

A6945 Wt. W11422/M1160 350,000 12/16 D. D. & L. Forms/C./2118/14.

Instructions regarding War Diaries and Intelligence Summaries are contained in F. S. Regs., Part II. and the Staff Manual respectively. Title pages will be prepared in manuscript.

WAR DIARY
or
~~INTELLIGENCE SUMMARY.~~
(Erase heading not required.)

Army Form C. 2118.

Place	Date	Hour	Summary of Events and Information	Remarks and references to Appendices
STEERHOEK	13/2/19		Major W. Russell arrived for duty. Taken on strength on 31.1.19.	
			Capt J. H. Swan reported for temporary duty with 1st Royal Irish Fusiliers.	[illegible]
	14/2/19		Route March	[illegible]
	15/2/19		Pt. Elliott A. RAMC. M.T. awarded the Military Medal	[illegible]
	16/2/19		Route March.	[illegible]
	17/2/19		Route March	[illegible]
	18/2/19		[illegible]	[illegible]
	19/2/19		Major S. C. Pickens detailed for temporary duty with 10th Fd. Amb.	[illegible]
	20/2/19		Capt A. E. Gravells reported for duty. Taken on the strength.	[illegible]
	21/2/19		Capt A. E. Gravells detailed to relieve Capt J H. Swan for temporary duty at No 10 C.C.S.	[illegible]
	22/2/19		Capt. J. H. Swan proceeded on leave from 23/2/19 to 8/3/19.	[illegible]
	23/2/19		Church Service 11 A.M.	[illegible]
	24/2/19		Route March	[illegible]
	25/2/19		Route March 4 Bay. horses transferred to M.G.C. Batt.	[illegible]

A6945 Wt. W11422/M1160 350,000 12/16 D. D. & L. Forms/C./2118/14.

Army Form C. 2118.

Instructions regarding War Diaries and Intelligence Summaries are contained in F. S. Regs., Part II. and the Staff Manual respectively. Title pages will be prepared in manuscript.

WAR DIARY
or
~~INTELLIGENCE~~ SUMMARY.
(Erase heading not required.)

Place	Date	Hour	Summary of Events and Information	Remarks and references to Appendices
STEENWERCK	26/2/19		Routine.	H.H.
	27/2/19	11.30	Major W. Russell M.C. attended conference at 137th F.A. re limitation and reorganisation of equipment of Field Ambulances.	H.H.
	28/2/19		Routine. 14 Y. and 5 Z horses & mules proceeded to LINSELLES Collecting Camp.	H.H.
				H. D.

A6945 Wt. W11422/M1160 350,000 12/16 D. D. & L. Forms/C./2118/14.

5

Mar 1919

Vol 42

140/3551.

War Diary

by

Lieut-Colonel H. S. Davidson. R.A.M.C.

Commanding 109th Field Ambulance.

March. 1919.

Instructions regarding War Diaries and Intelligence Summaries are contained in F. S. Regs., Part II. and the Staff Manual respectively. Title pages will be prepared in manuscript.

WAR DIARY
or
~~INTELLIGENCE~~ SUMMARY.
(Erase heading not required.)

Army Form C. 2118.

Place	Date	Hour	Summary of Events and Information	Remarks and references to Appendices
STERHOEK.	1/3/19.		Major J.E. Picken reverts to Captain on [illegible] of Field Ambulance "C" Section being disbanded.	[illegible]
	2/3/19	10.00	Capt J.E. Picken detailed for temporary duty with 153 Bde R.F.A.	
			Major Russell M.C. attended conference on [illegible] of Field	[illegible]
		11.00	Ambulances at 137 F.A.	
	3/3/19	10.00	Major Russell attended conference at 137 F.A.	[illegible]
	4/3/19	15.00	Capt A.F.R. Conder rejoined from temporary duty with 5th Labour Group	
	5/3/19	17.00	9 O.R. RAMC and 2 A.S.C. H.T. proceeded to Concentration Camp for demobilisation	[illegible]
	6/3/19		Routine	[illegible]
	7/3/19		Routine.	[illegible]
	8/3/19		Capt A.F.R. Conder detailed to proceed home on demobilisation	[illegible]
			9 O.R. detailed to proceed on demobilisation.	
	9/3/19		Capt A.F.R. Conder proceeded to U.K.	[illegible]
	10/3/19		Lt W.E. Perrott granted leave to U.K. from 10–24:3:19.	[illegible]
	11/3/19		Routine.	[illegible]

A6945 Wt. W11422/M1160 350,000 12/16 D. D. & L. Forms/C./2118/14.

Army Form C. 2118.

Instructions regarding War Diaries and Intelligence Summaries are contained in F. S. Regs., Part II. and the Staff Manual respectively. Title pages will be prepared in manuscript.

WAR DIARY
or
INTELLIGENCE SUMMARY.
(Erase heading not required.)

Place	Date	Hour	Summary of Events and Information	Remarks and references to Appendices
STEENHOEK	12/3/19		2 A.S.C. H.T. transferred to No 1 Coy Div^n Train	HR
	13/3/19		5 O.R. RAMC proceeded to Concentration camp for demobilisation	HR
	14/3/19		1 A.S.C. M.T. OR proceeded to 31st Div^n M.T. Coy for demobilisation	HR
	[illegible]		Capt Gravelle RAMC returned from duty with No 10 C.C.S.	HR
			Capt. J R Evans RAMC returned from leave	HR
			Capt S.E. Picken returned from Tempy duty with 153 R.F.A.	HR
	15/3/19		Major W Russell M.C. RAMC proceeded to report to D.M.S.	
			2nd Army.	HR
			Capt. Gravelle proceeded to U.K. for demobilisation.	HR
			Capt J H Lea proceeded to 43 M.A.C. as Officer Commanding	HR
	16/3/19		Church parade 11.15	
	17/3/19		The unit celebrated St Patrick's Day in true Irish fashion.	HR
	18/3/19		Routine	
	19/3/19		Capt S.E. Picken M.C. proceeded with 136 R. to H.Q. 2nd Army.	HR
			6 O.R. proceeded to Concentration Camp for demobilisation	HR
			Lt. W. E. Perritt rejoined from leave	

D. D. & L., London, E.C.
(A7883) Wt W809/M1672 50,000 4/17 Sch. 52a Forms/C/2118/14

Instructions regarding War Diaries and Intelligence Summaries are contained in F. S. Regs., Part II, and the Staff Manual respectively. Title pages will be prepared in manuscript.

WAR DIARY
or
~~INTELLIGENCE~~ SUMMARY.
(Erase heading not required.)

Army Form C. 2118.

Place	Date	Hour	Summary of Events and Information	Remarks and references to Appendices
STERHOEK	20/3/19		Routine	[initials]
	21/3		Routine	[initials]
	22/3		Routine	[initials]
	23/3	14.00	1 O.R. to Demobilisation Camp.	[initials]
	24/3	10.00	9. O.R. to Demobilisation Camp.	[initials]
		15.00	1 O.R. A.S.C. returned to 36 Div^n. Train.	
	25/3		Routine	[initials]
	26/3		Routine	[initials]
	27/3	10.00	3 O.R. to Demobilisation Camp. Unit now reduced to Cadre Strength + includes 2 O.R. R.A.M.C. surplus to provide for sick wastage, and 1 O.R. A.S.C. H.T. Of the three P.B. O.R. one is eligible for Army of Occupation.	[initials]
	28/3.	11.00	Heavy fall of snow during the night 6"-8".	[initials]
		21.00	Rum issue	[initials]
			Cpl. W. F. Quinn, D.C.M.; M.M.; awarded Decoration Militaire (2nd Class) + Croix de Guerre of Belgium.	[initials]
	29/3.		Routine	[initials]

D. D. & L., London, E.C.
(A7283) Wt W809/M1672 50,000 4/17 Sch 52a Forms/C/2118/14

Instructions regarding War Diaries and Intelligence Summaries are contained in F. S. Regs., Part II. and the Staff Manual respectively. Title pages will be prepared in manuscript.

WAR DIARY

or

~~INTELLIGENCE SUMMARY~~.

(Erase heading not required.)

Army Form C. 2118.

Place	Date	Hour	Summary of Events and Information	Remarks and references to Appendices
STEENHOEK.	30/3/19.	10.30	5 X mules sent to Linselles Collecting Camp.	H.P.D.
		11.00	Church Parade	
	31/3/19.		Routine	H.P.D.

D. D. & L., London, E.C.
(A7883) Wt W809/M1672 50,000 4/17 Sch 52a Forms/C/2118/14

Apr 1919

War Diary

by

Capt. S. P. Rea.

R.A.M.C.

Commanding

109th Field Ambulance.

April. 1919.

Instructions regarding War Diaries and Intelligence Summaries are contained in F. S. Regs., Part II, and the Staff Manual respectively. Title pages will be prepared in manuscript.

WAR DIARY
or
~~INTELLIGENCE SUMMARY~~.
(Erase heading not required.)

Army Form C. 2118.

Place	Date	Hour	Summary of Events and Information	Remarks and references to Appendices
STERHOEK	1/4/19.		Routine. S/S.M Brigham granted 14 days leave to Switzerland.	H.G.
	2/4/19.	10.00.	3 O.R. A.S.C H.T. transferred to 287 Coy. R.A.S.C. ST ANDRE.	H.G.
			1 O.R. A.S.C. H.T. reported for duty.	
	3/4/19		2 X Riders sent to [illegible] Collecting Camp.	H.G.
	4/4/19		Routine.	
	5/4/19		3 L.D. X Horses evacuated to 44 M.V.S. sick.	H.G.
	6/4	11.00.	Church Parade.	
	7/4/19.		O.C. received telegram to proceed on demobilisation.	H.G.
	8/4/19.	11.00	Routine	
	9/4/19		[illegible] handed over command to Lieut. Smith and proceeded for [illegible]	W.S.
	"		2 O.R. on leave	
	10/4/19		Routine	W.S.
	11/4/19		[illegible] proceeded on leave	W.S.
	12/4/19		1 L.D. X Horse to 36 M.G. Bn. Routine.	W.S.
	13/4/19		Church Parade 11.00 [illegible] on 1 with [illegible] Draughts 2 miles from M.G. Batt.	W.S.
	14/4/19		1. O.R. proceeded on leave to U.K. Routine	W.S.

D. D. & L., London, E.C.
(A7883) Wt W8cq/M1672 50,000 4/17 Sch. 52a Forms/C/2118/14

Instructions regarding War Diaries and Intelligence Summaries are contained in F. S. Regs., Part II, and the Staff Manual respectively. Title pages will be prepared in manuscript.

WAR DIARY
or
INTELLIGENCE SUMMARY.
(Erase heading not required.)

Army Form C. 2118.

Place	Date	Hour	Summary of Events and Information	Remarks and references to Appendices
Steenbeek	15.4.19	10.00	Parade 10.30 Inspection Routine	[illegible]
"	16.4.19	"	[illegible] on Strength [illegible]	[illegible]
"	17.4.19	"	Routine.	SPR
"	18.4.19	"	Routine.	SPR
	19.4.19	"	2 L. mules sent to LINSELLES Collecting Camp. One O.R. R.A.S.C. M.T. granted leave to U.K.	SPR
	20.4.19	"	Church Parade 11 a.m. Routine.	SPR
	21.4.19		Holiday.	SPR
	22.4.19		One O.R. RAMC granted leave to U.K. Routine.	SPR
	23.4.19		One O.R. R.A.M.C. granted leave to U.K. 41120 L. SERGT. D SERVICE promoted to Rank of ACTING SERGEANT with effect from 22.3.19. 54761 PRIVATE I. R. SMITH promoted to rank of ACTING CORPORAL with effect from 22.3.19. One mule received from 35th DIV. TRAIN and taken on strength.	SPR
	24.4.19		Proceeded to U.K. on 14 days leave and handed over Command to LT. W. E. PERRITT.	SPR

D. D. & L., London, E.C. (A7883) Wt W809/M1672 50,000 4/17 Sch 52a Forms/C/2118/14.

Army Form C. 2118.

Instructions regarding War Diaries and Intelligence Summaries are contained in F. S. Regs., Part II. and the Staff Manual respectively. Title pages will be prepared in manuscript.

WAR DIARY
or
~~INTELLIGENCE~~ SUMMARY.
(Erase heading not required.)

Place	Date	Hour	Summary of Events and Information	Remarks and references to Appendices
Sterhocke	25/4/19	10.00	Pay Parade Routine	W.D.
"	26	" "	1 O.R proceeded on leave to U.K. Routine 1 X H.D. Horse to Tourcoing Veterinary Camp	W.D.
"	27	11.00	Church Parade. Routine Escort proceeded to Havre re deserter	W.D.
"	28	" "	Routine	W.D.
"	29	" "	1 O.R. proceeded on leave to U.K. Routine	W.D.
"	30	" "	2 O.R proceeded for demobilisation 1 O.R proceeded on leave to U.K.	W.D.
			1 X mule taken on strength from 36 Divisional Train. Routine.	W.D.

30/4/19

[illegible] Lieut.
A/O.C. 109th Field Ambulance

D. D. & L., London, E.C.
(A7883) Wt W809/M1672 50,000 4/17 Sch. 52a Forms/C/2118/14

Confidential

War Diary

by

Captain S. P. Rea. R.A.M.C.

Commanding

109. Field Ambulance.

May 1919.

Instructions regarding War Diaries and Intelligence Summaries are contained in F. S. Regs., Part II. and the Staff Manual respectively. Title pages will be prepared in manuscript.

WAR DIARY
or
~~INTELLIGENCE SUMMARY.~~
(*Erase heading not required.*)

Army Form C. 2118.

Place	Date	Hour	Summary of Events and Information	Remarks and references to Appendices
[illegible]	1/5/19	10.10	Dr. Petrie R.N.S. 6 under arrest awaiting C.C.M. Routine	K.C.
"	2 "	"	1 O.R. proceed on leave U.K.	K.C.
"	3 "	"	Routine	K.C.
"	4 "	11.00	1 O.R. rejoined from temporary duty 31st [illegible] 1 O.R. proceeded on leave U.K.	K.C.
"			Church Parade 11.0 Routine	
"	5 "	"	Routine	K.C.
"	6 "	"	Pay Parade 11.0 Routine	K.C.
"	7 "	"	1 O.R. proceeded on leave U.K. Routine	K.C.
"	8 "	"	1 O.R. proceeded on leave U.K. Routine	K.C.
"	9 "	"	Cpl E.C. Rae rejoined from leave to U.K. 8 O.R. proceeded for demobilization	K.C.
"	10 "	"	1 O.R. proceeded on leave U.K. Routine	S.P.R.
"	11 "	"	1 O.R. proceeded on leave U.K. Routine	S.P.R.
"	12 "	"	1 O.R. admitted to 110 F.A. Routine	S.P.R.
"	13 "	"	1 O.R. proceeded on leave U.K. Routine	S.P.R.
"	14 "	"	CPL SMITH proceeded on leave to U.K. 4 O.R. 2 BRUSSELS for 2 days.	S.P.R.

D. D. & L., London, E.C.
(A7883) Wt W809/M1672 50,000 4/17 Sch 52a Forms/C/2118/14

Instructions regarding War Diaries and Intelligence Summaries are contained in F. S. Regs., Part II. and the Staff Manual respectively. Title pages will be prepared in manuscript.

WAR DIARY
or
INTELLIGENCE SUMMARY.
(Erase heading not required.)

Army Form C. 2118.

Place	Date	Hour	Summary of Events and Information	Remarks and references to Appendices
Sterlock	15	11am	Routine	SPK
Do	16	–	Routine	SPK
Do	17	–	Routine	SPK
Do	18	–	PTE RAE admitted to 62 C.C.S from 110 F A DRS	SPK
Do	19	–	PTE A.F. WILSON. R.A.M.C. embarked for demobilization 5.5.19. Struck off strength.	SPK
Do	20	–	Medical Equipment handed in to 31 Ad. Depot Medical Stores.	SPK
Do	21	2pm	2 "X" Mules sent to TOURCOING Animal Collecting Camp. No animals on charge now.	SPK
Do	22	–	New Cadre for R.A.S.C. H.T. 1 W.O. 1 SGT. 2 OR. 1 SGT and 4 O.R. Supers. sent to 287th Co. R.A.S.C. H.T. ST. ANDRE. PTE. A. SAVAGE granted leave from 24.5.19 to 7.6.19	SPK
Do	23	–	Routine	SPK
Do	24	–	Routine.	SPK
Do	25	–	DR. HOBSON. R.A.S.C. proceeded to 287 Co. R.A.S.C. PTE SOAMES proceeded on leave.	SPK

1577 Wt. W10791/1773 500,000 1/15 D. D. & L. A.D.S.S./Forms/C. 2118.

Army Form C. 2118.

Instructions regarding War Diaries and Intelligence Summaries are contained in F. S. Regs., Part II. and the Staff Manual respectively. Title pages will be prepared in manuscript.

WAR DIARY
or
~~INTELLIGENCE~~ SUMMARY.

(Erase heading not required.)

Place	Date	Hour	Summary of Events and Information	Remarks and references to Appendices
May 1919				
Sterkrade	26	10am	PTE McEVOY embarked BOULOGNE 6/5/19 for Demobilization. Struck off strength.	[illegible]
Do	27	-	L CPL CRAIG Deprived of L CPL'S stripe and 2 days pay.	[illegible]
Do	28	-	5 O R proceeded for Demobilization. 2 O R S HILL proceeded on leave. DRIVER NELSON G RASC MT deprived of 7 days pay. Court of Inquiry assembled re damage to Ambulance Car.	[illegible]
Do	29	-	Routine	[illegible]
Do	30	-	Routine	[illegible]
Do	31	-	Routine	

1577 Wt. W10791/1773 500,000 1/15 D. D. & L. A.D.S.S./Forms/C. 2118.

June 1919

140/35-8-
[illegible]

109th F.A.

Instructions regarding War Diaries and Intelligence Summaries are contained in F. S. Regs., Part II. and the Staff Manual respectively. Title pages will be prepared in manuscript.

WAR DIARY
or
~~INTELLIGENCE~~ SUMMARY.
(Erase heading not required.)

Army Form C. 2118.

V845

Ceased

Place	Date	Hour	Summary of Events and Information	Remarks and references to Appendices
Sterkrade	1/6/19	10am	1 O.R RASC H.T. proceeded to 287 COY RASC HT and is struck off strength.	SPR
Do	2	–	Routine	SPR
Do	3	–	1. O.R RASC proceeded to report to 287 COY RASC. CPL PATTON. RASC M.T. to OC 36 DIV. M.T. COY for demobilization	SPR
Do	4	–	3 O.R RAMC proceeded to 5 AREA Concentration Camp for demobilization	SPR
Do	5	–	Routine.	SPR
Do	6	–	Handed over Command of the unit to LT W.E. PERRITT. Authority ADMS. 5th AREA 187/20 dated 4th inst. 1 O.R. Struck off Strength 14/6/19	SPR
Do	7	–	1 O.R. RASC M.T. proceeded to 36th Coy M.T. for demobilization. Wagon handed in to [illegible]	W.E.P.
Do	8	–	~~[illegible]~~ – Routine –	W.E.P.
Do	9	–	Routine – Ashiary –	W.E.P.
Do	10	–	Pay Parade 09.30 [illegible]	W.E.P.
"	11	–	Dr Peters tried by F.G.C.M. for desertion at Marseilles	W.E.P.

1577 Wt. W10791/1773 500,000 1/15 D. D. & L. A.D.S.S./Forms/C. 2118.

Instructions regarding War Diaries and Intelligence Summaries are contained in F. S. Regs., Part II. and the Staff Manual respectively. Title pages will be prepared in manuscript.

WAR DIARY
or
INTELLIGENCE SUMMARY.
(Erase heading not required.)

Army Form C. 2118.

Place	Date	Hour	Summary of Events and Information	Remarks and references to Appendices
Steinbach	12/6/19	10.00	5 O.R. R.A.S.C. proceeded to 36 Div Train. Struck off strength	W.P.
"	13 "	" "	18 O.R. R.A.M.C. proceeded to St Andre Concentration Camp for demobilization	W.P.
"	14 "	" "	Ordnance equipment handed in to D.C.S. Corps unit disbanded	W.P.

W. [illegible] Lieut & Qr Mr R.A.M.C.
O.C. 109th F. Amb

1577 Wt. W10791/17

www.ingramcontent.com/pod-product-compliance
Lightning Source LLC
Chambersburg PA
CBHW080846010526
44114CB00017B/2378